SHAKESPEARE

FROM *Richard II* TO *Henry V*

Shakespeare

FROM *Richard II* TO *Henry V*

by

DEREK TRAVERSI

STANFORD UNIVERSITY PRESS • Stanford, California 1957

STANFORD UNIVERSITY PRESS, STANFORD, CALIFORNIA

© 1957 by the Board of Trustees of the Leland Stanford Junior University
All rights reserved
Printed in the United States of America

Library of Congress Catalog Card Number: 57-11673

Published with the assistance of the Ford Foundation

PREFACE

DIFFERENT plays of Shakespeare, conceived at different stages in his artistic development, call for a specific approach and lead to a distinctive interpretation. Some critics of a recent study of mine, on the last plays, were disturbed by what they regarded as an excessive stressing of their 'symbolic' content; in so judging, I believe that they both misapprehended the meaning of the term, as I used it, and depreciated the true originality of Shakespeare's achievement. Be that as it may, the historical plays call for, and here receive, a more directly 'dramatic' approach; considerations of language and verse are, as ever, relevant, but the meanings to which they point are closer than in the final comedies to normal conceptions of character and dramatic action. The plays here considered are not, perhaps, by the very highest Shakespearean standards, masterpieces; but they offer a consistently personal reading of contemporary ideas on history and politics, and illuminate, perhaps as clearly as any, the emergence of many of the distinctive themes of the still greater plays to follow.

The question of critical indebtedness is, as always, difficult to define. To claim independence from the findings of earlier writers would be absurdly presumptuous, and I am conscious of a considerable debt to the scholarly investigations of Professor J. Dover Wilson, Dr. E. M. W. Tillyard, and others; the debt remains, though no doubt much in the argument which emerges from the following pages would not commend itself to them in its emphasis and spirit. Critics of a more recent generation appear to have produced little that is really illuminating on these plays. I have owed something, however, to Professor L. C. Knights' essay (*Notes on Comedy*) published in *Explorations* (London: Chatto & Windus, 1946) and to some penetrating pages by Mr. John F. Danby in his book, *Shakespeare's Doctrine of Nature* (London: Faber and Faber, 1949). Other echoes no doubt exist, but I have not been explicitly aware of them in the act of writing.

Shorter studies on three of the plays here considered—*Henry IV*, Parts I and II, and *Henry V*—were published at different periods in *Scrutiny*, and permission to reprint parts of these is gratefully acknowledged.

DEREK TRAVERSI

Teheran
May 1957

Contents

Chapter One INTRODUCTION

THE HISTORICAL PATTERN FROM
RICHARD THE SECOND TO *HENRY THE FIFTH*

ANYONE approaching the study of Shakespeare's second, and greater, series of plays on English history must be acutely aware of treading controversial ground. Neither on the guiding conception of the series nor on its artistic merits has agreement been reached, so that spirited defences of the patriotic interpretation—like that put forward in more than one place by Professor J. Dover Wilson[1]—alternate with readings of a very different kind, less simple and positive in tone. The increased attention now given to the background of the plays in terms of contemporary political thought, though in many ways illuminating, has not been without dangers of its own. There is a very real risk that erudition, in relating these plays to their period, may end by obscuring their true individuality, the personal contribution by which they live as works of art. The true artist, when circumstances induce him to approach political conceptions, gives them a new human value in the light of his own experience; and it is this combination of old and new, the inherited theme and its individual re-creation, that confers upon Shakespeare's historical plays their distinctive and transforming interest.

This general observation, which applies in varying degrees to Shakespeare's earlier chronicles,[2] is still more true of the set of plays which, extending from *Richard II* to *Henry V*, represents his most extended treatment of material derived from English history. The starting point of the series is, in accordance with the inherited conception, an adapta-

---

[1] In *The Fortunes of Falstaff* (Cambridge: The University Press, 1943) and in his introduction to the two *Henry IV* plays and *Henry V* (Cambridge: The University Press, 1946 and 1947).

[2] Professor J. Dover Wilson, following earlier students of the *Henry VI* plays, has defended the view that these represent the reshaping for performance by Shakespeare's own company of plays originally written by other hands; but other investigation, such as that incorporated in Peter Alexander's important study, *Shakespeare's Henry VI and Richard III* (Cambridge: The University Press, 1929), tends to give Shakespeare greater credit for originality in his early writings.

tion to the exigencies of Tudor political thought of traditional conceptions of monarchy. The royal office is assumed to be divinely instituted,
the necessary guarantee of order in a state nationally and patriotically
conceived; the political thought expressed in these plays combines the
fervent nationalism of the day, fostered for practical ends by the ruling
dynasty, with sacramental notions of monarchy more venerable than
itself. In the period covered by this series, however, the emphasis rests
on the interruption of the relationship which should naturally exist,
according to the traditional view, between king and subject, on the
disastrous consequences of that interruption, and on the restoration of
ordered rule, after the uneasy interim of Henry IV's reign, on a more
secure, if more limited, basis under the authority of his son. The relevance to contemporary purposes of the lesson already drawn from the
events depicted by such chroniclers as Hall and Holinshed[3] was, beyond
doubt, a determining factor in Shakespeare's choice of subject.

As we follow the development of this closely integrated series,[4] we
are aware that the historical theme corresponds in its entirety to the plan
just indicated. It opens with the overthrow, in *Richard II*, of a king
whose hereditary position and claim to allegiance are in themselves
unchallenged by a usurper—Bolingbroke—whose action derives from,
though it is not excused by, crimes committed and at heart acknowledged by his victim. Chief among these crimes was the murder of
Edward III's son, Thomas, Duke of Gloucester, referred to by Shakespeare on several occasions[5] and more directly treated by an unknown
writer in the earlier play of *Woodstock*.[6] From the moment of Richard's
murder, the royal office, its reputation already tarnished by the unworthiness of its last legitimate holder, ceases to confer upon the king a natural,
spontaneous right to allegiance; its necessary authority will be restored,
if at all, on the basis of a more conscious, deliberate estimate of political
realities, and only after the consequences of the original crime have
worked themselves out through the body politic in disintegration and
bloodshed.

The fruits of usurpation in terms of civil strife are, indeed, amply
shown in the two plays devoted to the usurper's reign. Henry's desire
to rule well is countered throughout by the dubious origins of his power.

---

[3] Hall's *Chronicle* was published in 1548, Holinshed's in 1577.

[4] The continuity of the argument does not, of course, imply that the four plays were
originally conceived as a single unit, but simply that the later terms of the series recognized
the existence of the earlier. In point of fact, some three years separate *Richard II*, which
must have been written around 1595, from the two parts of *Henry IV* and *Henry V*.

[5] See more especially *Richard II*, I. ii.

[6] Edited by P. A. Rossiter in 1946.

Usurpation breeds rebellion in those who, after all, have only backed his claim for ends of their own, so that the new reign resolves itself into the king's inconclusive struggle against the selfish interests which he has himself fostered to gain access to the throne. This new situation is accompanied by a notable extension of the ground covered by the action. Beyond the remnants of the original feudal relationship between the king and his aristocratic vassals—a relationship which the act of rebellion has subjected to stress, taken out of the natural order of things—the range of political realities covered by these two plays is most notably widened. The political events depicted still take place, in the main, within the aristocratic limits where decisions are arrived at and the course of action determined; but the consequences of this action are expanded—as they never were in *Richard II*—to cover a more ample field. Disorder, no longer confined to the clash of courtly rivalries, spreads from these to cover the nation's life; and this disorder, which breeds within itself an increasingly explicit comment, the repudiation of those whose deeds have opened the way to its tragically conceived effects, is brought home most immediately to the king through the dissolute behaviour of his son.

This dissolution, however, though related to the diseased state of the body politic, is less real than apparent. Hal, brought up in the new order of things, represents rather a fresh beginning than a continuation of the sombre realities around him. It is true that his behaviour in the *Henry IV* plays is conditioned, at least in part, by the nature of the society in which he finds himself; but this situation, which is not of his making, does not weigh upon him with the limiting, constraining force that so imposes itself upon his father. His conduct is marked from the first by a sense that the traditional sanctions of monarchy are no longer immediately valid, that the implications of the royal office need to be reconsidered in a new world of uncertainties. This reconsideration, presented through the successive stages of the action, is a principal theme of the *Henry IV* plays. Hal is subjected to a process of education which finally enables him to assume, with full competence, the burden of authority in the circumstances which his father's act (and Richard's own previous unworthiness) has brought into being; and in this process, his own dispassionate nature, his readiness to see things as they are, plays a decisive part. When, at the end of *Henry IV*, Part II, his growth into responsibility is complete, the entire series is rounded off with the consolidation of a new political order concentrated on the person of Henry V, who possesses to a supreme degree his father's political capacity but whose authority has not been directly flawed by the dubious nature of its origins.

Thus far, the theme followed in this series of plays belongs, in its main outline, to the political commonplaces of Shakespeare's age. The overthrow and restoration of ordered rule under the royal fountainhead of authority are, however, no more than a part—albeit essential—of his purpose. The traditional story presented a further motive for development in the portrayal of Prince Hal, whose progress from dissolute heir apparent to responsible monarch gives a main thread of significant continuity to the series. It is, in fact, through his study of the Prince, and of his relationship to his father, that Shakespeare, by shifting his emphasis from the public to the personal aspect of his story, approaches the full originality of his conception. The question we come increasingly to ask ourselves, as we follow the various stages of the Prince's career, is one which, because it stands in evident relationship to realities in the moral order, has obvious dramatic possibilities: What are the personal, as distinct from the political, qualities that go to the making of a king? The answer is provided in several stages, each of which is at once based on contemporary notions of the political character and vastly extends the implications of these notions, passing from an affirmation of the necessity of monarchy to a searching analysis of the qualities and limitations of the public personality.

The study has been prepared for, mainly in its negative aspects, by the portrayal of Hal's royal predecessors. The failure of Richard, in the opening play, to exercise effectively the legitimate and divinely sanctioned authority which he alone, in the whole series, can indubitably claim, is shown as a reflection of grave personal weakness. This weakness, having precipitated his own tragedy and brought the royal institution into grave crisis, acts in turn as a conditioning factor in all that follows. Richard's fall and the usurpation of Bolingbroke emphasize between them the necessity of the political qualities for the successful exercise of kingship. By his possession of these qualities Bolingbroke justifies, as far as may be, his otherwise indefensible seizure of the crown; and a clear-sighted and dispassionate estimate of the varied motives which accompany the struggle for power, once the foundations of ordered rule have been called into question, is passed on by Bolingbroke as a basic condition of public life to his son.

The true interest of the conception, however, really begins at this point. The contrast with Richard has established, with what has for Prince Hal the validity of an axiom, the relevance of his father's political gifts; but the presentation of Henry's reign, in the two plays which follow, equally stresses its limitations. Henry IV's concentration upon the political aspects of behaviour, having brought him to the throne, leaves him as king with no sufficient substitute for the accepted sanctions of royalty which he has himself, as a usurper, subjected to outrage. These sanctions are founded, in the last analysis, upon personal and therefore human values, which he has neglected at his peril, and which now exact from him an unwilling recognition of which the son, as he approaches his father with increasing intimacy, cannot fail to be aware. The very concentration upon the political virtues that have enabled Henry to press successfully his claim to the throne becomes, once he has been crowned, a limiting factor, a weakness which, as he increasingly stresses it in his exchanges with Hal, is borne with a persistence akin to tragedy upon his son's thoughts.

In the light of these considerations the apparent contradictions which have so often been felt to underlie the presentation of the Prince's character become consistent and comprehensible. Hal, in his characteristically self-conscious aspiration to princely perfection, is less a free agent than the product of the preceding circumstances by which his own reactions have been shaped. He is presented to our consideration, not merely as an individual, but as the member of a family, whose qualities and defects he shares. The very considerable virtues which bring him finally to political success represent, in more aspects than one, the turning to practical account of inherited limitations. As the son of a usurper, Hal is deprived of the sanctions which the traditional monarch derived from unquestioned heredity, sanctions upon which Richard (to return to the starting point of the series, still alive in its later stages) too complacently counted to offset his personal unworthiness. This lack of traditional sanction, which had constituted his father's problem, becomes, in the political order, his opportunity. It enables him to propose to himself with full awareness ends which a traditional ruler can too easily take for granted, reconciling the legitimate authority which (more clearly than his father) he is in a position to exercise, with the insight and political skill needed to maintain it in a world of shifting and often cynical values. From the outset, the supreme quality inherited by Hal from his father and raised by his own practice to new levels of shrewd consistency is *detachment*: a *detachment* from traditional conceptions which he turns into the active intelligence so firmly applied by him to his relatively legitimate situation, but which is at the same time—and to forget this is to fail to respond to the balanced conception of the character—his limitation as a human being.

Once this situation has been grasped in its full subtlety, the process of 'conversion' which Shakespeare derived from his sources and which no doubt contributed in no small measure to the popularity of the series is seen in its true light. In a very important sense, there is in Hal's behaviour no true 'conversion' at all. The detachment which we have just asserted to be his distinguishing quality, his most important inheritance from his father, determines from the first moment his attitude in the tavern scenes of the two *Henry IV* plays. Whatever his father may fear, Hal is never truly subjected to the vices with which he associates for ends he has deliberately, and with full consciousness, made his own. From the first, he is only waiting the opportune moment for his self-revelation; this is plainly stated in his first soliloquy[7]—in which Shakespeare turns the lack of verisimilitude in his theme into a psychological virtue—and remains, from that moment, a principal key to his behaviour. Falstaff and his companions are, from this point of view, no more than living examples of the consequences of 'misrule,' of the anarchy which his father's action has, against his own intentions, promoted but which he has never, with his outlook confined as it is to the narrow sphere of courtly intrigue, properly understood. Henry V, unlike Bolingbroke, *will* understand it, because he has surrounded himself with it, has with set purpose gone so far as to *live* it in his own person; but when the time comes for his tavern friends to be discarded, that action will come easily to a man who has from the first declared his intention of turning away from them as soon as he has extracted, from his contact with them and by intimate observation, the knowledge he requires of men as they are, and—further—as soon as this rejection will appear in its full value in the public eye. That this sober estimate of public convenience implies increasingly some lack of human warmth is no doubt true, but it is no more than one example of the crux upon which all that is most personal in Shakespeare's presentation of the character turns.

The stages of Hal's 'public' redemption, to which the growing coolness of his relations with Falstaff are a background, are, roughly speaking, two; they correspond with sufficient exactitude to the two plays into which the *Henry IV* action is divided. The core of his successful affirmation, in Part I, as warrior and man of chivalry lies in the conflict between himself and Harry Percy. As a result of this conflict, a new and politically practical virtue asserts itself victoriously over a tarnished and inadequate conception of aristocratic 'honour.' Once more, the emphasis is placed upon the rise, under the new conditions implied by Bolingbroke's seizure of power, of a fresh and contemporary attitude to politics. Percy's 'honour,' presented in him as a sincere attribute, is none the less out of touch with the world in which it moves. It is, in its own despite, verbal in content, unable to offer an adequate alternative to the political

---

[7] *1 Henry IV*, i. ii. See pp. 57–58 below.

manoeuvrings which it repudiates but which have nevertheless replaced the traditional loyalties to which the leaders of the rebel faction, even as they follow the claims of self-interest, still ostensibly appeal. As such, it stands for an essentially gullible attitude towards life, and Percy himself, in a world where all affirmations of nobility call for scrutiny, has become the instrument of unworthy designs. Hal's conception of chivalry is, by comparison, self-reliant and workaday, conceived not in rhetoric or pride of caste, but in strict relation to the sober and necessary ends he has proposed to himself. At Shrewsbury, a dying tradition, shorn by the impact of new circumstances of the values which had originally justified it, meets a fresh conception of 'virtue,' founded on a less prejudiced estimate of practical possibilities, of the true nature of man as a political being, and inevitably succumbs. But behind the triumph of this new conception, justified and necessary as it is, there lies, as the following action shows, a sense of relativity, of inescapable hollowness.

This sense, indeed, looms increasingly large in *Henry IV*, *Part II*, where it is projected for Hal no longer in the simple sphere of active self-affirmation, in which he has proved himself strong, but in a more intimate, personal order. Having asserted himself as a modern prince in the exercise of the chivalrous virtues, and so laid the foundation of his future greatness, Hal is now faced with the more arduous necessity of subduing his own will, of making himself the instrument of a conception of justice which transcends all personal considerations and upon which his own authority—if it is to receive true acceptance—must rest. At this point he meets, squarely and for the first time, the true implications of his own nature and of the circumstances which have attended his own rise to political efficacy. It is this fact, above all others, which accounts for the notable change in feeling which distinguishes *Henry IV*, Part II, from the preceding play. The shadow of the traditional conception of monarchy, thrust aside by his father in the act of self-assertion which brought him to the crown, returns as the specific personal problem of the son. It is, indeed, the relation between the necessary impersonality of the king, little short of superhuman in its implications, and the self-assertion called for in a complex and shifting world that becomes in increasing measure the key to Hal's character and to the concept of political behaviour sketched in his development. Having overthrown Percy (a relatively simple triumph), the Prince needs—as the last stage in his preparation for kingship—to overcome himself, to attain the impersonality which his great office requires of him; and this is what is implied, against a sombre background of social realities more extensively presented than in the preceding plays, in his final reconciliation with the

Lord Chief-Justice. After this alone, Hal—ostensibly at peace with himself, confirmed in the exalted selflessness of his vocation—is ready to be crowned.

From this exposition of the development in Hal of a study of political perfection (perfection, be it stressed once more, which is neither more nor less than political), it emerges that the king can only be understood in relation to the realm over which he exercises his necessary, his indispensable authority. It is indeed the supreme achievement of this series of plays that, as the personal implications of the royal vocation in Hal are progressively unfolded, they are constantly related to the state of an England which at once reflects and conditions the central presentation of royalty. That this should be so is only natural, because—as we have suggested—these plays regard the king as being, by close analogy, the head of his realm, the incarnation of its purpose, and the summit of its accumulated strength. The 'moral' regeneration of Hal (which is, as we have seen, rather a growth in political understanding) is operated throughout in relation to the England he will govern; and the result is a picture of notable consistency and depth, in which each new element, as it is introduced into the action, falls into place in a complete and balanced artistic achievement.

Once more, and in accordance with the nature of the entire series, the complete truth emerges in relation to the various stages of the historical pattern. The 'viciousness' of Hal's early surroundings and of his unregenerate behaviour (which his own father, with less than complete understanding, accepts at its face value) reflects the disorder which was at once the cause and the result of Bolingbroke's usurpation; the aristocratic intrigues of the rebels, with their disruptive effect upon the unity of the state, find their reflection in the dissolution of the tavern scenes, supremely incarnated in the anarchy of Falstaff. From this disorder the Prince, even as he participates in it, stands aside in detached sufficiency. He deliberately sets himself to study it, to make himself realistically familiar, *on all levels*, with the conditions of his future rule; and the result is that the dramatic action takes shape, round his person, in a world in which Hotspur and Douglas, Falstaff and Bardolph, Poins and Pistol, each alive in his own right, live further as an integral part of the society which it is the king's vocation to mould into an active unity of purpose. It is the breadth of understanding which follows from this conception of his office—the refusal to be limited exclusively to court circles and values—that distinguishes Hal from his father, for whom the royal authority has always been confined in its exercise to the political manipulation of courtly appetites, and who has shown throughout a distinct contempt, related to, but essentially different from, his son's detachment, for everything that may be described as 'popular.'

In terms of this detachment, at least, the Prince and Falstaff represent contrasted poles, upon whose clash and subsistent interrelation the conception which animates these plays finally turns. To grasp the nature of the link that binds them together in diversity is to penetrate most closely to the central experience of the series. As Hal assumes his royal responsibilities, he inevitably turns away from his companion in dissolution, until the break is consummated in the final rejection.[8] That rejection is, from the point of view of his growth as a public figure, the necessary external consequence of his acceptance of his royal vocation; this requires a visible turning away from the 'misrule' which is the supreme enemy of true kingship, and without it his later triumphs would be inconceivable. In *Henry V*, the king, having finally and with complete self-consciousness assumed the barely human responsibilities of his office, is at last able to use the knowledge he has gained of men and affairs to lead a nation from which the figure of 'riot' has been finally expelled to his victorious enterprise in France.

The triumph of Henry V, however, though valid in its own right, equally confirms what has been implied by the presentation of his character throughout the series. The loss in human qualities which appears, in these plays, to be involved in the very fact of political success gives a tragic undertone to his triumphant progress. For what is at each stage, and in accordance with the initial conception, a realistic study of social dissolution is turned, by the most daring stroke of all, into a source of comic energy, a comment developed in parallel form upon the entire political action. It is here that the function of Falstaff enters into its full subtlety, combining the vicious rôle of the fat knight as misleader of youth and incarnation of anarchy with that of vivid human commentator on the detached inhumanity which political ability, once the natural bonds of an ordered society have been broken, seems increasingly to imply. This double conception of Falstaff, and its constant relationship to the various stages of the Prince's development is Shakespeare's supreme personal contribution to the historical material of these plays.

From this point of view, again, the Prince's attitude towards Falstaff develops notably in the course of the action. In Part I, as Hal observes in Falstaff the real consequences of anarchy and misrule (consequences which are shown, above all, in the Eastcheap robbery, in which the Prince, albeit in detachment, participates), he is confirmed in his political

---

[8] *2 Henry IV*, v. v.

vocation. At each stage, however, Falstaff provides, besides a living picture of disorder, a valid comic commentary. His function up to the battle of Shrewsbury is evidently in some sense a critical one, not altogether different, though vastly developed, from that of Faulconbridge in *King John*.[9] The Prince's reconciliation with his father is preceded by the parody of that reconciliation in the tavern,[10] in the course of which Falstaff, defending himself against charges which will ultimately prove fatal to him, symbolically assumes the throne of misrule; and the final victory over Hotspur is accompanied by the parody of warlike valour and by an implicit comment on the values of 'heroism' itself.[11] In neither case are we to equate mockery simply with seriousness, or parody with truth; but in each an aspect of reality relevant to a balanced judgement is being advanced. The linking through one personage of the serious to the comic action, so that a commentary on the one springs out of the limitation, the stressed corruption of the other, is the most original feature of the whole play.

In Part II, as the Prince directly faces the deeper implications of his vocation, a new and increasingly sombre note is struck in the avowedly comic scenes. Falstaff, in tune with his surroundings, grows notably in age and obvious decay. Losing a great part of the vitality which had distinguished him in the previous play, he becomes subdued to the quality of the life around him, in which senility, disillusionment, and impotence largely predominate. Equally, however, he shows at moments a new kind of tragic pathos which, presented without sentiment, is not incompatible with his growing monstrosity and which even his necessary subjection to justice cannot entirely obscure. His age, accentuating in him the elements of dissolution, also stresses a sense of death which is shared, finally and as one element in a complex effect, by the very order which has seen Henry's rise to power. The picture of an England in disorder, the background to the Prince's growth in political competence, expands from court and tavern, already conceived in parallel function, to include Gloucestershire, the local foundations of life in a rural society; and the sense of age and decay which accompanies this presentation (though it does not exhaust it) is a background to the increasingly sombre quality of Hal's own reflections and to the cynicism which has throughout marked the behaviour of the political leaders to whom success is in the process of becoming an end in itself.

---

[9] If one aspect of Faulconbridge finds fulfilment in the figure of Edmund in *King Lear*, another can be said to anticipate the comic spirit of Falstaff.

[10] *1 Henry IV*, ii. iv.

[11] *Ibid.*, v. iv.

Of the Prince himself we should not say that he is, by the end of the series, subdued to this new order of cynicism, against which, indeed, his royal actions are conceived as a decisive reaction. Yet his inevitable relation to this order colours his thought and has from the first conferred a certain sombre detachment from humanity upon his behaviour, which finds its supreme practical expression in the rejection scene (the necessity of which, however, is not in question). It is worth noting that Hal's final assumption of his royal duties is accompanied, as its necessary corollary, not merely by the banishment but by the death of Falstaff, with which the relationship between them concludes. In the double link which, at the heart of an England which these plays have progressively depicted in the widening scope of its varied social relationships, binds Falstaff to Hal as necessary sacrifice and vivid protest opposed to tried virtue and cold competence, we approach the true sense, the final originality, of this great series of plays.

Chapter Two RICHARD THE SECOND

THE STARTING point for a study of the series of plays that here concerns us is necessarily *Richard II*. It is true that the play stands in some respects apart from those which followed it; in style, as in date, it is clearly distinguished from the two parts of *Henry IV* and the final presentation of Henry V's triumphant progress. The separation, however, covers points of contact, confirmed by a series of references back to the play from its successors,[1] which establish it as an initial term for the later development. In Shakespeare's highly selective treatment of Richard's tragedy, we are shown the downfall of a natural, sanctioned conception of royalty, and its replacement, in an action the pattern of which leans heavily upon the traditional conception of Fortune's wheel, by a political force at once more competent, more self-conscious, and more precariously built on the foundations of its own desire for power.

If the plot of *Richard II* is deliberately simplified to point the central political conflict, its style is very curiously elaborate. The variety achieved by the play is largely conferred upon it by a poetic expression which aims with some consistency at the presentation of significant contrasts between opposed personalities and ideas. The presence of convention, of conscious literary artifice, is felt throughout; but within the limits which this presence imposes we can detect an attempt, consistently followed, to distinguish between past and present realities, to separate the dramatic re-creation of historical events from the comments occasionally passed upon them by characters upon whom a certain choric function is conferred,[2] and to set the legitimate but inadequate conception of feudal loyalty represented by Richard against the advance of a formidable but unsanctioned political energy. This effort to diversify artificial forms, to make the elaboration of contrasted styles respond to the tensions which constitute the true tragic theme, is possibly the most original feature of the play.

---

[1] These have been dealt with exhaustively by, among others, E. M. W. Tillyard in his book on *Shakespeare's History Plays* (New York: The Macmillan Company, 1946), and it seems unnecessary to go over the ground again.

[2] Such characters are John of Gaunt, the Queen, and, in one scene deliberately inserted into the historical action (III. iv), the Gardeners.

I

The action of *Richard II* opens on a note of high formality with the confronting of Bolingbroke and Mowbray under the eyes of their king. This formality has from the first a more than decorative purpose; it reflects a kingship which, alone in all this series of plays, combines legitimacy with the assertion of a sanction ultimately divine.[3] The courtly rivals here presented in the initial act of replacing unity by strife, allegiance by passionate self-assertion, are still acutely aware of being grouped in a pattern of loyalties dependent upon the crown; and to this awareness Richard responds by asserting the impartiality which his exalted central position implies. To Bolingbroke's salutation of his king,

> Many years of happy days befal
> My gracious sovereign, my most loving liege!

corresponds Mowbray's effort to cap it, to go a step further in the rhetorical expression of his devotion:

> Each day still better other's happiness;
> Until the heavens, envying earth's good hap,
> Add an immortal title to your crown!

The turbulent rivalries which, almost immediately after this assertion, break into open strife cast back on these professions a shadow of empty hyperbole which is, without doubt, part of the complete effect; but in themselves they imply a proper subjection, a recognition of the bonds of respect and service that bind a true subject to the office and person of his king.

As the scene proceeds, however, the presence of dangerous stresses beneath the pattern of courtly propriety is variously revealed. Although the contending nobles at first maintain the appearances of loyal respect, the formal statement of their allegiance stands in significant contrast to the blunt expressions of mutual defiance which immediately follow. The opening words of Bolingbroke's indictment, spoken 'In the devotion of a subject's love,' rise by stages to the expected gesture of allegiance; but only when he turns to accuse his rival:

> *Now*, Thomas Mowbray, do I turn to thee,
> And mark my greeting well;

are his emotions fully and directly engaged. Similarly, when his opponent replies, the last conventional expression of deference, 'And let him

---

[3] In Henry IV and Henry V, who follow Richard, the royal authority is still divinely sanctioned, but the claim to legitimacy is indelibly stained by the nature of its origins.

be no kinsman to my liege,' which has already been set against the directness of 'The blood is hot that must be cool'd for this,' is finally absorbed,
after 'I do defy him, and I spit at him,' in the clash of opposed wills.

More interesting than this emergence of rivalries is the emotional
quality of their expression. As defiance provokes defiance, the rhetorical
utterance of the contendents rises indeed, but less to manly directness
than to a pitch of strained and hysterical artifice. In Bolingbroke's challenge, the energy with which he has turned upon his rival is quickly
caught up, involved in a weakening convention:

> Thou art a traitor and a miscreant,
> Too good to be so and too bad to live,
> Since the more fair and crystal is the sky,
> The uglier seem the clouds that in it fly!   (1. i)

'Traitor' and 'miscreant' are direct and brutal enough in their effect;
but their bitterness is qualified by the balanced antithesis of 'good' and
'bad' which follows, and by the conventional contrast between the 'fair
and crystal' sky and the 'uglier' aspect of the clouds that 'in it' (and the
rhyme clinches the note of artifice) 'fly.' Similarly, in Mowbray's retort,
the rhetorical rhythm lifts the constructed period to a new level of
passion, only to leave it finally, after the tense, strained note of

> the trial of a woman's war,
> The bitter clamour of two eager tongues,

in a resolution characteristically weakened by overstatement:

> I do defy him, and I spit at him;
> Call him a slanderous coward and a villain:
> Which to maintain I would allow him odds,
> And meet him, were I tied to run afoot
> Even to the frozen ridges of the Alps,
> Or any other ground inhabitable,
> Where ever Englishman durst set his foot.   (1. i)

As in Bolingbroke's challenge, to meet which it has deliberately and self-
consciously risen, the expression of feeling here has prolonged itself
beyond its true content. After the opening insult, the tide of emotion,
half poetic and half conventional in accordance with the mode of this
play, is carried across the concluding lines with an elaboration that points
beyond the decorative content to a weakening of true sentiment.

If formal expression is, in this scene, continually balanced by a sense
of artifice and strain, part at least of the reason is to be sought in the
grounds of conflict between the rival lords. As the altercation between

them drops from the poetically passionate to the realities of policy there is a notable change of tone. The charges in Bolingbroke's indictment are solid enough. They include the embezzlement of royal revenues for 'lewd employments,' consistent intrigue, and, above all, the plotting of the Duke of Gloucester's death; the last accusation, most ominous of all, involves the king himself, the centre of the feudal structure of loyalty to which lip-service is still paid, in ambiguity and corruption. This is not immediately apparent, but it is noteworthy that this crime, the main-spring of the following tragedy, is denounced by Bolingbroke with an amplitude of utterance that separates it from the courtly niceties we have just witnessed and strikes the deeper, more directly choric effect so characteristic of the *Henry VI* plays:

> he did plot the Duke of Gloucester's death,
> Suggest his soon-believing adversaries,
> And consequently, like a traitor coward,
> Sluiced out his innocent soul through streams of blood:
> Which blood, like sacrificing Abel's, cries,
> Even from the tongueless caverns of the earth,
> To me for justice and rough chastisement.   (i. i)

The elaboration and the suggestion, in the solemn Biblical parallel, that this crime has a universal significance add a new and important note to the complete effect of the episode. Mowbray's reply, on the other hand, convincing and of a piece as a rhetorical reaction, is hesitant and uncertain in the sphere of fact. Part of the money received from the royal treasury was held back, though—it seems—to pay a debt contracted on another occasion. Gloucester was not slain by Mowbray, who yet neglected his 'sworn duty' in that case, and a plot against Gaunt's life is confessed to, though with affirmations of repentance and seeming reconciliation. This is clearly a world more complex than that of rhe-torical defiance and knightly conflict, and in it Richard, who still main-tains an attitude of royal impartiality, is more deeply involved than he admits.

Richard's increasing evasiveness, indeed, the failure—implied, if not yet stated—to impose his impartial judgement in relation to events which closely concern him, is the last notable feature that modifies the patterned formality of this introduction. His first brief interventions have been proper affirmations of royal detachment:

> Mowbray, impartial are our eyes and ears:
> . . . .
> He is our subject, Mowbray; so art thou:
> Free speech and fearless I to thee allow;

but as the accusations, rising in tone, implicitly approach his person, there is a suggestion, even in his early reaction—'How high a pitch his resolution soars!'—that he is conscious of treading dangerous ground. Almost imperceptibly, this suggestion undermines the apparent firmness of his stand. When Mowbray has answered defiance with defiance, it is noteworthy that Richard's gesture of royal peace-making should be expressed in terms of almost cynical aphorism:

> Let's purge this choler without letting blood:
>
> .   .   .   .
>
> Forget, forgive; conclude and be agreed;
> Our doctors say this is no month to bleed.

Is this to be ascribed to intelligence or to indifference, to superior under-standing or to a tendency to evade the decisions which the speaker's authority requires? Perhaps the answer to this question lies in the re-lation of these utterances to the poetic spirit of the entire episode. The varied use of poetic artifice for dramatic ends is characteristic of *Richard II*. The very elaboration of the conflicting expressions of defiance points to an emptiness which is filled, on the plane of action, by less respectable political motives; and Richard's own regality can turn, and will do so repeatedly, into a kind of bored indifference which is rooted in his weak-nesses. Neither the honour which the contending lords affirm they value above life,[4] and to defend which they thrust aside their duty of allegiance, nor Richard's own impartial royalty are altogether what they seem. In the world of lyrical rhetoric which surrounds the court action they are appropriate, but in the sphere of personal and political responsibility the reality is more obscure, less defined. Richard himself utters, perhaps, the supreme recognition of this at the close of the scene when, after asserting the authority which belongs to him as king—'We were not born to sue, but to command'—he breaks away from his own assertion in the following admission of helplessness: 'Which since we cannot do,' which is only partly covered by the conclusion 'to make you friends.'

The tournament scene itself (I. iii) is conducted in a similar spirit. As befits the occasion, it is surrounded with a formality which, at the same time as it contributes to the creation of an atmosphere 'mediæval,' chivalrous in spirit, points to a definite limitation. The last declaration of the contendents before what they imagine to be the resolution of arms

---

[4] See Mowbray's 'My life thou shalt command, but not my shame,' and the lines which follow, leading up to his affirmation:

> The purest treasure mortal times afford
> Is spotless reputation.   (I. i)

is marked, once more, by a deliberate and strained lyricism. For Bolingbroke, the approaching joust is a 'pilgrimage,' preceded by

ceremonious leave
And loving farewell of our *several friends*.

And his following speech, combining the note of youth and courtship
with the aristocratic image of falconry, reflects a courtier remarkably
unlike the Bolingbroke of the later scenes: a young warrior soaring on
the wings of his self-conscious poetry, subdued to a world which is that
of Richard's kingship, lyrically conceived, elaborate and thoroughly
theatrical in its courtliness. Mowbray's reply, contending verbally with
the exultation of his rival—

Never did captive with a freer heart
Cast off his chains of bondage, and embrace
His golden, uncontroll'd enfranchisement,
More than my dancing soul doth celebrate
This feast of battle with mine adversary

—is equally remote from realism, contributes to the building up of that
poetic expression of aristocracy which is the setting for Richard's self-
conscious and finally ineffective kingship. The very remoteness of this
type of utterance from the intrigue which we know to be taking shape
beneath it is at once a distinctive feature, the sign of a court still founded
on legitimate royalty, and an indication of hollowness.[5]

For, of course, the conflict to which these exchanges point never takes
place. The king's own position here is curiously wavering. Like Bolingbroke and Mowbray, in their response to the conventions of feudal
chivalry, he is in part acting a set rôle. His first action, as he interrupts
the rising tension and forbids the clash to which the upward flight of
intense emotion seems to be leading, is thoroughly respectable in its
motive:

our kingdom's earth should not be soil'd
With that dear blood which it hath fostered.

The king at this point is following his duty, exercising his authority in
the name of concord; and when, immediately after, he refers to

the eagle-winged pride
Of sky-aspiring and ambitious thoughts,

---

[5] The scene between John of Gaunt and the Duchess of Gloucester (i. ii) has been,
of course, deliberately sandwiched between the opening court episodes to recall past events
and to provide concrete illustration of this hollowness.

he is at once carrying on the soaring imagery of the contendents and placing it by establishing its origins in anarchy and unchecked ambition. In a later play, or even later in this play, the judgement would have been more explicitly conveyed, more firmly founded on the facts of character. Bolingbroke and Mowbray would have been less poetic, more 'concrete' in their presentation; we should have *seen*, exposed in detail, the designing motives which impel them, beneath the appearances of loyalty, to sterile conflict.

Here, however, the point is made without dramatic concreteness, as befits characters who have yet to step finally, by their own actions, from the framework of decorative allegiance which still limits their presentation. Meanwhile, the figure of Richard himself is strangely indefinite and contradictory. There is about his decision, as uttered, a sense of pose, of the self-conscious shadow rather than the substance of authority:

> It boots thee not to be compassionate:
> After our sentence plaining comes too late.

The decision thus somewhat flatly taken is the last which emerges as a true expression of royalty from this artificial world of allegiances so uneasily built on a real foundation of rivalries and hatreds. It is significant that the emotions of those most closely affected by banishment are couched in terms of courtly elaboration. When Gaunt consoles his departing son:

> Suppose the singing birds musicians,
> The grass whereon thou tread'st the presence strew'd,
> The flowers fair ladies, and thy steps no more
> Than a delightful measure or a dance,

he is in fact subduing feeling to expression, making of emotion a decorative subject rather than a reality. This he does as one who belongs to the past, whose loyalty is to a king for whom forms mean more than substance, who can rest, and often beautifully, on the unquestioned legitimacy of his inherited position, but who will fail to maintain it by the force of his own decisions. In Bolingbroke's reply to these consolations,

> O, who can hold a fire in his hand
> By thinking on the frosty Caucasus?

a firmer reality emerges tentatively through forms still conventional. Richard, in rousing his rival's hatred by banishing him, and in modifying his own decision by shortening the term of exile, has acted with typical inconsequence; from now on the style of the most individual parts of the play will be modified, so that what has been hitherto formality and pattern, based on the ostensible acceptance of traditional order, will give way to a new directness of action and expression.

The change in artistic intention, indeed, immediately makes itself felt. After the banishment of the contending nobles, Richard is introduced in the company of his favourites, and the presentation of the man begins to prevail over that of the feudal monarch. The sceptical tone of the conversation with Aumerle (1. iv) contrasts, no doubt deliberately, with the preceding aristocratic lyricism. 'And say, what store of parting tears were shed?'—the tone of the question invites the cynical reply which it in fact receives:

> Faith, none for me; except the northeast wind,
> Which then blew bitterly against our faces,
> Awaked the sleeping rheum, and so by chance
> Did grace our hollow parting with a tear.

This empty bitterness has its fitting counterpart in the distrust and fear which, immediately afterwards, emerge from Richard's account of Bolingbroke. The political game is already being played, and the king and his advisers have observed his rival's wooing of the common people, thus raising for the first time a theme to be repeated in *Henry IV*:[6]

> he did seem to dive into their hearts
> With humble and familiar courtesy,
> What reverence he did throw away on slaves,
> Wooing poor craftsmen with the craft of smiles
> And patient underbearing of his fortune,
> As 'twere to banish their affects with him.
> Off goes his bonnet to an oyster-wench;
> A brace of draymen bid God speed him well
> And had the tribute of his supple knee,
> With 'Thanks, my countrymen, my loving friends;'
> As were our England in reversion his,
> And he our subjects' next degree in hope. (1. iv)

The sense of 'politic' behaviour, not to say of calculation, is here set against the speaker's aristocratic contempt for 'slaves' and 'poor craftsmen,' as one world against another, and we should refrain from simplifying the issues as we consider the conflict. In Bolingbroke, no doubt, the virtues of reverence and humility have been transformed into the 'craft of smiles,' popularity has become an instrument of policy, and the

---

[6] Compare Henry IV's own account of his procedure in *1 Henry IV*, III. ii, and Worcester's accusations in the same play (v. i).

bending of the 'supple knee' a means to power; but it will, after all, be a feature of the plays to follow that the conception of England will be extended, in its social range, to allow a place for those whom Richard despises, and in Green's complacent dismissal of the future enemy—'Well, he is gone; and with him go these thoughts'—the shade of Nemesis is already evoked.

The calculation of Bolingbroke, indeed, needs to be set against the thriftless cynicism which Richard already shows, and which stands in such revealing contrast to his royal claims. Most damaging of all is the tone in which, at the end of the scene, he greets the news of Gaunt's sickness:

> Now put it, God, in the physician's mind
> To help him to his grave immediately!   (i. iv)

The assertion is even more grave in its implications than the obvious callousness would suggest. Gaunt, as we shall shortly see, represents on his deathbed the traditional spirit of England associated, for this play, with Edward III and his blood, and when Richard desires his death it is his own vocation that he is in fact setting aside. It is now clear how Shakespeare intends to incorporate into a coherent conception the seemingly contradictory material on which his play is based. On the one hand, it is his obligation (in Tudor times it could be called no less) to exalt the royal office, to set the king at the head of an aristocratic structure possessed of a splendour and luminosity of its own; on the other, the man who holds this office is, politically speaking, incapable and morally flawed, so that the portrayal of his fall may leave the monarchic principle itself substantially untouched. Out of this marriage of contrasted conceptions Shakespeare, at once fully contemporary and, within the framework of his times, freely intelligent, has embarked on the first stage of a study of political behaviour that will have universal implications.

The next scene (ii. i), in which Richard is confronted with Gaunt, confirms this interpretation. The famous speech on England, easily passed over as a rhetorical interlude, a set piece of poetic virtuosity, has a place of its own in the main development. Stylistically, its heightened lyricism is linked in spirit to the early court scenes and belongs, like them, to a past which has already succumbed to the inner hollowness that undermines it. In this sense, the elegiac note of Gaunt's elaborate prologue to his main utterance,

> The setting sun, and music at the close,
> As the last taste of sweets, is sweetest last,

anticipates, beyond the speaker's own death, the passing of an order which Richard's own authority, its proper support, cannot in fact maintain. The prevailing imagery of the final prophecy, with its insistence upon jewels as symbols of value ('this precious stone set in the silver sea') and upon the association of royalty and beneficent fertility ('this teeming womb of royal kings'), is in some sense related to the previous references to the sons of Edward III;[7] and, as in their case, the poignancy of the reference indicates death and loss in the present. The speech is further marked by a persistent Christian content which at once contrasts with Richard's present cynicism and anticipates the religious note which will be associated, in his later tragic speeches, with the spectacle of royalty overthrown. As Gaunt's words rise to their highest intensity in the contemplation of sacred majesty, England becomes

> this *teeming womb* of royal kings,
> Fear'd by their *breed* and famous by their *birth*,
> Renowned for their deeds as far from home,
> For *Christian service* and *true chivalry*,
> As is the sepulchre in stubborn Jewry
> Of the *world's ransom*, blessed Mary's son.   (II. i)

The connection with themes to be developed in this play, and in those to follow, is rich and varied. England, in its state of unity, is, as it were, an anticipation of perfection ('This other Eden, demi-paradise'), and the substance of its blessed state is conveyed through a sublimation of the chivalry which survives, as a shadow blemished with strife and egoism, in Richard's own court. The reference to the Holy Sepulchre, again, will be taken up repeatedly in the later action. Bolingbroke, as Henry IV, will see in his projected crusade a symbol of the dedicated unity which political realities will never allow him to establish under his own rule, and the presence of a Christian aspiration will be balanced, in Richard's own tragic utterances, by a sense of betrayal, the shadow of the gesture of Judas, which will accompany him through his decline. 'This land of such *dear souls*, this *dear, dear* land': Beneath this poignant assertion of patriotism there lies a sense of spiritual value, the expression of a tragedy, reflected in Gaunt's own death, which finds in the religious reference a universal expression.

---

[7] See *Richard II*, I. ii:
> Edward's seven sons, whereof thyself art one,
> Were as seven vials of his sacred blood,
> Or seven fair branches springing from one root.

The following denunciation of Richard, seen against this background, acquires a deeper, more ample significance. The exchange between the two is nicely balanced, like so much in this play, between feeling and artifice:

> GAUNT: I mock my name, great king, to flatter thee.
> RICHARD: Should dying men flatter with those that live?
> GAUNT: No, no, men living flatter those that die.
> RICHARD: Thou, now a-dying, say'st thou flatterest me.
> GAUNT: O, no! thou diest, though I the sicker be.
>
> (II. i)

The ideas of flattery and truth, health and sickness, life and death are here interwoven in a way which, beyond the obvious artifice, has its relation to the complete conception. Gaunt is dying, indeed, and the world of patriotic certainties associated with the descendants of Edward III with him, but Richard too, in his apparent health, is on the way to decline, and his sickness, moreover, will be that of his country. The whole exchange is at once elaborate, artificial ('Can sick men play so nicely with their names?'), and, beneath its elaboration, a means to convey the state of contradiction, poised between the duty of loyalty and the need for renovation, in which the realm finds itself.

Against this background the final denunciation put into Gaunt's mouth ('Landlord of England art thou now, not king') is seen in its full meaning. England is described, by contrast with the previous lyricism, as in a state of sickness which is that of the monarchy itself:

> Thy death-bed is no lesser than thy land,
> Wherein thou liest in reputation sick.

It has been Richard's crowning irresponsibility to commit his 'anointed body,' the health of which so closely shapes that of his realm, to 'those physicians that first wounded thee.' Finally, a further elaborate image identifies the royal state with that of the country of which the king is the indispensable head:

> A thousand flatterers sit within thy crown,
> Whose compass is no bigger than thy head;
> And yet, incaged in so small a verge,
> The waste is no whit lesser than thy land.   (II. i)

The crown is at once diminished to the unworthiness of its wearer and expanded in identity with the realm of whose unity it is both symbol and guarantee; whilst the disease which Gaunt on his deathbed sees concentrated in the royal person before him is at the same time a symptom of the corruption of order and rule in the body politic.

Gaunt's closing words, besides stressing his own weakness and the approaching death of the order which survives in him, return, by way of contrast, to the theme of the true kingship represented by his father which Richard, by his part in Gloucester's death, has helped to undermine. As usual on the introduction of this subject, the expression is heightened to a note of sombre fatality:

> O spare me not, my brother Edward's son,
> For that I was his father Edward's son;
> That blood already, like the pelican,
> Hast thou tapp'd out and drunkenly caroused.

The repetition of 'brother Edward's son' and 'father Edward's son,' backed by the strong choric rhythm, takes us back in style to the *Henry VI* plays and is, indeed, conceived with a similar sense of doom. An older and more worthy order is dying with Gaunt. That order was associated with the rule of Edward, the spilt blood of whose son is given a religious significance by the reference to the sacrifice of the 'pelican'; set against this sacramental implication, in terms of drunken carousing, is the spirit of Richard's rule, the substitution of his empty subtleties and those of his favourites for the direct honesty of Gloucester, 'plain well-meaning soul.' The spilling of 'Edward's blood' has been, in fact, an act of sacrilege, whose consequences outreach even murder and involve both the unworthy king and his realm in a single adverse fatality.

Richard's reaction to this denunciation confirms the moody, contradictory facets of his nature. These have already expressed themselves, in Gaunt's presence, through the sultry petulance of 'lunatic lean-witted fool,' and are now further confirmed by the outburst which follows his departure:

> let them die that age and sullens have;
> For both hast thou, and both become the grave.

Immediately afterwards, however, this bitterness is seen to imply an intimate recognition of his own state and of the baseless fiction of loyalty which surrounds him. When York seeks to turn his anger by affirming Gaunt's love for him, comparing that love, with unconscious irony, to that professed by Bolingbroke, Richard's reply penetrates for a moment to an anticipation of his own future:

> Right, you say true: as Hereford's love, so his;
> As theirs, so mine; and all be as it is.

This mood of disillusioned fatalism, in which insight and a touch of self-indulgence are so typically mingled, is essential to Richard's nature.

It is one more sign that the character is emerging in its own right, taking its place in what is coming to be no longer a conventional presentation of chronicle events but the analysis of a situation full of contradictory possibilities. From the point of view of the complete conception, this is perhaps the most important statement so far achieved. Richard himself participates in the pathos which marks the death of the order which his own acts are in the process of overthrowing and in which he feels his own fate involved:

> The ripest fruit first falls, and so doth he;
> His time is spent, our pilgrimage must be.

But, as the facile rhythm indicates, the sentiment is turned to a purpose finally cynical, to be dismissed as such by the brief 'So much for that' which follows. To set an incipient note of tragic disillusionment side by side with the puerile callousness which prompts Richard, in the very shadow of Gaunt's death, to seize his revenues, is to respond to a character and a situation which are growing in close relationship to the exposition of their full reality.

Richard's growing instability is followed immediately by a notable change in the attitude of those who have so far professed allegiance to him: a change which amply confirms his sense that the ground he treads is hollow. In York's defence of Bolingbroke's rights, traditional feudal ideas merge almost imperceptibly into the defence of selfish interests. On the one hand, the claim of lineage, the rights of normal inheritance, are being defended by 'the last of noble Edward's sons'; on the other, a world of covetousness and mutual distrust is already feeling its way towards the overthrow of legitimate authority. Bolingbroke, so York argues, is Gaunt's son, and the hereditary principle which should render his property untouchable is one on which the crown itself also rests:

> for how art thou a king
> But by fair sequence and succession?

To insist on confiscation would be, in terms of expediency, to 'lose a thousand well-disposed hearts' and to inspire in York himself

> those thoughts
> Which honour and allegiance cannot think.

What is in York indecision, a clash of loyalties, is soon seen to involve in others a more direct awareness of threatened interests. After Richard has left, Northumberland adopts a tone which will be associated with his name in the following plays; the king is 'not himself,' and the envious counsels of his flatterers will translate themselves into acts ' 'Gainst us, our lives, our children, and our heirs.' The true implications of the rivalries with which the play opened are now emerging in their double nature. If the disintegration of loyalty proceeds from the unworthiness of its royal fountainhead, it is none the less in the form of unwarrantable resentment, the maintenance of selfish positions, that it extends itself.

Disintegration, indeed, is the final impression left by this scene with which the first stage of the play draws to a close. In the mounting indignation of the nobles we may see reflected the breaking unity of the English state. The episode ends, significantly, after Northumberland's remarkable phrase,

> even through the hollow eyes of death
> I spy life peering,

with the announcement of Bolingbroke's return. The action is now embarked upon the dual course which it will follow to the end of the play. The return of Lancaster, as he will from now on call himself, is simultaneously a necessity, if the foundations of order are to be restored upon the firm, conscious exercise of authority, and an expression of rebellious selfishness, defeating its own purposes by the unnatural nature of its claim. The contradiction thus indicated between means and ends, between Lancaster's desires and the manner in which he usurps the crown, will dominate the following history.

II

From this moment to the first, and crucial, encounter between Richard and Bolingbroke, the scope of the play is narrowed to a conflict of personalities. The tragic impotence of the king is balanced by the purposeful advance of his rival towards the ends he has proposed to himself. The exchange between the Queen and Richard's favourites (II. ii) uses typically 'conceited' language to introduce the peculiar melancholy which, after Gaunt's death, surrounds the king. To the Queen's foreboding, her sense of the imminence of 'some unborn sorrow, ripe in fortune's womb,' Bushy offers an intricate 'philosophic' consolation, which is at once conventional and analytic, empty, and, almost in spite of itself, descriptive:

> Each substance of a grief hath twenty shadows,
> Which shows like grief itself, but is not so;
> For sorrow's eye, glazed with blinding tears,
> Divides one thing entire to many objects;

> Like perspectives, which rightly gazed upon
> Show nothing but confusion, eyed awry
> Distinguish form: so your sweet majesty,
> Looking awry upon your lord's departure,
> Finds shape of grief, more than himself, to wail;
> Which, look'd on as it is, is nought but shadows
> Of what is not.   (ii. ii)

A first estimate of this passage will probably stress the elements in its expression which are least real, most intolerably artificial. There is, however, more than this to be said. First, and most obviously, the artifice is that of a courtier, professionally dedicated to flattery and expert in pursuing indirect paths to conviction; second, the elementary distinction between the 'substance' of grief and its 'shadow' becomes, in the expression, something more intricate, more closely connected with the melancholy, half real and half artificial, which accompanies Richard throughout his tragedy. The 'substance' of grief is attended by multiple 'shadows,' just as the effect of tears is to split the unity of vision into 'many objects,' each a partial reflection of the original whole; and the value placed upon the vision thus constituted is a matter of 'perspective,' of gazing 'rightly' or 'awry' to distinguish—by a paradox implicit in the deceptive nature of things—either true chaos or the illusory appearance of 'form.' In this way, flattery and the scepticism which so persistently emerges from Richard's words are gathered into a single ambiguous utterance which corresponds to the present reality of his state.[8]

After this brief interlude the action at once returns to the onward march of events. The news of desertion and flight, remorselessly pressed, turns the 'shadow' of grief most brutally into its substance. Northumberland, Percy, and Worcester desert the king's declining cause, and the Duchess of Gloucester, relic of a happier and more simple age, dies; York alone is left poised in indecision, unwilling to betray but unable to devote convinced loyalty to a cause that he already judges to be beyond hope:

> what a tide of woes
> Comes rushing on this woeful land at once!
>
> . . . .
>
> I should to Plashy too;
> But time will not permit: all is uneven,
> And everything is left at six and seven.   (ii. ii)

---

[8] It is interesting to compare the use of metaphor in this speech with that, notably similar, in the early political scenes of *2 Henry IV*. See pp. 109 ff. below.

The apparent crudity of the style should not blind us to the effort, elementary as it is, to make words and rhythms follow the movements of
thought and feeling in their confused state. 'Time will not permit' either
indecision or the very disloyalty which reason urges against conscience;
on a note of disorder and despair, itself the reflection of Richard's own
state both as tragic individual and unworthy king, the scene ends, having
prepared the way for Bolingbroke's return.

That return reveals by contrast (ii. iii) a nature aware of its ends
and clear-sighted in its acceptance of the means to obtain them. To the
flattery implied in Northumberland's commendation of his 'fair dis-
course' which has made 'the hard way sweet and delectable,' Lancaster
replies with blunt brevity:

> Of much less value is my company
> Than your good words.

This is indeed a different figure from the Bolingbroke of the early dispute
with Mowbray, a figure who has stepped out of the conventional frame
of 'aristocratic' poetry and is in process of becoming the political leader
whose unerring instinct for the practical will contrast so decisively with
that of the king he is about to overthrow. It is as if Bolingbroke had been
up to now a figure subdued to the decorative splendour of his rival's
court and so less than perfectly himself; from the moment of his return,
released from the glamour that surrounds Richard as anointed king, he
will take the direction of affairs into his own capable hands and seize
the crown at which he already aims.

His progress towards his goal is as cautious as it is sure. For the
moment, his ends are wrapped in cultivated courtesy and in the carefully
worded expressions of gratitude with which each of the defecting courtiers is successively greeted. Percy, still too young to participate in the
intrigues of his elders, too young even to remember having seen Bolingbroke before his exile, is greeted with effusive thanks and an indication,
tactfully worded, of recompense to come:

> And as my fortune ripens with thy love,
> It shall be still thy true love's recompense.

The speaker is careful to lay emphasis upon the dependence of his future
'fortunes' on the 'love' of those who have come to greet him, at the same
time as he suggests—almost in a tone of self-depreciation—that the 'fortune' so achieved will in due course bear fruit in compensating graces.
Percy's offer of service is, of course, steeped in an unconscious irony
which looks forward to the future:

> My gracious lord, I tender you my service,
> Such as it is, being tender, raw, and young;
> Which elder days shall ripen and confirm
> To more approved service and desert.[9]

The 'nature' of this 'ripening' and of the 'service' here promised will be made clear at Shrewsbury when Hotspur, grown to a mature warrior, will not be Henry's 'servant' but the most redoubtable of his enemies.

To make himself dependent in appearance whilst in reality reaching out to the exercise of authority is, at this stage, Bolingbroke's secret; and his deferent attitude to Ross and Willoughby, who follow Percy in their offer of allegiance, confirms this. Even the senile, indecisive indignation of York is met with a calculated reasonableness, a judicious appeal to family sentiment:

> You are my father, for methinks in you
> I see old Gaunt alive.

The effect of this approach upon York, who has already in his heart chosen the path of betrayal, is immediate. 'I have had feeling of my cousin's wrongs'—the family relationship is once more stressed before he confesses his helplessness,

> I cannot mend it, I must needs confess,
> Because my power is weak,

and sanctions his defection after his own manner by declaring himself 'neuter.' Bolingbroke's suave reply, 'we must win your grace to go with us,' already indicates that such neutrality is impossible. In the spirit which here increasingly prevails, scruple divorced from action is no more than a confession of incapacity to influence the course of events; and York fittingly ends the scene on a note of sententious fatality: 'Things past redress are now with me past care.'

The short episodes which follow reflect further the disintegration of Richard's authority and the ruthlessness of Bolingbroke's march to power. The desertion of the Welsh forces (ii. iv) is greeted by Salisbury with a reference to the setting sun which, from now onward, is increasingly associated with Richard's declining royalty:

> Thy sun sets weeping in the lowly west,
> Witnessing storms to come, woe and unrest.

---

[9] It is worth noting that Hotspur will recall this episode on the eve of embarking on rebellion. See *I Henry IV*, i. iii, and p. 62 below.

Opposed to this tendency is the indictment of Bushy and Green (III. i) in confirming which Henry reveals aspects of his nature which will reappear, as part of the family character, in the plays to follow. In his separation of spiritual and political responsibilities:

> Bushy and Green, I will not vex your souls,
> Since presently your souls must part your bodies,

Bolingbroke is already the father of Henry V; solicitude in the spiritual order can exist side by side with the inflexible execution of justice, but the one must not interfere with the practical necessities of the other. These necessities, moreover, make it expedient that the sentence should be justified before it is carried out:

> to wash your blood
> From off my hands, here in the view of men
> I will unfold some causes of your deaths.

That in this particular case Henry is an instrument of justice is not to be doubted; but the anxiety to seek public justification for his necessary ruthlessness will be passed on by him to his son and may well, on future occasions, find more dubious causes on which to exercise itself. For the moment, the inflexible final command—'My Lord Northumberland, see them dispatch'd'—is immediately, and significantly, followed by an expedient gesture of consideration to Richard's queen ('Take special care my greetings be deliver'd') and by the practical aphorism which brings the scene to a close: 'Awhile to work, and after holiday.'

It is no accident that this blunt dedication to the purpose in hand is followed (III. ii) by the reappearance of Richard. His first speech, in reply to Aumerle's welcome on the coast of Wales, points already to a significant contrast. The sentiments flow easily, not to say with facility, into poetic forms at once powerful enough to move and superficial, conventional enough, to induce a suspension of complete acceptance. 'I weep for joy' are his first words on returning to his kingdom; they are followed by an elaborate personification of inanimate nature, by which the hoofs of rebel horses 'wound' the 'dear earth,' his restoration to which becomes in turn, by a further extension of fancy, the reunion of 'a long-parted mother with her child' who 'plays fondly with her tears and smiles in meeting.' The tears and smiles are, of course, those of Richard himself, who at once expresses tragic feeling and plays with his emotions, 'weeping, smiling' as he greets the land which, even as it inspires him to genuine love, is the occasion for a display of self-conscious sentiment. The importance of this lies, as we have said, in the growing subjection of poetic feeling to a presentation of character. The judgement which Richard's words prompt in us is not, indeed, to be simply made. After Bolingbroke's practical coldness, we shall find attractive and human the ability to express feeling; but the suggestion of convention and the very ease with which feeling flows point to a limitation, indicate a character too ready to exploit his own emotions, to live with a certain complacency at the centre of a tragic situation which his own weakness, practical incompetence, and a kind of unconscious cynicism have brought into being. As usual in Shakespeare, here perhaps nearer his mature self than he had yet been, the weight of judgement and sympathy needs to be evenly distributed. The truth, if such we are to call it, lies not in any one point or person, but in a balance of contrasts which we, as spectators, are intended to maintain.

This characteristic ambivalence is stressed in the later part of Richard's speech, where his references to his enemies are, beneath their conventional quality, charged with potential hysteria. By so elaborately invoking 'spiders' and 'heavy-gaited toads,' 'stinging nettles' and 'lurking adders,' Richard reduces tragedy to melodrama; what in one of the earlier chronicle plays would have been a sign of poetic inadequacy, of undue reliance upon conventional sensationalism, is in the process of becoming a revelation of character which the contrast with Bolingbroke will qualify, set in its true light. Beneath the artifice and the pathos alike, we feel the speaker's distraught and essentially morbid, febrile imagination, which is as much part of his nature as the ability to respond with tragic dignity to his situation as a betrayed king. His emotions, indeed, may be said to have an unconsicous as well as a conscious content; and this gives the character, beneath its conventionality and its public significance, a depth and complexity perhaps greater than those of any other figure drawn by Shakespeare at this stage in his dramatic development.

The weaknesses thus indicated in Richard amount, in terms of action, to an incapacity in the face of practical necessity which the words of his followers at once underline. The Bishop of Carlisle, whilst echoing the doctrine of divine kingship which Richard, not without a touch of complacency, has made his own, adds an indication to the effect that God helps those who help themselves,

> The means that heaven yields must be embraced,
> And not neglected;

which is supported by Aumerle's even blunter statement: 'He means, my lord, that we are too remiss.' Richard takes up the assurance whilst neglecting the warning. Assuming the conception of divine vocation, which is by right his, he turns it into a poetic image of the sun rising and putting to flight the accumulated shadows of night; but the summons to action is laid aside. The affirmation of divine sanction is indeed moving, more so perhaps than Richard himself as king can be:

> Not all the water in the rough rude sea
> Can wash the balm off from an anointed king.

To fail to give due weight to this assertion is to misinterpret the nature of Bolingbroke's crime, which is not merely personal treachery and murder but the overthrow of an order divinely sanctioned in the name of inordinate ambition. Yet, in the light of the consistent presentation of the royal character, there is more than this to be said. The king who thus places his trust in the divine protection is he who has been involved in Gloucester's death and who has 'farmed out' his realm to pay for the extravagances of his favourites; he is also the Richard who, in the sphere of practical politics, can seek in a telling phrase the substitute for action and who will shortly find, when confronted with the rise of a new political force, that verbal felicity, even when allied to abstract right, is not enough.

The fall from exaltation, indeed, comes with dramatic rapidity. It is consistently presented in terms of character, a swing from the preceding confidence to the broken directness of 'Have I not reason to look pale and dead?' From this moment such reaction as takes place is partial and rhetorical—

> I had forgot myself: am I not king?

—whilst the predisposition to pessimism is constant and the receiving of Scroop's further instalment of bad news takes place even before the news is uttered:

> Say, is my kingdom lost? why, 'twas my care;
> And what loss is it to be rid of care?
>
> . . . .
>
> Cry woe, destruction, ruin and decay;
> The worst is death, and death will have his day.

The verbal consolation, so facile and typical of Richard in his moments of trial, passes into a vision of universal chaos which is itself a hysterical evasion of the truth. When the news itself has been uttered, the expression of Richard's overwrought emotion is set against the hard, direct tone of the references to Bolingbroke's return,

> covering your fearful land
> With *hard bright steel* and hearts *harder than steel*.

Against this, even the assertion of legitimate royalty loses force in the practical order, and the collapse releases, not for the first time, sub-conscious images of hysteria. 'Vipers,' 'dogs,' and 'snakes' are the means through which Richard's helpless loathing is expressed; but this time, in direct contact with adversity, they are further associated with a sense of betrayal allied to expressly religious symbols. The 'snakes' are in his 'heart-blood warm'd,' the traitors 'Three Judases, each one thrice worse than Judas' who, in making—as Richard believes—their peace with his rival, have condemned their souls to destruction. The effect is once more simultaneously one of hysteria, emotional excess, and of true tragedy; of an inadequate king failing to respond to his situation and of the sacred institution of monarchy betrayed in the perverse following of self-interest.

These outbursts lead finally, in the culminating speech of the scene, to a full expression of despair. As always, a certain conventionality per-sists in the tone of Richard's lament, but can be felt in the process of giving way to a stronger current of emotion:

> let us sit upon the ground
> And tell sad stories of the death of kings:
> How some have been deposed; some slain in war;
> Some haunted by the ghosts they have deposed;
> Some poison'd by their wives; some sleeping kill'd;
> All murder'd. (III. ii)

Basically, of course, this is a traditional catalogue of the misfortunes that, by the compensating action of the wheel of Fortune, accompany the exaltation of royalty. The examples are familiar, even commonplace, but in the flow of the expression, the rise of the voice to the longer period in 'Some haunted by the ghosts they have deposed,' and the fall to 'All murder'd,' we find conveyed simultaneously a true tragic sense, a notion of the insignificance which surrounds the pomp of royalty, and this par-ticular speaker's capacity to dwell on his own tragedy, exacting from his plight a sad refinement of sensation. The effect, indeed, is, beneath its obvious precedents, one of some complexity. Richard, true to character, at once expresses his tragedy through the application to his own case of accepted commonplaces (which live more than conventionally in the expression) and finds a certain emotional gratification in contemplating his state; so that it is not surprising that the speech, after the grave beauty to which it rises in the contemplation of the vicissitudes of royalty, falls away into hysteria and self-pity:

> Cover your heads and mock not flesh and blood
> With solemn reverence: throw away respect,
> Tradition, form and ceremonious duty,
> For you have but mistook me all this while:
> I live with bread like you, feel want,
> Taste grief, need friends: subjected thus,
> How can you say to me, I am a king?   (III. ii)

The appeal in the opening phrases is still to the traditional sanctions that accompany the royal office, to the 'reverence,' 'form,' and ceremony that surround a legitimate king; but it is at the same time an appeal theatrically conceived, a turning of tragedy to self-exhibition which at once attains, in the broken rhythms of the final lines, a real pathos and covers a weak man's resentment at what are, for him, the incomprehensible turns of fate.

It is finally on the weakness that Carlisle insists when, as Richard ceases to speak, he utters his practical rejoinder:

> My lord, wise men ne'er sit and wail their woes,
> But presently prevent the ways to wail.

It is notable though that even here the emphasis is rather on the acceptance of death than on any true reason for hope:

> Fear, and be slain; no worse can come to fight:
> And fight and die is death destroying death;
> When fearing dying pays death servile breath.

The elaboration here has its roots in emotions which Shakespeare's mature work will develop. If this be consolation at all, it is rather in embryo the self-deceiving comfort of Macbeth than a source of true encouragement. It fits the mood in Richard against which it seeks to react, producing first a facile recovery—'An easy task it is to win our own'—and finally, when Scroop brings the news of York's betrayal, an equally facile plunge into despair:

> Beshrew thee, cousin, which didst lead me forth
> Of that *sweet way* I was in to despair!

To the last, Richard's expressions are loaded with memories of tragic effects too easily obtained by lesser writers in their plays; but the facility, besides surpassing itself at the best moments to achieve a genuine sense of tragedy, is at the same time a revelation of weakness. The capacity, even at this early stage, to associate detachment and tragic intensity in a personal development of conventional means of expression is possibly the most individual aspect of the play.

The scene which at last brings Richard and his rival face to face (III. iii) is conceived with a remarkable sense of the dramatic possibilities of contrasted character. From the first, the hard clear tone of Bolingbroke's dispositions, concentrated exclusively on the definition of facts, is opposed to the elaborate play on sentiment that belongs naturally to Richard. The background to this contrast is, appropriately enough, the cynical attitude of the courtiers who have deserted their former allegiance to rally to the new power; there is a wealth of meaning behind Northumberland's brief reply to York's protest against the omission of the royal title:

> Your grace mistakes; only to be brief,
> Left I his title out.

Both Richard and York himself are, by implication, here dismissed: Richard because he has shown himself unable to hold power, in a world where only power counts, and York because, having deserted his master, he is unwilling to lay aside entirely the memory of his former respect. Bolingbroke is neither deceived by the flatterers of the new power nor impressed by those who hesitate between their former and their new allegiance. When York reminds him of the continuing jurisdiction of the 'heavens,' his reply is both a gesture of acceptance to principles which, ready as he is to pay lip-service to them, are in his world finally irrelevant and, by implication, an expression of contempt for those who can neither renounce the desire for power nor devote themselves wholeheartedly to obtaining it:

> I know it, uncle, and oppose not myself
> Against their will.

The conventional gesture to the established moral sanctions, which only interest him in so far as they further his political ends, introduces a feature that Bolingbroke will show throughout his career and hand on, in some degree, to his son.

After this introduction, the iron tone of the following challenge confirms the entry into the action of a new, decisive power. The 'brazen trumpet' of Bolingbroke's messenger sends 'the breath of parley' into the 'ruin'd ears' of Richard, pitifully sheltered in the 'rude ribs' of his ancient castle. Henry, even in the act of asserting the reality of his power, maintains the form of allegiance. He maintains it, however, *provided* that he is restored to his former position. 'If not,'

> I'll use the advantage of my power
> And lay the summer's dust with showers of blood
> Rain'd from the wounds of slaughter'd Englishmen.

For all the artificiality of the comparison, these words anticipate the events to follow. These 'showers of blood' will follow Bolingbroke to the end of his reign; and his tone here, combining menace with a disclaimer of responsibility, is that which Henry V will adopt before the citizens of Harfleur.[10] The forms of service conceal the realities of domination, and the 'tender' show of 'stooping duty' is stressed almost subserviently to cover the bare grasping of power that underlies it. All this, however, is no more than appearance. 'Be he' (Richard) 'the fire, I'll be the yielding water'; the suggestion of compliance covers a real inflexibility of aim, and the 'raging fire' turns out to be a hectic flame doomed to extinction. Henry's true attitude, astute and severely practical, is conveyed in the injunction—'March on, and mark King Richard how he looks'—which immediately precedes his challenge.

Richard's appearance on the battlements is marked by a change in poetic tone which, once again, cannot be less than deliberate. Bolingbroke himself, as he takes up the sun image so frequently linked with royalty in this play, confirms it. He compares Richard's advent to that of the sun rising from 'the fiery portal of the east' in a glory which is, however, 'blushing discontented,' prelude to a passage which, 'bright' though it be, is to its setting in 'the occident.' York's comment equally confirms the sense of majesty in decay. 'Yet *looks he* like a king,' he says, conscious of the gap that already separates appearance from reality; and again:

> alack, alack, for woe,
> That any harm should stain so fair a show!

It is precisely this 'stain,' this 'harm,' that is about to be represented, the reality beneath this 'show' that is to be brutally revealed.

In the situation thus carefully prepared, Richard's assertion of the divine foundation of his authority cannot be, immediately, other than empty, devoid of practical reality. Only after his fall has been consummated will his fate appear as the universal tragedy, the reversal of true order, that his own words have, albeit hysterically, evoked. The call to allegiance is a gesture which, even as he makes it, Richard knows to be vain; although, vain as it is, it is backed by the dignity of anointed royalty

---

[10] *Henry V*, III. iii. See pp. 182–83 below.

and touches, as it looks forward to the future, upon a main theme of the entire action:

> Tell Bolingbroke—for yond methinks he stands—
> That every stride he makes upon my land
> Is dangerous treason: he is come to open
> The purple testament of bleeding war;
> But ere the crown he looks for live in peace,
> Ten thousand bloody crowns of mothers' sons
> Shall ill become the flower of England's face.   (III. iii)

The realities of civil war will be more immediately, less poetically evoked, in the plays to follow; but the stress laid on this warning, at this decisive moment in Richard's fortunes, confirms the close unity of conception that animates the entire series.

The following exchange between Richard and Northumberland carries on the use of poetic convention for increasingly subtle dramatic ends. Northumberland, bringing what is in effect his master's ultimatum, covers it in a wealth of stylistic affectation that announces its own emptiness, points to the worthless nature of the final offer of 'faithful service.' Richard, on his side, is perfectly aware of his situation. To Bolingbroke's offer to pay allegiance if his demands are satisfied, an offer presented in terms of the values of feudal loyalty—

> Thus swears he, as he is a prince, is just;

and confirmed by Northumberland in a phrase that has a touch of irony,

> And, as I am a gentleman, I credit him

—he replies with assumed meekness; but, even as he speaks, he knows that reality is undermining the content of his words:

> We do debase ourselves, cousin, do we not,
> To look so poorly and to speak so fair?

and the realization inspires him for a moment to a vain project of defiance which, as he is well aware, can only end in death. Aumerle alone, who sees Richard's surrender as a means of gaining time, shows some sense of political reality:

> let's fight with gentle words,
> Till time lend friends and friends their helpful swords.

Even this suggested stratagem, however, is finally nullified by Richard's own sense that the flow of events, derived from his own weakness, is leading inexorably to a tragic conclusion:

> O God, O God! that e'er this tongue of mine,
> That laid the sentence of dread banishment
> On yon proud man, should take it off again
> With words of sooth! O that I were as great
> As is my grief, or lesser than my name!
> Or that I could forget what I have been,
> Or not remember what I must be now!   (III. iii)

Here, at least, the utterance is simple, direct enough to pass beyond artifice and pretence to penetrate to the true extent of a royal tragedy.

More typically, however, Richard's sense that the revocation of his original judgement will undo him expresses itself in what he knows to be, even as he speaks, 'idle talk.' This is apparent in the elaborate self-exhibition of 'What must the king do now? must he submit?'

> I'll give my jewels for a set of beads,
> My gorgeous palace for a hermitage,
> My gay apparel for an almsman's gown,
> My figured goblets for a dish of wood,
> My sceptre for a palmer's walking staff,
> My subjects for a pair of carved saints,
> And my large kingdom for a little grave,
> A little little grave, an obscure grave;
> Or I'll be buried in the king's highway,
> Some way of common trade, where subjects' feet
> May hourly trample on their sovereign's head;
> For on my heart they tread now whilst I live;
> And buried once, why not upon my head?   (III. iii)

In these lines, and in those which follow, artifice, weakness, and pathos are variously interwoven. It is interesting to compare the spirit of this utterance with that, partially similar, of Henry VI's nostalgia for the simple life when faced with the horrors of civil war.[11] The artificial construction is parallel, but is put to ends substantially different; for in Richard, far more than in Henry, it is a kind of pathetic self-pity, as much the exhibition of sorrow as grief itself, that prevails. The words combine poetry, still in a conventional mould, with a firm sense of character. This is not merely the utterance of a defeated king, but of one particular dramatic figure in whom self-contemplation and pathos are strangely joined in the consideration of defeat. Knowing that he is lost, Richard exploits his doom self-consciously; but his artifice is at once moving, as related to a royal tragedy, and sufficiently realized in terms

[11] *3 Henry VI*, II. v.

of character to evoke that pity which only the emotions of a person can give. For Richard, even as he 'plays the wanton' with his woes, is aware that this is precisely what he is doing:

> Would not this ill do well? Well, well, I see
> I talk but idly, and you laugh at me.

The speaker's feeling, precisely by being aware of its artificiality, becomes more real than that of Henry VI, less confined to the literary order—in which, however, it has its origins—and more capable of arousing pity.

The end of this episode confirms the situation of its central figures by giving them external projection. Brought back to reality by Northumberland's blunt request 'may it please you to come down,' Richard takes up the sun image already applied to him by Bolingbroke:

> Down, down I come; like glistering Phaethon.

The image adds to the presentation of an individual tragedy the universal implication proper to the ruin of a king. The meeting with Bolingbroke, which follows, brings power, still cloaked in the appearance of loyalty, face to face with helplessness, with what Northumberland, with characteristic cruelty, calls the fondness of a 'frantic man.' Henry, kneeling with external deference to his 'gracious lord,' calls on his followers to 'show fair duty to his majesty.' Richard, not content to respond to these signs of courtesy, penetrates more directly to the bare facts of his situation:

> Up, cousin, up; your heart is up, I know,
> Thus high at least, although your knee be low.

To the newcomer's realistic 'I come but for mine own,' he replies with a realism still more direct, 'Your own is yours, and I am yours, and all,' to follow it, most realistically of all, with his rejoinder to Bolingbroke's empty offer of service:

> Well you deserve: they well deserve to have,
> That know the strong'st and surest way to get.

The distance travelled by Richard since the early scenes of courtly pageantry is never more apparent than at the moment of pronouncing this phrase, in which his personal tragedy is seen as the foundation for the political development to follow.

III

From the moment of Richard's descent, 'like glistering Phaethon,' into the 'base court' his fate is substantially sealed. The last part of the play confirms his fall, investing it with the tragic quality that surrounds the misfortunes of an anointed king, and consummates the ruthless process of his rival's rise to power. After the short scene (III. iv), conveying the Queen's meeting with her Gardeners, which clearly answers to a certain 'symbolic' design, using an elaborately prolonged metaphor to underline the relationship between Richard's tragedy and the disorder of his realm, the return to the main action (IV. i) is marked by a further access of realism, the fitting accompaniment of the new power. The quarrel between the lords, occasioned by Bagot's accusation of Aumerle for his part in Gloucester's death, is both elaborate in expression and detached, realistic in presentation. Aumerle, in spite of his defiance, is aware of weakness; the lords who turn against him, invoking 'truth' and 'honour,' already have an eye to their future good. On either side, the expression is overpitched, strained as though conscious of its own falsity; the ringing rhetoric—in which an echo, as it were, of the opening scenes can still be detected—turns into a shabby interchange of snarl and countersnarl which only Bolingbroke is detached enough to watch without illusion. When he intervenes, with a pacifying gesture to insinuate Mowbray's return, it is left to Carlisle to evoke the values implied in his former rival's crusading venture and—at the same time—to announce the crusader's death. The counterpart of his announcement, valid in the present, is York's proclamation of Bolingbroke as king, briefly accepted by the latter with his 'In God's name, I'll ascend the regal throne.'

The proclamation is immediately followed, in accordance with the main design, by Carlisle's assertion of Richard's divine right, and by his prophecy which looks forward to a future of civil war:

> And if you crown him, let me prophesy:
> The blood of English shall manure the ground,
> And future ages groan for this foul act;
> Peace shall go sleep with Turks and infidels,
> And in this seat of peace tumultuous wars
> Shall kin with kin and kind with kind confound;
> Disorder, horror, fear and mutiny
> Shall here inhabit, and this land be call'd
> The field of Golgotha, and dead men's skulls.   (IV. i)

The speech presents a community of style with the patriotic utterances of Gaunt, and the culminating reference to Golgotha will shortly be echoed by Richard himself. Its careful elaboration is intended to stand out against the blunt realism of Bolingbroke, here triumphant in the very process of creating for itself the cause of future tragedy. That realism, meanwhile, takes control in Northumberland's sharp comment,

> Well have you argued, sir; and, for your pains,
> Of capital treason we arrest you here,

which Henry caps by summoning Richard himself and by pointing openly to the political ground of his whole proceeding:

> Fetch hither Richard, that in common view
> He may surrender; *so we shall proceed*
> *Without suspicion.*

Finally, Henry's realistic estimate of his position is made clear in his sharp admonition to the arrested lords:

> Little are we beholding to your love,
> And little look'd for at your helping hands.

From the first moment, the new king is shrewdly aware of the unsure foundations upon which his power rests.

The entry of Richard, stressing the note of treachery supremely associated, not for the first time,[12] with the evocation of Judas, is characteristically poised between pathos and emptiness. His situation is genuinely pathetic, and the emotion stands out, up to a point, against the cold purposefulness that surrounds him; yet it is impossible not to feel that the comparison of the crown to a deep well in which two buckets alternately rise and fall is too shallow to carry the weight of feeling which the speaker desires to lay upon it. It is no accident that Richard's elaborate renunciation of rights already surrendered is set against his rival's plain insistence on the end in view:

> I thought you had been willing to resign.
> . . . .
> Are you contented to resign the crown?

In Richard's attitude, complex and contradictory by comparison, the germs of many later Shakespearean developments can be discerned. Pathetic and yet too self-conscious to be entirely tragic, sincere and yet engaged in acting his own sincerity, possessed of true feeling and elaborately artificial in expressing it, Richard is the distant predecessor of more than one hero of the mature tragedies, who suffer in acute self-consciousness and whose tragedy expresses itself in terms that clearly point to the presence of the weakness that has been, in part, its cause.

---

[12] See *Richard II*, iii. ii, and p. 32 above.

The utterances of the deposed king turn, indeed, not merely on natural grief, but on a sense of vanity—*nothingness*—which the very artificiality of its expression confirms and, paradoxically, deepens:

> Ay, no; no, ay; for I must *nothing* be;
> . . . .
> Make me, that *nothing* have, with *nothing* grieved,
> And thou with all pleased, that hast all achieved!
> Long mayst thou live in Richard's seat to sit,
> And soon lie Richard in an earthy pit!   (IV. i)

We must feel here that the word nearest to the speaker's heart is, after all his elaborations, *nothing*, and that his mood issues in an intense craving for death; but the nothingness—it must be added—is also reflected, in the last analysis, in Bolingbroke's absorbing pursuit of power. Richard's attitude to political responsibility is, of course, extreme, in a sense self-indulgent; but it is also relevant, and not least to the usurper who is now, with little but devices of policy in his mind, replacing him on the throne. *Nothing, nothing*: in the long run any relevant political conception will have to face the challenge implied in that word, and confirmed by the behaviour shown in this play. As we read these elaborate expressions of feeling, we realize that the intricate rhetorical devices of the earlier plays and of Shakespeare's contemporaries are in the process of being turned, definitely though still without complete consciousness, into an instrument for the simultaneous expression of different aspects of reality.

The accusation of Richard by Northumberland, which now follows, emphasizes the royal tragedy rather than the personal disaster. Having abdicated, he has drawn upon himself sympathy; isolated and helpless, he appears less as the self-indulgent monarch than as the victim of a betrayal which his failings cannot excuse. To his final, exhausted 'What more remains?' there corresponds, however, not pity, but the remorseless persecution of the accusation against him:

> No more, but that you read
> These accusations and these grievous crimes,

followed by an admission that the real end of this proceeding is to justify the usurper in the eyes of the world:

> That, by confessing them, the souls of men
> May deem that you are worthily deposed.

Surrounded by this ruthless calculation, Richard's weakness becomes subsidiary to his tragedy as king deposed; his reply to Northumberland raises to a fresh level of poignancy the Christian reference which, more especially from now on, runs as a principal thread of feeling through the tragedy:

> Nay, all of you that stand and look upon,
> Whilst that my wretchedness doth bait myself,
> Though some of you with Pilate wash your hands
> Showing an outward pity; yet you Pilates
> Have here deliver'd me to my sour cross,
> And water cannot wash away your sin.   (IV. i)

Our reaction to this is necessarily double. Richard is still exhibiting his emotions, playing with feelings the seriousness of which we cannot, in view of his weaknesses and consequent responsibility for his state, fully accept; and yet the betrayal, based on the calculation that everywhere surrounds him, is indefensible and its effect deepened by the fact that it is a king whom his subjects, sworn to loyalty, are deserting.

Richard himself is not without insight in his misfortunes. When he says, in reply to Northumberland's pitiless 'My lord, dispatch; read o'er these articles,'

> Mine eyes are full of tears, I cannot see:
> And yet salt water blinds them not so much
> But they can see a sort of traitors here,

the play with images cannot cover the fact that a truth is being expressed. It is the tragedy of betrayal, as well as that of fallen royalty, that is being enacted round his person; and the treachery, moreover, is doubly personal because Richard, by his past irresponsibility, has betrayed himself before he was in turn betrayed:

> Nay, if I turn mine eyes upon myself,
> I find myself a traitor with the rest.

Richard has betrayed the office which he has unworthily held, and the betrayal has bred treachery around him. Bolingbroke, in due course, will prove to be similarly divided between the political virtues that are his to a degree never possessed by Richard, and a desire for power which is ominously shared by the court of time-serving and ambitious lords who accompany his rise to authority. The conception, in all its possible variety, is only sketched and faintly indicated here; but the whole series of following plays will be largely occupied with exploring it.

Beneath the conventionality of Richard's expression at this stage lies, indeed, a genuine effort to define his relation to the tragic course of events. This culminates in his request for a looking-glass, in which once more artificiality, conscious self-exhibition, and true self-exploration are typically blended. Henry, now secure master of the situation, contemptuously accedes to the latest emotional trick of his victim, whilst Northumberland, as ever, ruthlessly presses the charge:

> Read o'er this paper while the glass doth come,

and stresses the political motive behind his disapproval of his master's careless concession:

> The commons will not then be satisfied.

When the mirror is at last brought, Richard contemplates his features with a kind of tragic self-analysis. This opens, as he breaks the glass, in a typically artificial statement: 'How soon my sorrow hath destroy'd my face'; but the comment offered by Bolingbroke points to a deeper contrast between shadow and reality, which is not without tragic content:

> The shadow of your sorrow hath destroy'd
> The shadow of your face.

This in turn produces from Richard, beyond the play on the related concepts of 'shadow,' 'sun,' and 'substance,' an indication of the deeper roots of his tragedy:

> Say that again.
> The shadow of my sorrow! ha! let's see:
> 'Tis very true, my grief lies all within;
> And these external manners of laments
> Are merely shadows to the unseen grief
> That swells with silence in the tortured soul;
> There lies the substance.

One can trace in Shakespeare a process by which literary artifice, expanding in complexity and psychological correspondence, becomes an instrument of self-analysis; and the person of Richard, as revealed here, represents an important stage in this process. The outer forms of grief are 'shadows' of the 'substance' within, in Richard as they will later be in Hamlet;[13] between the tragic content of the two characters there is, of course, no comparison, but a process of development may possibly be traced by which the literary artifice of the one is transformed into the true complexity of the other. Once more, the later plays in the series will throw light upon the nature of this transformation. For the moment,

---

[13] Compare *Hamlet*, I. ii:
> But I have that within which passeth show;
> These but the trappings and the suits of woe.

Richard's expression of tragedy leads to the final breakdown which accompanies his request for 'leave to go'

> Whither you will, so I were from your sights,

in which the measureless bitterness of his situation is simply expressed.

By the opening of the last act, the central dramatic contrast has been fully developed, and the result, as the action moves towards its foreseen conclusion, is a certain drop in tension. To Richard in his decline, the felicity he formerly enjoyed appears as a 'dream' from which he has now awakened to 'the truth of what we are':

> A king of beasts, indeed; if aught but beasts,
> I had been still a happy king of men.   (v. i)

These meditations are interrupted once more by the entry of stern reality, in the form of Northumberland, who arrives to convey the deposed king to Pomfret. Richard's reaction, prophetic in tone, is linked with the later development of the series:

> The time shall not be many hours of age
> More than it is, ere foul sin gathering head
> Shall break into corruption: thou shalt think,
> Though he divide the realm and give thee half,
> It is too little, helping him to all;
> And he shall think that thou, which know'st the way
> To plant unrightful kings, wilt know again,
> Being ne'er so little urged, another way
> To pluck him headlong from the usurped throne.
>
> (v. i)

Here, at last, Richard penetrates to a vision of the pitiless nature of political processes in the world of 'beasts' to which he has become, too late, alive. The action in *Henry IV*—the counterplay of intrigue between powers haunted by past guilt in the form of a trustless present—is here foreshadowed. Henry, having taught his associates to overthrow a king, will always fear that the lesson may be turned against himself; and his friends, in turn, will at once anticipate the consequences against themselves of this fear, and crave to extend the power which they have so precariously won. After this prophecy which Northumberland grimly accepts—'My guilt be on my head, and there an end'—the final parting of Richard and his queen is a thin, artificial affair which leads us, however, further along the road of the foreseen tragedy.

The following scene, in the Duke of York's palace, points equally to the inevitable conclusion. York's account of the contrasted entries into London of Bolingbroke and Richard stresses, on the one hand, the former's politic submission to the populace—

> he, from the one side to the other turning,
> Bareheaded, lower than his proud steed's neck,
> Bespake them thus: 'I thank you, countrymen'

—and, on the other, the desertion of Richard, on whose '*sacred* head' dust was thrown, and in the reference to whose 'gentle sorrow,' 'grief and patience,' we may perhaps see that echo of the Christian passion which, whilst never applicable to the person of the victim, seems none the less present in Shakespeare's treatment of the betrayed king. The suggestion has already been implied in Richard's own references to Judas; but as his tragedy moves from the realm of sentiment towards a dreadful reality, so does it gather emotional force. We are moving into a harsh world of political realities, in which conscience and human feeling have small place: the world to which York refers when he says:

> But heaven hath a hand in these events,
> To whose high will we bound our calm contents.
> To Bolingbroke are we sworn subjects now.   (v. ii)

The mood is one of fatalism rather than of acceptance, of subjection to events rather than of a true concordance with them; but whether the issues which 'heaven' will bring to birth are propitious or otherwise, time alone will show. Meanwhile, the first sign of the new order, developed in a spirit that recalls the conscious formalism of the *Henry VI* plays, is York's readiness to impeach his son for treason to his new master. Sweeping aside his wife's plea, and apparently unmoved by the prospect of being left heirless, he is ready to sacrifice his own blood for a usurper who has only used him as an instrument and who will from now on distrust him as a possible rival. Fear is the mainspring of his action, as it is a sign of the new order; it is as though Richard's recent prophecy were already on the way to becoming reality.

The reappearance of the new king (v. iii), with his suggestion that his son is a 'plague' hanging over him in punishment for sin, also introduces a theme prominent in later plays. It is not, however, developed, nor is the mention of the 'sparks of better hope' also seen by his father in Hal's behaviour. The cynicism of the dissolute prince's attitude to the Oxford jousts is, as Percy describes it, not without meaning:

> His answer was, he would unto the stews,
> And from the common'st creature pluck a glove,
> And wear it as a favour; and with that
> He would unhorse the lustiest challenger   (v. iii)

This, perhaps, is more significant than may appear. The Prince's reaction is at once an assertion of his own degradation, and a sardonic comment on the decorative but empty tournament world which the events of this play have so effectively shattered. Besides the obvious show of dissolution in Henry's son, the report implies a repudiation of verbal dignities in a world in which the most venerable concepts—including that of 'honour' itself—are becoming subject to compromise: a world of chivalry already in decay under Richard and finally killed by his rival's accession. The Prince will, in due course, make the best of the new order of unprejudiced realism, more limited and less artificial than its predecessor, into which he is born; his activities, in the next play, in the taverns and streets of London will testify at once to the baseness around him, in which he participates, and to the greater breadth and firmness, when compared with Richard and even with Hotspur, of his contacts with life.

All this, however, belongs to the future, and the main action is conducted, in the meantime, on a perfunctory level, as in the following contest between York and his duchess for his son's life. On this, indeed, Henry seems to say the last word with his brief:

> Our scene is alter'd from a serious thing,
> And now chang'd to 'The Beggar and the King,'

where the incredible theatrical effect is surely placed. The whole of this part of the play suggests that the author's interest in his creation, temporarily exhausted after the presentation of contrasted orders and personalities, was now flagging.

Richard's last long speech (v. v) returns to, and in some sense sums up, the personal tragedy now being wound up against the growing sombreness and disintegration of which he has been at once the cause and the victim. Like so much else in this play, it gives a peculiar impression of convention shading almost imperceptibly into a sustained attempt at self-analysis and the expression of true feeling. The opening parallel,

> I have been studying how I may compare
> This prison where I live unto the world,

is thoroughly artificial; the rhythm falls to an accustomed beat, and the succession of ideas is rather mechanical than revealing. The reference to the Christian axioms, which follows, though it has parallels in the play, is scarcely less abstract; the general impression is of aphoristic wisdom using familiar illustrations—the prisoner in the stocks, the actor on the stage—to point an attitude which strikes us less as a tragic reflec-

tion than as an academic exercise in poetic pessimism. Only as the speech
moves to its climax is a deeper note attained, a more felt reference to a
universal human situation touched upon, when Richard returns to the
idea of *nothing* which has been so persistently present as a background,
expressed and implied, to his thoughts:

> whate'er I be,
> Nor I nor any man that but man is
> With nothing shall be pleased, till he be eased
> With being nothing.

Here, at least, in the balance of 'any man that but man is,' followed by
the echo of 'pleased' and 'eased,' and the opposition of 'nothing' to
'nothing,' is a serious attempt to make expression respond to feeling,
in something like a tragic statement about life. It is noteworthy, moreover, that this increase in depth is immediately followed, most improb-
ably in terms of realism, by the playing of 'music,' in what we may
consider a first dim indication of one of the mature Shakespearean
symbols. The harmony, suitably contradictory in its effects, like the
speaker's thoughts—

> how sour sweet music is,
> When time is broke and no proportion kept!

resolves itself, in an attempt at more subtle analysis, into a complicated
parallel:

> here have I the daintiness of ear
> To check time broke in a disorder'd string;
> But for the concord of my state and time
> Had not an ear to hear my true time broke.

Beneath the artificial balance of the phrasing, the speaker is at least
attempting to make a valid statement of his condition, and in the observation which follows—'I wasted time, and now doth time waste me'—
he almost succeeds. Even the elaborate expression has a certain justification in terms of character, as the utterance of one who has habitually
acted on his royal stage, observed, as it were, the effect of his attitudes
with an eye to public effect and personal gratification:

> Thus play I in one person many people,
> And none contented.

The devices of this speech, to be fully convincing, would need to be filled
out with personal experience to a degree never here attained; but, imperfect as it is, the meditation does foreshadow later developments in

the presentation of the tragic hero. Certainly, the murder which follows is, by comparison, no more than a pedestrian piece of melodramatic writing. Perhaps Richard's last individual word is spoken in the bitter comment to the Groom on the value of human titles and honours: 'The cheapest of us is ten groats too dear.' This is at once legitimate comment and the confirmation of a character, the evaluation of an inhuman political situation and the expression of a king who has always tended to find in an effective show of cynicism a refuge from the collapse of his self-indulgent sentiments.

The final scene (v. vi) rounds off the play in a mood of foreboding and the anticipation of thwarted purposes. Already it is clear that Boling-broke's crime, tacitly admitted as such, will bring neither personal nor political peace. The 'latest news,' announced by his own mouth, is that the 'rebels'—not now his own supporters, but those who have in turn risen against his usurped power—have 'consumed with fire' the town of Cicester. On all sides, executions respond to renewed civil strife; the heads of numerous 'traitors'—so called by he who has just ceased to be such—are on their way to London, and the spiritual power, hence-forth to be increasingly involved in political intrigues, is curtailed by the death of the Abbot of Westminster and by the banishment of Carlisle, in whom Henry himself recognizes the presence of virtue:

> High sparks of honour in thee have I seen.

Upon this catalogue of mischance and cross-purposes the murderers of Richard enter with his body, not to be commended for their 'deed of slander,' but yet to pin bluntly upon their master the guilt to which he himself admits:

> EXTON: From your own mouth, my lord, did I this deed.
> BOLINGBROKE: They love not poison that do poison need,
> Nor do I thee: though I did wish him dead,
> I hate the murderer, love him murdered.

Beneath the careful balance of the phrasing, the presence of 'the guilt of conscience' is firmly asserted in the new king, and his last words announce the intention, which will accompany him as an unfulfilled aspiration to his death, to redeem this 'guilt' by a spiritual enterprise in 'the Holy Land.' This aspiration, the failure to fulfil it, and its trans-formation into a more limited political purpose, are the themes of the plays to follow.

Henry the Fourth, *Part I*

TO PASS from *Richard II* to *Henry IV*, Part I, is to be aware of a remarkable growth in significant complexity of structure. The scope of the action initiated in the earlier play is notably widened, approached with a considerably greater breadth of view and a fresh maturity of vision. The presentation of Henry's kingship in the new play is, of course, conditioned by previous events. It is his expressed desire to rule well by the necessary exercise of royal authority; but the desire is flawed by the presence of inner contradictions connected with his own past actions. In point of fact, Henry's conception of kingship is barely shown except as an aspiration, the background to a feudal order torn from its natural framework of allegiance and reduced to a clash of selfish interests destroying the national unity in the pursuit of power. This clash is in turn related to one between the traditional virtues of chivalry—still verbally honoured, but in great part deprived of their true value—and a more conscious exercise of political intelligence based on unprejudiced initiative and an awareness of the permanent threat of anarchy. The growth of this new conception is associated, in the dramatic action, with the overthrow of Hotspur and the changing relation of Prince Hal—the central figure in this play and those which follow—to his father.

The complete conception of *Henry IV*, Part I, however, embraces even more than this. The development into full consciousness of the effective political Prince, impressive, necessary, and limited by the very exercise of his virtues, is set against the background of the English realm, a kingdom threatened by anarchy on the popular as well as the aristocratic level. It will be Hal's special vocation to conjure this threat, restoring unity to the society of which he is to be the anointed head; but—meanwhile—it will be part of his political preparation to participate in the state of his future realm, to study its condition in detachment, to reject what his intelligence finds to be corrupt in it whilst converting himself, by conscious effort and choice, into the supreme embodiment of political virtue. And finally—by the most daring stroke of all—in his intensely rich and varied relationship to Falstaff, Hal will himself be-

in some sense evaluated, subjected to comic criticism by the life, dis-
orderly and excessive though it be, which he has necessarily to reject.

I

The expository scene which opens the play shows Bolingbroke already
weighed down, as the concluding scenes of *Richard II* have anticipated,
by thoughts of anarchy and civil war. The very opening line,

So shaken as we are, so wan with care,

corresponds in its deliberate irregularity of rhythm to the speaker's *felt*
reaction to the chaos which threatens his kingdom. The public state, in
short, is reflected in personal insecurity, an impression of momentary
calm snatched out of a condition of peril. 'Find we a time for frighted
peace to pant': the king feels, as it were, *physically*, in his own body, the
sense of relief which his every action will, from this moment, strive to
make permanent.

The relation to the main conception of this state of precarious rest
is stated in the body of the speech. Its background is the bitter memory
of 'civil butchery,' of strife between enemies 'All of one nature, of one
substance bred,' clashes within the body politic that can only serve to
wound and destroy it. The nature of these clashes is conveyed through
a heightening of emotion which has its own dramatic justification; for,
when Henry speaks of 'short-winded accents of new broils,'

To be commenced in strands afar remote,

the breathless urgency of 'short-winded' stands out from the rhetorical
period which follows, and the prophetic vision which looks forward to
the time, so intensely desired, when

No more the thirsty entrance of this soil
Shall daub her lips with her own children's blood,

conveys at least as much a sense, strained and almost hysterical, of exhausted emotion as an affirmation of the ends at which the king in his
new authority is aiming. Artifice and rhetoric, in other words, have at
this point a dramatic function of their own, corresponding to a struggle
in Henry's mind, not merely between past and present, but between the
aspiration and the reality of his kingship. Finding his country still
'shaken' by civil disasters to which his own actions have supremely
contributed, it is his desire to propose a higher aim in following which
the factions so recently at one another's throats may find a common
ground of unity. In this spirit Henry calls his barons, united under the

'blessed cross,' to the liberation of the Holy Sepulchre. The crusade will serve both to calm the political passions which he has himself exploited to reach the throne and to provide a foundation for the unity which, as king, he now sincerely desires.

It is here that Shakespeare, still using traditional conceptions, begins to unfold a personal interpretation of his theme. In calling for a crusade Henry is moved by motives in which selfish calculation is oddly mixed with a true desire for the common good. As crowned king he genuinely wishes to unite his subjects in a worthy and religious enterprise; but as usurper he hopes, in words used by him at a later stage, to 'busy giddy minds with foreign quarrels,'[1] and so distract attention from the way in which he came to the throne. Once more, the emotional quality of the expression is revealing. Henry proposes his crusade in language which breaks through the conventions of public rhetoric with an effect, often to be repeated in his utterances, which we can best call nostalgic:

> Therefore, friends,
> As far as to the sepulchre of Christ,
> Whose soldier now, under whose blessed cross
> We are impressed and engaged to fight,
> Forthwith a power of English shall we levy;
> Whose arms were moulded in their mothers' womb
> To chase these pagans in those holy fields
> Over whose acres walk'd those blessed feet
> Which fourteen hundred years ago were nail'd
> For our advantage on the bitter cross.   (I. i)

The depth and intensity of the religious feeling is not in question, as is not its relation to an intimate, personal sense of the wounds caused by civil war. The one, indeed, is a product of the other. Henry, exhausted and already more than a little burdened with his guilt, lifts his eyes from the immediate prospect of past and future discord to a remote purity of purpose. The religious tone is one of emotional compensation, of the casting off of a personal burden of sin. In other words—and here Shakespeare's thought is clearly working on contemporary readings of history—Henry's genuine desire to play properly his royal part is flawed past mending by the way in which he came to the throne. His murder of Richard, a crime—as we have seen—not merely against common humanity but against the divine foundation of order centred on the crown, fatally engenders the strife which he now aims at ending. Such, after the opening indication of Henry's own position, is the reality revealed

---

[1] *2 Henry IV,* IV. v.

by this scene. No sooner has he affirmed his purpose than 'heavy news' comes 'all athwart' from Wales to force for the first time what will turn out to be a lifelong postponement of the crusading project. The reign which opens with the summons to a holy enterprise will end, after years of weary disillusionment, with death in a room 'called Jerusalem' which is fated to be his nearest approach to the Holy Land;[2] and in between it will have seen little but rebellion, plot and counterplot, and battles in which victory serves only to sow the seeds of further civil strife.

If the principal conception of the play were contained in the preceding analysis its interest would lie only in the skill with which Shakespeare had unfolded a completely traditional scheme. His real purpose, however, far from ending here, begins at this point. Its true originality first appears when the political is reinforced by a personal interest. Henry is punished for his past sins, not only as king in the weariness which his opening words betray, but as father in the most intimate concerns of his life. Once more, the initial exposition points to a principal theme of the later action. The news of Hotspur's reported victory at Holmedon leads Henry less to rejoice than, by a typical contradiction, to 'sin' in envy:

> there thou makest me sad and makest me sin
> In envy that my Lord Northumberland
> Should be the father to so blest a son,
> A son who is the theme of honour's tongue;
> Amongst a grove, the very straightest plant;
> Who is sweet Fortune's minion and her pride:
> Whilst I, by looking on the praise of him,
> See riot and dishonour stain the brow
> Of my young Harry.   (I. i)

This contrast will be presented in a variety of lights during the course of the play. Hotspur's 'honour,' which Henry here covets for his son, will be shown to have its limitations, related to the moral weakness of the cause he is shortly to make his own, and the Prince's dissolute life will appear as a cover for the mixture of political ability and practical virtue which will bring him eventually to success; this virtue, however, will be in turn revealed as a reflection of the family character in a son whose behaviour makes him, in the early stages, an instrument for his father's mortification. It is here that Shakespeare, still using inherited material, begins to show the true originality of his purpose. For Prince Hal, destined to become the incarnation of political competence and to achieve all his father's ends, will only be fully reconciled to him on his

---

[2] See *2 Henry IV*, IV. v.

deathbed; and Hotspur is already, by his refusal to surrender his prisoners, on the way to becoming a rebel. Henry's disappointment, thus
initially indicated as an intimate source of tragedy, is ultimately related
to unresolved contradictions, upon which the main action will throw
light by a variety of significant contrasts, in the family nature.

These, however, are themes for future development. Their equiva-
lent in the external action is the first crossing of Henry's declared purpose. Unity is countered by rebellion, past victory by present defeat and
the beginnings of a new rising in the North. By the end of the scene,
Henry is obliged to shelve his opening statement of purpose:

> for this cause awhile we must neglect
> Our holy purpose to Jerusalem.

'Holiness' is not of the political world of this play, but belongs to some
dim, unattainable future; the burden of royalty lies in a continual
struggle against the forces, related to the origins of its own power, which
so persistently thwart its unifying purpose.

The two scenes which follow branch out from this introduction to
lay the foundation for the main construction of the dramatic action.
Both, indeed, have been anticipated in the opening, and more particularly in Henry's speech, just quoted, on the obstacles which obstruct his
patriotic ends. On the 'political' level we are shown (1. iii) the process of
rebellion, foreshadowed by Henry himself, taking shape in the form of
open rivalry, and involving Hotspur's emotional conception of 'honour'
in ambiguous subtleties beyond its depth; and in Hal's tavern we are
brought into contact with the dissolution which so disturbs his father
and which is at the same time a projection of disorder in the state and
the starting point for that transformation in his son which is the central
theme of the entire play. Immediately after Henry's abandonment of
his crusading project, the play turns (1. ii) to what appears at first sight
a totally different world. It is, however, and among other things, rather
the same world seen from another point of view. Among the features
which distinguish *Henry IV* from *Richard II* is the effort, initiated at
this point, to represent dramatically the various levels of English society;
we have only to compare the presentation of the people in the prose
scenes of this play with the elaborate artifice of the Gardeners in *Richard
II*[3] to appreciate the difference in scope and purpose between the two
works. The Gardeners belong to a world of poetic convention, and their
appearance is intended to confirm an elegiac mood and to point a

[3] See *Richard II*, III. iv.

sophisticated moral in a world of courtly elaboration; but the tavern scenes of *Henry IV*, in both its parts, introduce, within dramatic limits, the real people over whom the king rules and who are variously affected by his decisions. This realistic purpose, however, is in turn connected with the themes already stated. This is the world in which Prince Hal has apparently chosen to repudiate his princely responsibilities, and from it emerges, in the figure of Falstaff, at once a supreme presentation of 'riot and dishonour'[4] and a comment, valid if not exhaustive, upon the shortcomings of the political order. Through Falstaff's relationship to the Prince the connection between the tavern world of popular incident and the political world of high utterance and divided purpose is drawn gradually closer as the action proceeds.

The full possibilities of this connection only emerge slowly in the course of the play. Among the signs of Shakespeare's maturing powers in *Henry IV*, Part I, is the presence of different styles, reflecting purposes that eventually converge upon a central intention. Falstaff's opening question—'What time of day is it, lad?'—is at once a challenge to the serious action and an indication of his limitations. Falstaff, as the Prince brings out in his elaborate reply, repudiates time. Time is no concern of his, as it will be in ever increasing measure of the politicians who will become—as we shall see—its victims; but the very fact that he repudiates it implies that he will himself have to be repudiated before the Prince can take up a vocation in which he will be at once conscious of time and, in some sense, its slave. The contrast implied in the shift from 'courtly' blank verse to the direct familiarity of prose touches in this way the heart of the conception.

The contrasted movements of style, indeed, which can be detected in the course of this scene repay careful study. They indicate at once the nature of the relationship by which Falstaff is bound to the Prince. His disintegrating, destructive attitude is compatible with the use, by himself and those around him, of an utterance euphuistic, if we may call it so, in its exuberance, but in which the artificiality of that convention becomes, at certain moments, the vehicle for an overriding, cumulative vitality. Something of this vitality communicates itself at first to the Prince, who, in responding to Falstaff, echoes his unmistakable idiom for the first and almost the last time in this scene:

What a devil hast thou to do with the time of the day? Unless hours were cups of sack and minutes capons and clocks the tongues of bawds and dials the signs of leaping-houses and the blessed sun himself a fair hot wench in

---

[4] The phrase has just been used by Henry. See p. 52 above.

flame-coloured taffeta, I see no reason why thou shouldst be so superfluous
to demand the time of the day.   (I. ii)

This exuberance, firmly founded on common realism, is new in Shakespeare, and as profound in effect as anything in the play. When Falstaff
takes up the spirit of it, turning to distinctive use the conventional
attributes of thievery—the idea that thieves are 'squires of the night's
body,' 'Diana's foresters . . . governed, as the sea is, by our noble and
chaste mistress the moon'—a significant relationship of contrasts is
already growing up between himself and his royal companion. As Falstaff's imaginative energy asserts itself in irresponsibility, which is one
aspect of the disorder which haunts royalty in these plays, so does the
Prince—who began, as we have seen, with a certain echo of that energy
—withdraw into detachment, into a refusal to be committed, that is
equally typical. Falstaff's spacious, irresponsible reference to the moon
is balanced by Hal's realistic estimate of the prospects of robbery:

. . . the fortune of us that are the moon's men doth ebb and flow like the
sea, being governed, as the sea is, by the moon. As, for proof, now: a purse
of gold most resolutely snatched on Monday night and most dissolutely spent
on Tuesday morning; got with swearing 'Lay by' and spent with crying
'Bring in;' now in as low an ebb as the foot of the ladder, and by and by in as
high a flow as the ridge of the gallows.   (I. ii)

From the imaginative fancy of the devotees of thievery as 'the moon's
men,' governed by the varying tides of fortune, to the reality of the
gallows the conception of a single, logically defined sequence imposes
itself. The bringing back of Falstaff's phrase to dispassionate reality
and implied condemnation is typical of the Prince. From the first, Hal
is presented in detachment from Falstaff. There is in his future development no real conversion, no fundamental change of attitude, because
the moral estimate of his temporary companions is from the beginning
firmly in his mind. The divergence of spirit thus indicated within
common means of expression belongs to the central conception of the
play.

In this way, the Prince is immediately dedicated to the world of
political necessities, and so partakes of the character of his family. No
doubt his attitude is inevitable, essentially just; and yet we may feel in it,
not only the repudiation of anarchy and dissolution which his whole
career will assume, but an implied criticism. The contrast, indeed, is
progressively deepened in the course of the exchange. Falstaff's observations leap from one subject to another, reducing each to relative value
in an attitude that refuses to accept submission; the wisdom of experi-

ence is qualified—'he talked very wisely, but I regarded him not'—and
so is virtue as he parodies it: 'now am I, if a man should speak truly, little
better than one of the wicked. I must give over this life, and I will give
it over.' The parody of the virtue which would save him, which is at
the same time a criticism of righteousness too easily affirmed, is an essential attribute of Falstaff. The Prince's reply shows him alternately touch-
ing on the excesses he is about to repudiate and passing on Falstaff's
professions a comment not far removed from the sardonic: 'I see a good
amendment of life in thee; from praying to purse-taking.' Both attitudes
are part of the truth, and in their light the necessary rejection of Falstaff
and the Prince's gradual hardening in his vocation can already be foreseen.

For it is necessary, in considering the effect of these scenes, to arrive
at a balanced estimate of the part played in them by Falstaff. No doubt,
in arriving at this estimate, we need to take not a few traditional elements
into account.[5] Falstaff bears about him elements of the buffoon, the Vice
of the mediæval stage, and incarnates the temptations against morality
and duty which the young king-in-the-making will be required to abjure.
He is not, however, altogether bound by limitations of this kind. If his
creator set about the presentation of him with these ends in view, it is
clear that the character began almost immediately to evade these limitations, to dominate, in spite of his real monstrosity, a world in which there
is certainly nothing more vital than himself. The Falstaff of *Henry IV,*
Part I, besides representing the vices which Hal must put aside, increasingly transcends the political action in which he moves and provides a
vital comment upon it. He serves, in some sense, as a connecting link
between two worlds, the tavern world of comic incident in which he is
at home and the world of court rhetoric and political decision to which
he also has access. So situated in two worlds and entirely confined to
neither, he passes judgement on the events represented in the play in the
light of his own superabundant comic energy. Working sometimes
through open comment, sometimes even through parody, his is a voice
that lies outside the prevailing political spirit of the play, that draws its
cogency—though of a limited kind, condemned even as it is expressed
for being partial, for the sin of mistaking the part for the whole—from
the author's own insight expressing itself in a flow of comic energy.
From this standpoint, and without overlooking the essential perversity
of his values, we may say that he represents all the humanity which it
seems that the politician must necessarily exclude. That humanity is
full of obvious and gross imperfections which are such, indeed, as—left

---

[5] These elements have been well studied by J. Dover Wilson in *The Fortunes of Falstaff.*

to themselves—must end by destroying the life they claim to affirm; but the Falstaff of this play, whilst he shares these imperfections and is indeed their supreme incarnation, is not altogether limited to them. His keen intelligence, his real understanding, his refusal to be fobbed off by empty or hypocritical phrases—these are characteristics that enable him to transcend his world and to become the individual expression of a great and completely serious artist. In this transformation of traditional material we approach the very heart of the conception that animates this play.

The entry of Poins, with news of the projected robbery, shows the Prince turning still further towards an attitude of self-sufficiency. Falstaff, as he persuades him to belittle himself, makes typical mocking use of set phrases, in which a Puritan note is deliberately struck. The parody of Puritan values, indeed, which there is no reason why we should not associate with Falstaff's supposed origin in a satire on the Lollard Oldcastle, is necessary to the complete effect. His words repeatedly ridicule as frigid and insincere the conceptions of virtue in relation to which he is himself condemned; and, on the other hand, the moralizing content which they repudiate is in some sense linked with the strain of conscious self-control which is one element at least in the Prince's own success. When Falstaff describes himself as 'little better than one of the wicked' and announces, ironically, his own conversion, he is at once ridiculing the idea of such conversion (which Hal will shortly assert, anticipating his own formal declaration, as a necessary public gesture) and admitting implicitly the existence of a background against which the limitations of his own dissolute vitality stand out; for Falstaff is at once to be condemned in the light of any conceivable set of moral values and escapes condemnation, repudiates the thin and theoretical strain which accompanies the attempt to impose moral values verbally upon life itself. The Prince, in turn, as he reacts to Poins's proposal, hesitates between a certain self-conscious dignity—'Who, I rob? I a thief? not I, by my faith' —and a condescension that comes, after this, more than a little out of place: 'Well then, once in my days I'll be a madcap.' Thus each—the Prince and Falstaff—imply by the mere fact of their existence a criticism of the other. The exuberance of Falstaff's utterance cannot disguise the fact that his is a disintegrating, ultimately a corrupting outlook; but the vitality of his reactions indicates, by contrast, a sense of thinness, of self-confident calculation in his princely associate. The latter impression is more than confirmed by Hal's first soliloquy.

The soliloquy, indeed, once more links the comic to the 'serious' political action. It touches on a theme anticipated by Bolingbroke and stressed throughout as a constant feature of the Lancastrian character:

the tendency to live for public effect, to grade behaviour to the reaction that it is desired to produce in the world. This, in turn, follows naturally from the subordination of personality to the public function. It might almost be said that the motives which condition the family behaviour throughout the trilogy are revealed, at this early stage, in the Prince's intimate expression of his thoughts. These spring in part from the nature of the material inherited by the dramatist. In writing his play, Shakespeare's freedom of conception was faced with what might seem at first sight a grave limitation: the necessity of squaring his account of the Prince with a traditional story as naïve in its moral assumptions as it was familiar in its details. The Prince, as he appeared in the popular account, was an outstanding historical example of the dissolute young man who, when faced by grave responsibilities, underwent a kind of moral conversion and finally made good in the great sphere of action to which he was called. The story, thus conceived, was too familiar to be ignored by a practical dramatist; but, on the other hand, its conception of character and motive was too naïvely optimistic to appeal to a Shakespeare already moving towards the mood in which he was shortly to produce *Hamlet.* Faced with this dilemma he chose to accept the very improbability of the story and turn it to account. The Prince, from his first appearance, has substantially made his choice; he looks forward to a reformation which, just because it is a little too good to be true, is partly moved by a political calculation which reflects his father's character. If his nature is to change, as he now announces, it is because a transformation of this kind will attract popularity; for 'nothing pleaseth but rare accidents.' The whole process of 'reformation,' as he describes it, has a surface quality which his own words emphasize. It belongs to the *public* life and is seen 'glittering' with metallic speciousness over previous faults 'like bright metal on a sullen ground'; and its purpose is, above all, to '*show* more goodly' and 'attract more eyes.' The 'conversion,' thus transformed from an edifying example to an instrument of policy, enters into the permanent characteristics of the House of Lancaster. The future Henry V, destined to become in due course an incarnation of the political virtues (which are in no sense to be despised), begins by consciously abstaining from the finer aspects of human nature, those which require intimate, inner conviction as opposed to the public display of moral qualities; for behind Shakespeare's acceptance of a traditional story lies the sense, which grows as the action develops, that success in politics implies a moral loss, the sacrifice of more attractive qualities in the distinctively personal order.

The tracing of a common destiny working itself out through character in the actions of the House of Lancaster is, thus considered, an essen-

tial part of the main conception. It is not, however, the whole. As the
action advances, we become aware that the individuals whose behaviour
is represented in the play form part of an embracing unity; their virtues
and faults, successes and failures, are interdependent aspects of a world
which, considered in its totality, amounts to a representation of the
political state of England. This becomes apparent in the following scene
(I. iii) in which, after the opening exposition of Henry's intentions and
of the contrary fatality which interrupts them, the warring parties who
divide the coming action are brought together to show the split between
them in the process of coming into being. At the same time, in the personal order, and after the demonstration, just witnessed, of Hal's political
detachment, the contrast with Hotspur, the object of the king's envy,
begins to take shape in relation to public events.

The king's opening affirmation of authority, indeed, comes significantly after his son's soliloquy. It is in accordance with the family
character, a clue both to its success and its limitations, that he should
speak of his own blood as

> too *cold* and *temperate*,
> Unapt to stir at these indignities;

the protest of self-control, coming from a king and inseparable from his
office, is no doubt justified, but the expression of it and the unction of
Henry's reference to himself as having been in the past 'smooth as oil,
soft as young down' are not without meaning. Although this sense of
a surface of control covering a natural spontaneity suppressed in its
normal outlets need not be overstressed, it corresponds to a factor repeatedly indicated as present in the family character.

In Worcester's reply, Richard's prophecy of future strife[6] is in process
of becoming a sinister reality. If Henry's kingship is rendered sterile
in its higher aspirations by the circumstances which accompanied his
seizure of the crown, a similar frustration accompanies those who, having
helped him to the throne to further their selfish ends, now wish to curb
his power. The part played by the rebels in Henry's assumption of office
is a chief point in the presentation of their case. Worcester refers to

> that same greatness too which our own hands
> Hath holp to make so portly.

A little later, Hotspur puts the relationship in less flattering terms, when
he describes his associates as the 'base second means,' 'the cords, the
ladder, or the hangman' involved in the late king's murder and is at
pains to emphasize that what they have done was committed 'in an

[6] *See Richard II*, v. i, and p. 44 above.

unjust behalf.' Desire for power prompted the rebel leaders to crime, and now mutual fear makes inevitable the clash between the usurper and those who formerly served his ends. Henry, aware that his position has been criminally obtained, must suspect that those who once followed their interest to dethrone a king may do so again; and the rebels (or the more reflective among them) understand that he must think in this way, and that they themselves can therefore never be safe. The result is an endless mutual distrust, the consequences of which finally conclude, in this play, at Shrewsbury.

The whole scene, turning upon this contrast, is admirably worked out in terms of character. The first part is dominated by a contrast between Henry and the very Hotspur whom he has already compared so favourably to his own son. Hotspur's first speech, describing the courtier who brought him the king's request for his prisoners after Holmedon, is finely conceived in the comic spirit; this is the man of action at his best, still sure of the validity of his own values, direct, incisive, impatient of artifice and intrigue. Already, however, it implies, beneath its attractiveness, an estimate of character. As Hotspur's emotions run away with him, we become aware of the speaker's impulsiveness, the tendency to be led by feeling into courses that will eventually bring him to ruin in an unworthy cause. For the moment, however, it is the impression of generosity, the repudiation of 'base and rotten policy' that prevails. The following clash of wills which leads to the king's departure is more conventional in its rhetoric, and it is not until the conspirators are left alone that their respective personal qualities begin to find definition.

What takes place, indeed, in the rest of the scene is the subjection of Hotspur's impulsive directness to the labyrinth of political behaviour. His first reaction to the king's final demand for the prisoners is stated with an emphasis that betrays the tendency, innate in him, to develop his emotions in excess of their cause, to assert himself with an intensity that finally betrays weakness:

> An if the devil come and roar for them,
> I will not send them: I will after straight
> And tell him so;

but Northumberland's immediate intervention counsels 'pause' and heralds, with the entry of Worcester, the change from emotional conflict to statecraft and the devices of 'policy.' In the rest of the scene, the entanglement of Hotspur proceeds, and the impulsiveness which has so far served mainly to contrast him with Hal, and to bring out the un-

generosity of those around him, is revealed in a light of growing absurdity. For him, the support of Mortimer is a means by which Richard's
betrayers may 'redeem' their 'banish'd honours,' and so 'restore' themselves

> Into the good thoughts of the world again;

and Worcester is subtle enough to play upon his impulsiveness when he
stresses the 'matter deep and dangerous,' 'full of peril and adventurous
spirit,' of the plot he is about to unfold. In his emotional reaction, Hotspur introduces for the first time the abstract 'honour' which represents
at once the strength and the weakness of his position, the honesty which
marks him out among his fellow conspirators and the emotional instability which leads him to be carried away by unconsidered feeling:

> Send danger from the east unto the west,
> So honour cross it from the north to south,
> And let them grapple.   (i. iii)

'Honour,' thus conceived, is in the process of converting itself, for Hotspur, into an emotional stimulus which, as it is mentioned, rouses an
infallible response in high-sounding rhetoric. As he progressively loses
his grip on reality the impulsive warrior becomes the instrument of the
unscrupulous politicians around him. It is not difficult to see, in these
rhetorical speeches, an anticipation of certain qualities which will later
find expression in the subtle blend of 'nobility' and impotence which
characterizes some of the mature tragic heroes. Othello, Antony, and
Coriolanus, each in his own distinctly different way, reflect in their
rhetoric a tendency to justify themselves, or to conform to an idealized
presentation of their own behaviour in the very moment of failure; and
if Hotspur is less subtly conceived, less various in his motives, the balance
of true emotion and emptiness, the reliance on a noble conception barely
developed beyond its verbal value reflects the essential moral adolescence
which, to some degree and maintaining all the necessary differences, he
shares with them. This adolescence makes him the victim of a 'policy'
from which his own conception of 'honour' is completely excluded.

Worcester's comments, indeed, both on his nephew's outburst and
the following apostrophe,

> By heaven, methinks it were an easy leap,
> To pluck bright honour from the pale-faced moon,

are incisively satirical:

> He apprehends a world of figures here,
> But not the form of what he should attend.

Hotspur, indeed, lives finally in a world of 'figures' which, as his emotions are increasingly engaged, prevails over the robust common sense of his first long speech and will make him eventually a figure strangely poised between the tragic and the comic, the heroic and the absurd. In the discussion which follows he is turned from a warrior into a schoolboy, unwillingly subjected to rule by elders who alternately humour and chide him. His outbursts of indignant impatience are met by Worcester's concentration on the matter in hand, and are invariably followed by an equally boyish repentance. To the last he sees Bolingbroke as 'a vile politician' and recalls the public humility of his earlier behaviour in terms which stress, in typical Shakespearean imagery, the note of servile dishonesty:

> what a *candy* deal of courtesy
> This *fawning* greyhound then did proffer me!
> Look, 'when his infant fortune came to age,'
> And 'gentle Harry Percy,' and 'kind cousin;'
> O, the devil take such cozeners![7]   (I. iii)

The immediacy of the presentation, and the presence of images repeatedly associated by Shakespeare with dishonesty and the world of flattery, guarantee sufficiently that Hotspur is here making a valid criticism; and yet the broken ineffectiveness of his conclusions—'I cry you mercy,' 'I have done'—coming after these outbursts is not less germane to the character. In drawing the parallel with the Prince which is, by common consent, a main theme of the play, these strains of personality are not irrelevant.

Worcester, with all the politician's contempt for the man of war, gradually involves his nephew in his web of intrigue. He persuades him first to give up his prisoners, retaining only the son of Douglas; and, having done this, he turns from Hotspur, for whom he will have no further use till the moment of action comes, to his fellow conspirator Northumberland:

> Your son in Scotland being thus employ'd,
> Shall *secretly into the bosom creep*
> Of that same *noble* prelate, *well-beloved*,
> The archbishop.

The ambiguity which balances the idea of a serpent creeping into a prelate's bosom against the implications of 'noble' and 'well-beloved' is typical of Worcester's world. Hotspur, out of his depth, salutes this

---

[7] Bolingbroke's speech has already been reported, of course, in *Richard II*, II. iii.

contrivance, in words strangely adapted to the facts, as 'a *noble* plot,' whilst Worcester, exposing the true nature of his endeavour, reveals its foundations as lying in guilt and expediency:

> 'tis no little reason bids us speed,
> To save our heads by raising of a head;
> For, bear ourselves as even as we can,
> The king will always think him in our debt,
> And think we think ourselves unsatisfied,
> Till he hath found a time to pay us home.   (I. iii)

Fear, in this world, breeds fear, and produces the very rebellion which fear itself, working through a conscience of guilt, would desire to avoid. The end of the scene shows Worcester, characteristically, as about to '*steal* to Glendower and Lord Mortimer,' seeking in dubious unity the remedy to 'much uncertainty.' Northumberland it leaves, not less typically, unsure of himself and of the future ('we shall thrive, *I trust*'), and Hotspur, a stranger in this world of intrigue and calculation with which he is none the less ready to compromise his 'nobility,' clings to the supposed certainties of action with a rhetorical gesture which is really an evasion of the choices in which he finds himself involved:

> Uncle, adieu: O, let the hours be short
> Till fields and blows and groans applaud our sport!

These are, indeed, Hotspur's only constants to guide him through a world of shifting uncertainties; how inadequate they are, how opposed in their adolescent simplicity to the controlled self-awareness of the Prince, the following events will show.

II

The opening scenes of *Henry IV*, Part I, so far considered, have principally presented the political action, relating to its origins in crime and mutual distrust the collapse into factious rivalry which threatens the English state. At this point, by a device which will become increasingly frequent in Shakespeare's greater plays, the interest shifts, in the scenes leading up to the exploit on Gadshill, to embrace a comic parallel to the central theme. This change of vision has a double purpose; it vastly extends the social range covered by the play, presenting a popular reflection to the prevailing crisis of authority, and provides the necessary background for the further development of Hal's character and for the activities of Falstaff. It is true that Falstaff has already been introduced in relation to the Prince; but before the full sense of that relationship can become apparent, he must be seen in action, at once supremely manifesting in his person the corruption abroad in the state and offering, by the astonishing vital paradox implied in his conception, an essential criticism. The series of episodes now initiated leads first to the robbery of the king's servants, itself a clear manifestation of disorder, and then, after the exposure of Falstaff in the tavern, to a parody of the reconciliation between the king and his prodigal heir which is shortly to be presented as the turning point of the entire action.

The dialogue between the Carriers, which sets the tone for what follows, is expressed in terms of deliberate sobriety. The comic touches, such as they are, are uniformly dispiriting in tone; the horse is a 'poor jade . . . wrung in the withers,' peas and beans are '*dank* as a dog,' Robin Ostler 'never joyed' after the rise in the price of oats, and such comedy as exists is connected with the stale 'chamber-lie' which 'breeds fleas like a loach.' Against this background, Gadshill and the Chamberlain convey the true sense of the scene when they discuss, obscurely but with implied cynicism, the 'patrons' who guarantee their safety in the dubious adventure now afoot. What is for both these shady instruments a 'profession,' a means to live, is for their betters, close to the fountainhead of authority, a frivolity undertaken for 'sport sake' by those who are ready, should the need arise, to shelter crime from justice in the defence of 'credit.' The emphasis throughout is on depredation; the 'commonwealth' has become the 'boots' of those that 'ride up and down on her,' whose impunity depends on the corruption of impartial authority, on the fact that 'justice' (so called) 'hath liquored her.' The prevailing vision is dispassionate and disillusioned. The final dismissal—implied in Gadshill's phrase, 'Go to; "homo" is a common name to all men'— of the difference between 'true man' and 'false thief' balances tolerance against cynicism, echoes a traditional expression of humane values in the very act of subjecting them to cynical distortion. The spirit thus given a passing expression will be taken up, given a new and distinctive context, in the fallen but exuberant humanity of Falstaff.

The robbery itself, so prefaced, is an active manifestation of disorder. It is not entirely an accident that the object of a theft in which the heir to the throne apparently connives is expressly described by Bardolph as money on its way to the king's exchequer. The essence of the adventure lies in the contrast between Falstaff's participation, shameless, corrupt, and ridiculous by turn, and the Prince's characteristic blend of diversion and detachment. Falstaff's behaviour, which so clearly exposes him to ridicule, is in part saved by the power to turn his disabilities to laughter, as in his humourous assumption of 'youth': 'young men must live.' The phrase is typically various in content, simultaneously a sign of imaginative energy (but spoken by a man himself touched with physical decay) and an implied criticism of the type of slogan that has in all ages condoned the operations of anarchy and 'appetite.' Falstaff is distinguished, within his dedication to dissolution, by the agility of his reactions, by the capacity to confer upon his own monstrosity, in the expression, an unexpected, impossible normality. In the act of committing a crime, he hopes to 'die a fair death,' but fears that he may have to ''scape hanging' for 'the killing' of Poins; and in grotesquely suggesting that he has been bewitched, given 'medicines,' to make him unable to forswear the company of that 'rogue,' another unexpected turn offers him a verbal loophole of escape from the condemnation which he has brought upon himself. All this leads finally to yet another of those satirical references to conversion which so abound in his utterances: 'An 'twere not as good a deed' (*but* 'as drink,' be it noted) 'to turn *true man* and to leave these rogues, I am the veriest varlet.' By the time he has strengthened his complaint with the final condemnation of the 'stony-hearted villains' around him, and with the devastating irony of 'a plague upon it when thieves cannot be true one to another,' both Falstaff's own situation and that of his companions in robbery have been involved in a complex series of comic inversions.

The essence of these inversions, and the key to Falstaff's function in the play, lies in the combination of death with life, irresponsibility with seriousness, the implicit presence in his utterances of the values which, even as he derides them, he in some sense accepts as his norm. This should not, however, lead us to neglect his limitations. Falstaff is still primarily the incarnation of 'misrule,' the coward, the traditional *miles gloriosus* exposed to ridicule in a particularly unsavoury situation. His triumphs, such as they are, depend on the evasion of facts, whereas the superiority of the Prince, who remains throughout this episode on the margin of events, rests on the dispassionate observation of them. The contrast between the two attitudes, so close to the spirit of the play, begins to take shape at this point. After the trick played upon him we are told of Falstaff by the Prince that he '*lards* the lean earth as he walks along.' The image is, of course, appropriate to the incarnation of 'riot,' open debauchery, and exorbitant 'misrule.' The Prince, in his clear-sightedness, imposes his vision of things; but this peculiar type of physical imagery, the product of a certain calculated and superior vulgarity which also belongs to the character, will be echoed at various stages of the later action. Its relation to Falstaff's 'fleshly' inversions of the spirit of Puritan morality is very close to the central conception.

Although this part of the play is concentrated on the 'comic' as opposed to the 'serious' action, the brief return to Percy (II.iii) both maintains the necessary connection between the two (for the comic scenes are parallel, in their commentatory value, to the political developments) and takes us a step further in estimating the character of Hotspur, himself conceived as a foil to the Prince. Percy's reading of his fellow-conspirator's letter shows him once more as the man of action out of his depth in the world of 'frosty-spirited' calculation into which his emotions have led him. No doubt he is right to dismiss his correspondent as a 'cowardly hind'; but equally certainly his own confidence will prove, in the event, baseless and his action in exposing himself to the betrayal he clearly anticipates, the height of folly. The expressions of repudiation—'I could divide myself and go to buffets, for moving such a dish of skim milk with so honourable an action!'—are admirably alive and, within their limiting naïveté, attractive; yet this is clearly a speaker who will be constantly carried away by his emotions, and whose lack of self-awareness can easily touch on the absurd.

This impression is confirmed by the following exchange with his wife, where the foundations of his character are more intimately presented. Hotspur's love for his wife is as much beyond question as is the true affection he rouses in her. It marks him out favourably in a play from which this emotion is otherwise almost entirely excluded; but the 'manliness' which emerges from Lady Percy's account of his dreams, the boyish stress on heroics and the instruments of war, have a feverish strain which, reflected in the 'beads of sweat' and 'strange motions' which agitate his sleep, is less than mature. Behind Percy's aggressively masculine restlessness and the light-hearted (and untrue) concealment of his feelings, there is, besides an unwillingness to subject his actions to rational scrutiny, a strain of adolescence which is in no small part the cause of his ruin:

> I care not for thee, Kate; this is no world
> To play with mammets and to tilt with lips:
> We must have bloody noses and crack'd crowns,
> And pass them current too.

The contrast with Lady Percy's reply—'since you love me not, I will not love myself'—so direct and true, is a sign of the gap in maturity which separates this unformed warrior, boyishly devoted to a half-defined concept of 'honour,' from his wife. If the assumption that the serious business of life is no more than a matter of 'bloody noses' and 'crack'd crowns' be the practical outcome of the cult of 'honour,' then there is in that outlook something lacking. It implies, indeed, a perpetuation of adolescence, a refusal to grow out of an eternal boyhood, self-centred in the simplicity of action, which will be shown, on a vastly developed scale, by some of Shakespeare's later heroes—Coriolanus and, to a certain degree, even Othello—but which is here offered more simply as an alternative to the Prince's self-sufficiency. It confirms, moreover, that the rebels, whose cause is founded on anarchy and selfishness, cannot possess, even in their most attractive personality, genuine moral stature. Of Hotspur's own spirit, the horse, the 'roan,' to which he so repeatedly refers in exclusion of a wife more balanced, more possessed of insight than himself, is a true and ironic symbol.

The scene which follows (ii. iv), returning to the 'low' action at Eastcheap, is, besides being the longest, one of the most important in the whole play. During the course of it, the various aspects of the complete action, thus far separately presented, are so drawn together that their relationships are seen to be mutually revealing. The episode on Gadshill, recently worked out in reality to Falstaff's discomfiture, is now gone over in retrospect and modified, in the process, by the comic imagination of the victim. The Prince carries on his jest at the expense of his companion, who simultaneously admits his defeat and evades it, transforms it into something different; and finally, in the incident in which the whole episode culminates, both combine to enact, in comic anticipation, the crucial meeting between father and son, at which the latter will accept the responsibilities imposed on him by birth, and the former find some compensation for the disappointment which his own past actions have inflicted on him.

The opening exchange between the Prince and Poins, besides stressing once more the temporary nature of the former's attachment to his base surroundings, throws a peculiar light upon his characteristic detachment. The relationship of Prince Hal to those around him, invalidated by the peculiar mental reservation which accompanies it, is necessarily incomplete. He is, to all appearances, capable of meeting his 'low' associates on their own level; but his attitude towards them, when he expresses his true feelings to Poins, who accompanies him throughout as a shady double, a baser reflection of his limitations, shows a revealing strain of condescension: 'I have sounded the very base-string of humility. Sirrah, I am sworn brother to a leash of drawers; and can call them all by their christian names, as Tom, Dick, and Francis.' The attitude is, to put the best interpretation upon it, one of patronage; the speaker, conscious of his superior station—'though I be *but* Prince of Wales': what can the 'but' imply, if not the opposite of its self-conscious fellow feeling?—expresses himself complacently to his dubious associate as he contemplates the success of his 'condescension.' The confidence with which he moves among the 'lower' orders is no more than an anticipation, one-sided if we will, still untouched with the dignity conferred by the royal office, of one of the outstanding personal qualities of the future Henry V. It is also clearly related to his father's efforts to insert himself into popularity and accounts for the tone of the patronizing references, which at once follow, to the limited vocabulary of the 'under-skinker' and to 'the pennyworth of sugar' he has just accepted from him. The tone is proper to a character in whom a necessary reformation is combined with an outlook consistently limited to the practical.

This opening incident, in itself unimportant, sets the tone of the comic action to follow, and establishes the nature of Hal's relation to Falstaff. If his character is that of a man whose intelligence is placed at the service of his public interests, he is none the less capable of responding to the comic situation with an energy of his own; this is apparent in his explanation, still to Poins, of the spirit in which he has undertaken the jest against Francis. He is, he says, full of 'all humours that have showed themselves humours since the old days of goodman Adam to the pupil age of this present twelve o'clock at midnight.' It is important to see in the Prince one of the outstanding political qualities: that of responding to human situations in their variety whilst maintaining a final detachment. If the politician is not so much a man of intellectual subtlety and moral discernment as one who can envisage with clarity the end of his activities and devote all his energies to its attainment, the Prince is a complete example of the type. Throughout this scene, he shows himself ready and able to respond to the prevailing comic spirit, to assume successively a number of parts with the intention, finally, of reducing them to absurdity; and in this Falstaff is his double, uninhibited by the need of conforming to a political pattern.

The Prince's first observations, indeed, throw light upon one of the principal contrasts of the entire action: that between himself and Hotspur, whose prowess and 'honourable' attitude have been so unfavourably compared, by Henry IV himself, with his own neglect of duty. His sense of the limitation of this 'honour' is one of the principal touchstones of Hal's developing character. His intelligence is of the kind that, operating entirely on the political level, sees through all pretences and evasions to the realities beneath them. Hotspur's reputation does not blind him to his failings, and when he now describes him he at once conforms to his own assumption of a cynical tone—appropriate to the 'humours' of his tavern associates—and stresses the lack of imagination which we have just witnessed in his rival's attitude to his wife. Hotspur is the man who 'kills me six or seven dozen of Scots at a breakfast' and then complains of his 'quiet life,' like Douglas whose prowess in battle is filled out, in the popular imagination, with adornments which strike Hal, in his ironical detachment, as simply absurd:

PRINCE: He that rides at high speed and with his pistol kills a sparrow flying.
FALSTAFF: You have hit it.
PRINCE: So did he never the sparrow.   (II. iv)

Once more, as so often in Shakespeare, we are to avoid taking sides. The Prince and Hotspur, opposed at this stage as the conventional incarnation of 'honour' and its seeming opposite, are in fact in some sense complementary figures. Hotspur's 'honour' is real, more real than the Prince in this mood would admit; its poetic expression at its best moments guarantees its validity, and the Prince is, thus far, the poorer for his lack of it. The implied criticism, however, is also real, related to aspects of the character already presented. It is worth noting, as confirmation of the continuity of conception that links this scene to the main action, that Hal stresses his rival's treatment, so recently presented, of his wife; the 'roan horse' appears once more, and the inarticulate replies of the man who despises words are reproduced, separated indeed from their redeeming tenderness, but none the less relevant. The criticism proceeds from an intelligence limited thus far by the lack of virtues which the comparison with Hotspur still suggests, but already able to probe the real weaknesses of his rival. For Hal, Percy is an enemy, but his attitude would hardly have differed had he been an ally. In either case, the firm if limited judgement would have been based on the same clear and narrow principles of expediency. With this attitude brought to life, vivified by the prevailing comic intention, we are introduced to the true spirit of this scene.

The next stage in the confronting of contrasted and mutually illuminating attitudes which make up this episode is provided by the exposure of Falstaff and his companions. To the Prince their entry has been a confirmation of the carnival spirit—'Call in ribs, call in tallow'—which dwells on the fleshliness it must shortly reject; but it also introduces comedy of a less obvious kind. In the re-creation of the Gadshill robbery, two different attitudes meet. For the Prince the episode has been a source of entertainment, a conscious turning aside—like the by-play with the 'drawers'—from responsibility in the course of which he has stooped very close to that 'preying upon' the commonwealth at which Gadshill first hinted. For Falstaff, on the other hand, this sordid episode becomes, as he relives it, an imaginative manifestation of the free spirit of comedy, a release from the ties of law which will not be finally valid (for he is, after all, eventually exposed), but which meanwhile represents itself in the most various ways. Here, as always, until he is curbed by the imposition of fact, Falstaff represents life, the refusal to be bound by moral categories which, necessary in themselves, are so often limited, even selfish in their particular application. His imagination habitually transcends his situation, escapes its immediate cause to rise to a generality of statement that is, in his mouth, at once grotesque and variously true. So it is with his denunciation of the 'cowardice' of his fellows. To discuss whether Falstaff is or is not a coward is finally irrelevant, because the character is not, at these moments, conceived in terms of realistic motive at all; it is rather that the categories of cowardice and valour have become, while he speaks, momentarily irrelevant. So much is this so that social necessity leads finally to his elimination, but will run the risk, in eliminating him, of killing the vitality it needs. To put the matter in another way, we feel at these moments an affinity with Falstaff as he rejects the common categories of virtue; but—we must add—by these categories, in spite of him, life must finally be lived, and only in the light of their necessity is the protest against them comprehensible.

'Is there no virtue extant?' In asking this question, Falstaff takes us beyond his own behaviour, is carried (and, while he speaks, carries us with him) by his exuberant imagination to make a statement that appears in his mouth monstrous, yet has relation, imaginatively speaking, to the sombre political world around him: 'there is nothing but roguery to be found in villanous man.' This again leads to a deploring of the death of 'good manhood' upon 'the face of the earth,' and to a picture of himself which, realistically grotesque as it is, yet lives by the sheer imaginative energy that goes to the expression of it:

There live not three good men unhanged in England; and one of them is fat and grows old: God help the while! a bad world, I say. I would I were a weaver; I could sing psalms or any thing.   (II. iv)

The imaginative range here is as far beyond the Prince as it is, in its kind, beyond any other character in the play. In the first place, comedy—monstrous, impudent, and grotesque—plays on the threat of the gallows which repeatedly shadows Falstaff, and continues to touch—but in a comic tone—on a note of pessimism. In the second, that same note is given personal illustration in terms of the fatness that is at once the outward sign of Falstaff's dissolution and his most obvious comic attribute; and then, having changed himself verbally into an object of pity, he touches in passing upon an impression of himself as a moralist deploring the ways of a degenerate world. The inversion of Puritan values is, indeed, constant in Falstaff, an essential element in his stupendous complexity of outlook. Falstaff at once comments on strict conceptions of 'virtue,' reducing them to the grotesquely insincere, and is shown, by his repudiation of them, as limited, lacking in a necessary moral dimension, which his associate, the Prince, in repudiating him, will appear to attain, but principally as an instrument of policy. Falstaff, for whom virtue implies negation and hypocrisy, and the Prince, master of the political situation but humanly flawed by the very success of his identification with his office, are bound together in a common destiny; and the final term in that destiny will turn out to be the 'rejection' from which neither really recovers.

Falstaff's account of the Gadshill adventure, and his subsequent exposure, are in the main self-explanatory. As always, two worlds, two contrasted attitudes to life, are brought into play. Falstaff's comic imagination plays upon the incident, transforming it at will and making of it, at least in part, a satire on the exaggerations of heroic warfare. 'Eight times thrust through the doublet, four through the hose . . . I never dealt better since I was a man': so might one of the warriors in the 'serious' action glorify his own prowess. The same expansive comic energy, using the effects of the popular stage to superb effect, has just produced the picture of Falstaff, in his own words, as beating the future king out of his kingdom 'with a dagger of lath' and driving his subjects before him 'like a flock of wild geese.' The astonishing variety of attitudes present in the utterances of a single man, combining this comic extravagance with insistent references to deliquescence and decay—the sun melting 'the dish of butter,' in the Prince's phrase, and the presentation of himself, in his own, as 'a shotten herring'—each image balancing its fellow and each, in refusing to be taken seriously, killing the false seriousness around it, is the key to Falstaff's function in the play.

Always, however, this positive comic aspect is balanced by its contrary. As Falstaff's imagination expands, moving away from the original sordidness of the Gadshill incident, so does the dry precision of the Prince take pleasure in exposing the facts of the case; and the exposure, again most typically, leads to that insistence upon sweat and grossness—'thou clay-brained guts, . . . thou whoreson, obscene, greasy tallow-catch'—which is at once the true reverse of Falstaff's exuberant fleshliness and a sign of the compensating vulgarity which, in these comic scenes, so persistently attracts Hal's cold-blooded, efficient way of thought. Once more the relationship between the two men brings out the character of each in its most extreme form. As Falstaff sees that his story is not accepted, he deliberately exaggerates it; the 'two rogues in buckram' become 'eleven,' not clearly because he expects to be believed—the palpable nature of the lie guarantees it against acceptance—but because he intends, by turning the episode to comedy, to remove it altogether from the realm of fact. As Falstaff's imagination grows, swells into the deliberately incredible, the Prince's reaction concentrates upon the element of physical disgust which the presence of his companion so persistently rouses in his colder, more fastidious nature.

To the end of the episode, however, Falstaff, opposing to concentration his nimble imaginative quality, eludes his pursuer. The escape is based on a refusal to accept as valid that 'reason' which is, for the Prince, the breath of political life, and which even in the tavern he only self-consciously lays aside. The clash of personalities ends, as usual, in a deliberate exaggeration on either side of the contrasted physical qualities which incarnate their respective natures. On the side of Falstaff, as seen by the Prince, we have 'this *sanguine* coward,' 'this huge hill of flesh,' images which expand, affirm themselves, and, at the same time, convey the speaker's disapproval; on the side of Hal, as pictured by his disreputable associate, we have 'you starveling, you elf-skin, you dried neat's tongue, you bull's pizzle, you stock-fish,' and the rest. Both are exaggerations, exaggerations respectively of warm corruption and cold efficiency, each revealed through its physical qualities; but it is certain that, with the argument on this level, Falstaff will have the best of it, and the Prince, to reassert himself, has to return to his own realm of cold fact and reason: 'when thou hast tired thyself in base comparisons, hear me speak but this.' Hal's dominion is, in the long run and even in his moments of tavern expansion, that of the 'plain tale'; Falstaff's is that of the comic fantasy playing upon reality, transforming it even in the acceptance of its own corruption. As seen by the Prince through the eyes of sober fact, which are finally relevant, Falstaff at Gadshill 'carried his guts away' and 'roared for mercy . . . as ever I heard bull-calf'; and once the dispute has been carried to this sphere, Falstaff can only recall his imaginative exploits and return to the 'play extempore.' The ascribing of his cowardice to 'instinct,' implying a mock bow to the princely status which Hal has been in this scene degrading, leads to the equally typical inversion of the scriptural admonition: 'watch to-night, pray to-morrow.' It is the essence of Falstaff's comic spirit, in playing upon familiar concepts, to invert them, and to extract from the inversion a distinctive, irreducible vitality.

The arrival of a messenger from the court, with news of the northern rebellion, at once prepares for the interruption of the tavern action, in which the Prince will henceforth play a steadily diminishing part, and gives Falstaff a new opportunity to apply his comic spirit. The tavern is not the world, implies indeed at this point an impossible rejection of the world; but the interruption opens the way for yet another significant contrast. The reactions of Falstaff and the Prince to the news are set once more in opposition. The Prince, concentrated as ever upon the practical, suggests, after something of a gibe at his 'father' and 'mother' that is not particularly attractive in him, that the messenger should be dismissed with a bribe: 'Give him as much as will make him a royal man.' Falstaff, on the other hand, turns the moral theme of time and old age to his own comic purpose: 'What doth gravity out of his bed at midnight?' Both act in accordance with their own natures. The Prince, devoted to the concrete, the practical, will eventually become the representative of a morality dedicated to political ends; Falstaff, in whose phrases life thrusts through all barriers and confinements, will be at once intensely alive and impatient of necessary order. The one will achieve his ends at the expense of some aspects of humanity; the other, while remaining human to the last, will end by distorting humanity itself to his own monstrous image, making it necessary for the moral instinct to disown him to escape the threat of complete anarchy.

Not, however, until the parody of the interview between Henry IV and his son is the connection between the 'serious' action and its 'comic' underplot made finally clear. The episode is of course a comic anticipation of the real one to follow;[8] it is moreover an anticipation critical in type, bringing out certain flaws in the central situation which it exposes to comic scrutiny:

FALSTAFF: . . . this chair shall be my state, this dagger my sceptre, and this cushion my crown.
PRINCE: Thy state is taken for a joined-stool, thy golden sceptre for a leaden dagger, and thy precious rich crown for a pitiful bald crown!

(II. iv)

The juxtaposition of the two speeches is not without meaning. Falstaff, typically, starts from the humble objects around him and, maintaining his comic purpose, subjects them, albeit in parody, to a certain imaginative transformation. The chair becomes 'my state,' the false dagger a 'sceptre,' and the cushion a 'crown'; whilst for the Prince, who follows the inverse process in his concentration upon the real, the same state is restored to its true nature as a 'joined-stool,' the 'golden sceptre' to a dagger of 'lead,' and the 'rich crown' to the 'pitiful bald crown' of ad-

[8] *1 Henry IV,* III. ii, and pp. 80–84 below.

vancing years. The process on either side is not without relation to the main conception.

As much can be said of Falstaff's following parody. He begins by referring to his imaginative power (drink-inspired, however) as capable of stirring 'the fire of grace' in his audience and goes on to stress the comic nature of what is to follow by calling for sack 'to make my eyes look red'; so inspired, he proceeds to parody the excesses of the old melodrama 'in King Cambyses' vein.' The theatrical quality of his parody is further stressed by the Hostess' reference to the 'harlotry players,' which sets the tone for what is to come. Falstaff's behaviour after ascending his mock throne is, as we have said, a parody by anticipation of the scene to follow, in which Henry IV's relation to his son is brought to the centre of the whole play; it is also a mock enthronement of 'misrule' in the spirit of carnival and leads finally to its necessary exposure. His description of the Prince, using the supposed words of his father, contains a sardonic caricature of the family nature: 'That thou art my son, I have partly thy mother's word, partly my own opinion, but chiefly a villanous trick of thine eye, and a foolish hanging of the nether lip, that doth warrant me.' It is not thus, of course, that Henry does actually speak to his son, nor is the relationship between them of this kind; but the disillusioned clarity, even the coarseness of Falstaff's description, corresponds to something really present in the family nature, that makes itself felt repeatedly in the Prince's attitude towards his tavern life—especially in association with Poins—and is related to the detachment which is one ingredient of his political sense. For, in spite of all, there is more than a little relevance in the question put by Falstaff into Henry's mouth: 'Shall the son of England prove a thief and take purses?'

If this were Falstaff's last word, however, he would be something less than the great comic creation he is. It is the essence of the character that it should at once convey dissolution and, in the manner of conveying it, provide it with a vitality that transcends it. Thus, having made—in parody—a serious moral point, and having backed it up—but in euphuistic hollowness of phrase—with the commonplace that 'pitch . . . doth defile' and 'so doth the company thou keepest,' he goes on to put into Henry's mouth an account at once comic, and so *not* to be taken at its declared value, and full of human feeling. When he points to himself as the 'virtuous man' whom the Prince should keep by him, he is clearly saying the opposite of what Henry will and *must* say; and yet the following description carries enough life with it for us to realize that the circumstances which demand Falstaff's banishment also involve a turning aside from life, a loss which no necessity, political or even moral, can make altogether irrelevant. For Falstaff, as he presents himself for this particular purpose (and his imagination can compass many presentations for many, even contradictory, ends), is

A good portly man, i'faith, and a corpulent; of a cheerful look, a pleasing eye, and a most noble carriage.

For all its admitted comic quality, there is no mistaking the positive, life-reflecting tone of this description. The speaker is imaginatively identified with his words even as he laughs at himself through the qualities he seeks to convey. When he makes the king say he sees 'virtue' in his eye, he is clearly mocking himself, and the image of the tree which is known by its fruit reaffirms the specific religious undertone, which is here at once an object of ridicule in its Puritan implications, and a measure or standard; and yet when he stresses age in himself, 'inclining to threescore,' it is, potentially at least, a real pathos that he is reducing to absurdity, and humour of this kind can only proceed from a certain honest candour of approach. 'Goodly' and 'cheerful' in his portliness, we can neither accept Falstaff as representing a sufficient view of life nor dismiss him as irrelevant. He is there, at the heart of the play, and his comments, though never all the truth, are always relevant to its complete definition.

This emerges clearly enough when it becomes the Prince's turn to parody his father. In contrast to Falstaff, he brings to his parody that concentrated intensity which is part of his largely amoral nature. Shakespeare has already, in this same scene, revealed this quality in apparently petty turns of phrase. When Falstaff, commenting on the news of the rebellion, refers to the critical state of the realm in words that suggest the presence of corruption—'you may buy land now as cheap as stinking mackerel'—his reply is characteristic:

. . . if there come a hot June and this civil buffeting hold, we shall buy maidenheads as they buy hob-nails, by the hundreds.

Spoken of itself in a tavern, phrasing of this kind might be passed over; but the type of feeling that prompts it makes its presence felt too often to be ignored. The Prince's dismissal as 'civil buffeting' of a crisis so close to his royal state is, however temporary or even assumed, scarcely edifying, and the reference to 'maidenheads' is prompted by an attitude to the flesh, almost contemptuous, that is paralleled elsewhere. Falstaff himself is the butt of an intense grossness that is surely relevant to the character; in this parody of the relationship between father and son, the Prince heaps upon him such a list of epithets as 'bolting-hutch of beastliness,' 'swollen parcel of dropsies,' 'huge bombard of sack,' and 'stuffed cloak-bag of guts.' It is noteworthy, in an episode so variously related to popular traditions, that the king's supposed denunciation should turn largely on the association of Falstaff with familiar conventions. If the 'roasted Manningtree ox with the pudding in his belly' derives explicitly from a popular feast, the further evocations of the 'reverend vice,' 'grey iniquity,' and 'vanity in years' clearly require, for their appreciation, a backward glance to the familiar figures of the 'morality' tradition. This variety in his traditional and popular derivations, indeed, largely accounts for the unique fascination exercised by Falstaff; it is as though many anonymous figures, consecrated by established custom and related to living popular traditions, were brought together, at once united and transformed, in this great figure of swelling, if unregulated, vitality and comic vigour.

From participation in this wealth of life the Prince is, by the very responsibilities of his position, largely excluded. We have only to compare the spirit of his denunciation with Falstaff's equally material, but more human, exuberance to see that a deliberate contrast is being pointed. As usual, the terms of the contrast are far from simple. The tone adopted by the Prince is no doubt a necessary correction to Falstaff's grotesque emphasis upon 'godliness' and 'noble carriage'; it certainly brings out a true aspect of his 'three score years of aging villany,' and the repudiation is undoubtedly necessary if the Prince is to fulfil his vocation. The truth, however, is so stated as to bring out certain less attractive qualities in the speaker, qualities which may assist him in gaining his political ends but are not thereby made more humanly acceptable. The insistence upon utterances so lacking in the spontaneous imaginative warmth that characterizes Falstaff's fleshliness is certainly intentional. It is as though Hal, whose every action tends to calculation, felt for his companion the semi-conscious repulsion inspired in the coldly practical intellect by something which it can neither understand, ignore, nor, in the last resort, use. The Prince, in echoing Falstaff's idiom, brings to it a cold, efficient intensity that points to an underlying aversion. The flesh, with which the finished politician needs to reckon, is nevertheless an object of repulsion to him. Beneath the burlesque and the rowdiness we may already look forward to the final rejection.

Falstaff, indeed, in a plea not less pathetic for being a parody based on monstrous presumption, finally justifies himself in terms of human normality:

If sack and sugar be a fault, God help the wicked! if to be old and merry be a sin, then many an old host that I know is damned: if to be fat be to be hated, then Pharaoh's lean kine are to be loved.

(II. iv)

The plea is steeped in sentiment, even in the exploitation of feeling, and to that extent it cannot be admitted; but, as an approach to human qualities that Hal is the poorer for having to exclude, it is supported by a religious reference that attains, through and in despite of open parody, a force of its own. Once more, the expression of the plea turns, in its most effective moments, on an inversion of the familiar Biblical phrases dear to the Puritan mind; but it is now directed to the service of a morality which even the speaker's grotesque enormity cannot entirely undo. This morality justifies, at least as part of the complete effect, Falstaff's final appeal against dismissal: 'banish plump Jack, and banish all the world.' Banish Falstaff, in other words, and banish everything that cannot be reduced to an instrument of policy in the quest for a success that is, in its absence, haunted by a sense of emptiness. It is true to the Prince's nature and to the tragedy of his family that he can already reply without hesitation, speaking in anticipation of his own future action as much as in parody of his father's present attitude: 'I do, I will.'

The news, carried by Bardolph, of the arrival of the Sheriff and the subsequent comedy, which shows Falstaff as sufficiently self-possessed to sleep behind the arras when his life, as he has himself confessed, hangs on the Prince's willingness to shield him, otherwise adds little to what has gone before. It ends with Hal's statement that 'we must all to the wars,' pointing to the change of spirit that now overtakes the action. From this time on, neither the Prince nor Falstaff will be devoted entirely to their life of comic freedom, and their actions, like those of everyone else in the play, will look forward to the resolution at Shrewsbury.

III

By the end of the great tavern scene, the two principal threads of the early action—the serious and the comic, the aristocratic and the popular—have been brought together, presented as mutually illuminating. Thus united they lead to a scene (III. ii) of central importance to the whole play, in which the king and his son are at last confronted and the choice between public vocation and private dissolution, ordered royalty and the chaos of 'misrule,' finally made. Upon this choice depends in turn the health of the English polity, already presented in its various elements as subjected to the disorder which emanates from its head, from the suspect origins of Henry's kingship. This decisive meeting is placed between two episodes which indicate between them, and each in its own way, the point of decisive change reached by the action as a whole. The first (III. i), focussed principally on Hotspur, stresses the growth of mutual recrimination in the rebel camp as a counterpoise to Hal's reconciliation with his father; in the second (III. iii), the Prince and Falstaff meet in their tavern surroundings for the last time (in this play) and the sub-jection of the comic action to warlike events is finally confirmed. From this point, the various strands of the conception, now united, will run together to meet in the arbitrament of war.

The first scene, therefore, returns to the political action and to the rebel camp. After Hotspur's first revealing admission—'I have forgot the map'—the scene moves on to a clash of personalities between himself and Glendower. The latter opens with an attempt, typically pretentious, to flatter his associate, which serves merely to irritate Hotspur and to provide an initial occasion of discord:

> GLENDOWER: as oft as Lancaster
>   Doth speak of you, his cheeks look pale and with
>   A rising sigh he wisheth you in heaven.
> HOTSPUR: And you in hell, as oft as he hears Owen
>   Glendower spoke of.   (III. i)

It is not in Hotspur's nature to respond in kind to Glendower's elaborate compliments. His retort, with its barely concealed impatience, produces one of the Welshman's expressions of poetic self-esteem, a statement that the earth shook at his birth, to which Hotspur replies with a frank dis-belief. Glendower persists in his fantastic claims, and Hotspur in his mulish refusal to be diplomatic, until the Welshman's final boast that he can 'command the devil' is met with the blunt 'tell truth, and shame the devil.' The two leaders irritate one another mutually in a way that bodes ill for the success of their cause.

Thus far Hotspur, though scarcely politic, has come well enough out of the exchange; but when the discussion passes to political negotiation his own failings are stressed. If Glendower is a mixture of superstition, vanity, and incompetence whose self-regard prompts him to look every-where for insults, Hotspur, the soul of 'honour,' is not only ready to carve his own country into the spoils of war but to quarrel over the division; and, when at last he has forced Glendower to agree, he admits in effect that his obstinacy has been the product of ill-tempered spleen:

> I do not care; I'll give thrice so much land
> To any well-deserving friend;
> But in the way of bargain, mark ye me,
> I'll cavil on the ninth part of a hair.   (III. i)

Here, at least, the reverse aspect of Hotspur's 'generosity' is remorselessly revealed. Having risked the unity of the enterprise to which he is in fact committed, he is able, having got his way, to thrust aside the occasion of his anger with an easy 'I do not care,' and an equally specious show of munificence; but the stubborn obstinacy echoed in his final words, and the pursuit of his feud with Glendower to a point at which it places the common interest in jeopardy, are undoubtedly revelations of an unstable and immature outlook.

The clash of opinions, which at once follows, between Hotspur and the shadowy Mortimer is used to present similar dissensions from yet another standpoint. The situation, still centred on Hotspur, is characteristically exposed through the varied reactions of those who participate in it, all relevant and illuminating, none finally valid. Hotspur's irritation with Glendower smoulders on in bluff, contemptuous impatience. So much talk about 'a moulten raven' and 'a ramping cat,' so much 'skimble-skamble stuff': this is a form of honesty which, at its best, can penetrate to the reality beneath political intrigue and which turns, at its worst, to obtuse and obstinate insensibility. To Mortimer, at all events, whose royal claim has served as a pretext to bring together these headstrong, rapacious conspirators, such disagreements foreshadow ruin. His attempt to reconcile his supporters is marked by the kind of courtliness that goes with gullibility:

> In faith, he is a worthy gentleman,
> Exceedingly well read, and profited
> In strange concealments; valiant as a lion
> And wondrous affable, and as bountiful
> As mines of India.

It is not difficult to see here a naïve, fatuous willingness to be impressed, taken in by the tall story, which is Mortimer's main contribution to the set of political portraits so realistically presented in this scene. A claim to authority so weakly sustained is in itself no match for Bolingbroke's disillusioned political competence; nor can it hope to impose unity upon the rival greeds and warring egoisms into which rebellion, following the compulsions of its own nature, finally disintegrates.

It is left, as usual, to Worcester to provide a distinctively 'politic' comment on these exchanges. Hotspur is reproved for

> Defect of manners, want of government,
> Pride, haughtiness, opinion and disdain,

qualities all presented, as befits the speaker, in terms of their unhappy public consequences; for of these faults he goes on to say:

> The least of which haunting a nobleman
> Loseth men's hearts and leaves behind a stain
> Upon the beauty of all parts besides,
> Beguiling them of commendation.

The rebuke is in perfect accordance with the political tone of the play, which both parties in the action ultimately share. In Worcester (who is in this not altogether unlike Henry, being indeed a disloyal image of his king) the moral qualities associated with 'nobility,' with elevated social standing and traditional distinction of 'blood,' have exclusively a public value; the attitude is one which, besides reflecting the duplicity which necessarily accompanies rebellion, is finally related to the uncertainty, the need to maintain an insecure public reputation which derives for both sides alike from the tarnished nature of Henry's own royal claim.

The end of the scene points a comic contrast between Mortimer's 'romantic' interlude with his wife, in which Glendower's 'magic' devices seek to bridge the gap of language between them, and the ironic comments of Hotspur and Lady Percy. Slight as it is, the episode continues to indicate flaws in character with economy and relevance. Hotspur's concealment of tenderness, of which he is made ashamed by the excessively facile emotions before him, once more suggests an incomplete attitude to human relationships:

> Swear me, Kate, like a lady as thou art,
> A good mouth-filling oath, and leave 'in sooth,'
> And such protest of pepper-gingerbread,
> To velvet-guards and Sunday-citizens.

The comment contains at once a true criticism of the false conventions which surround Mortimer's 'romance' and an implied exposure of the speaker's own limitation to a set of prejudices imposed upon him by character and class alike. The traditional aristocrat's pride in his own plain-speaking, and his contempt for the pretensions to breeding self-consciously assumed by the lower orders are here combined in an admirable portrait from which neither detachment nor a certain affection are absent. In its modest way, this piece of 'popular' comedy already reflects the mature Shakespearean capacity for extracting a variety of meanings from the dramatic presentation of human relationships.

With the movement of the scene from Wales to London (iii. ii), from the rebel quarters to the private councils of the king, the relation of the 'personal' to the political theme is at last directly explored. The confronting of Henry with his son, and the latter's acceptance of his royal vocation has, of course, a 'public,' rhetorical value which the traditional story imposed. The king's opening words, however, modify this conception to include issues of a more intimate kind. Prince Hal, destined to become the incarnation of political virtue, is in his unregenerate state a 'scourge' in the hands of God, a reminder to his father of the 'displeasing service' performed by him in the past:

> I know not whether God will have it so,
> For some displeasing service I have done,
> That, in his secret doom, out of my blood
> He'll breed revengement and a scourge for me;
> But thou dost in thy passages of life
> Make me believe that thou art only marked
> For the hot vengeance and the rod of heaven
> To punish my mistreadings.   (III. ii)

The stressing of the theme of retribution corresponds already to an intimate sense of tragic fatality. The 'doom' is 'secret,' the 'revengement' obscurely bred out of the sinner's own blood to chastise him for his public fault; and yet the sense of guilt which burdens the speech is presented, in accordance with the speaker's character, as related to his overmastering sense of expediency. What Henry condemns in his son is finally a public, a political blemish. His preoccupation is with the 'low' and 'inordinate' nature of desires that do not correspond to the princely standing of his heir; Hal's 'attempts' are 'poor,' 'bare,' 'lewd,' and 'mean,' his pleasures 'barren,' and the essence of his faults is a surrender to 'rude society' which prejudices his 'greatness' and is incompatible with the obligations of his 'princely heart.' From the very first the tragic quality of Henry's most intimate reflections is associated with the public, visible nature of the vocation he has dubiously assumed and which is already turning into the consuming burden of his life.

Henry's second and longer speech, which follows his son's first slight effort to clear himself, penetrates more deeply to the intimate nature of his tragedy. The words in which he points bitterly to the contrast between Hal's youth and his own show a remarkable and characteristic blend of feeling and political calculation. The former indeed shades almost imperceptibly into the latter, lending it the modifying presence of true emotion. That Henry is genuinely moved by his son's behaviour, that he feels 'tenderness' for him and has 'desired to see him more' is beyond doubt; without the presence of such feeling, indeed, the sense of tragedy which his utterances convey would be inconceivable. Yet, as we follow the long speech, the suspicion grows upon us that the only true *moral* criterion of this king has been, from the beginning, *political* effectiveness. His early ambitions, once so confidently pursued, have become the limiting conditions which pursue the House of Lancaster throughout this series of plays, and which even his son's future triumphs will not entirely transcend. It is necessary, of course, in pointing to this limitation, not to exaggerate its relevance. The royal vocation is, by its nature, lived in the public eye; but the emphasis on appearance, on popularity as a determining factor in behaviour confirms a family trait already touched on by the Prince in his opening soliloquy and reflected, from time to time, in the detachment with which he views his 'low' associates. Political virtue, in other words, can easily become private limitation, and the sense of this limitation, related to the memory of crimes committed for personal ends, is in itself a source of tragic feeling.

The exchange between father and son is, in short, coming to life in terms of a consistent reading of character and heredity. As Henry, looking back over his past, compares his own attitude with Richard's prodigality, the speech gathers life, attains a fuller and more varied expressive power:

> The skipping king, he ambled up and down
> With shallow jesters and rash bavin wits,
> Soon kindled and soon burnt; carded his state,
> Mingled his royalty with capering fools,
> Had his great name profaned with their scorns
> And gave his countenance, against his name,
> To laugh at gibing boys and stand the push
> Of every beardless vain comparative,
> Grew a companion to the common streets,
> Enfeoff'd himself to popularity;
> That, being daily swallow'd by men's eyes,
> They surfeited with honey and began
> To loathe the taste of sweetness, whereof a little
> More than a little is by much too much.
> Soon when he had occasion to be seen,
> He was but as the cuckoo is in June,
> Heard, not regarded; seen, but with such eyes
> As, sick and blunted with community,
> Afford no extraordinary gaze,
> Such as is bent on sun-like majesty
> When it shines seldom in admiring eyes;
> But rather drowzed and hung their eyelids down,
> Slept in his face and render'd such aspect
> As cloudy men use to their adversaries,
> Being with his presence glutted, gorged and full.
>
> (III. ii)

In length and variety of expression alike, the speech confirms its fundamental importance in the development of the political conception. The
vigorous criticism of Henry's predecessor, 'the skipping king,' draws
freely on vernacular phrasing—'*carded* his state,' 'capering fools,' 'shallow jesters and rash *bavin* wits'—to reflect the speaker's keen interest in
the intricacies of political behaviour. The rhythms still follow, basically,
the common blank verse pattern; but the increasing tendency of the line
to overrun its limits, the greater length and complexity of the periods,
and the coincidence of stress with the powerful accumulation of emphatic
words and phrases ('soon kindled and soon burnt,' 'carded . . . mingled
. . . profaned,' 'sick and blunted,' 'glutted, gorged and full') point to
the existence of a deeper and more varied interest. That interest is, as
we have said, essentially political in type and, as such, a constant feature
of the Lancastrian outlook; it is also a key both to the success which has
accompanied the family (for Richard's failings, here so forcibly and truly
described, amount to a degradation of royalty) and to its limitations.

Behind this statement, indeed, associated with the political virtues
as the intimate, personal flaw which has already manifested itself supremely in the readiness to contemplate murder as a means to power,
Shakespeare is careful to convey a note of falseness and moral complexity.
The speech opens in calculation, turns with preference on an estimate
of the public effect of 'virtuous' discretion:

> By being seldom seen, I could not stir
> But like a comet I was wonder'd at;
> That men would tell their children 'This is he;'
> Others would say 'Where, which is Bolingbroke?'

The use of modesty to arrive at a position of pride, of concealment to
produce universal attention, is deeply implanted in this essentially, exclusively, public personality. The ambiguity of the following phrases
amply confirms the initial effect. Bolingbroke, in his own words, '*stole*
all courtesy from heaven,' 'dress'd' himself in a humility which is clearly
less a moral virtue than a device of policy. For Henry the criterion of
morality has always tended to be success; and, that being so, it is not
surprising that his son should have learnt to separate feeling from the
necessities of political behaviour and that filial tenderness, real as it is
in him in his moments of deeper sincerity, should exist side by side with
a readiness to subject personal considerations to public achievement. In
the realization, born of bitter experience, that the quest for this achievement can also be an illusion, lies the secret of the tragic note which
dominates the king's later years.

The comparison of his son with Hotspur, with which Henry concludes his harangue and reveals the latest news of the rebellion, is scarcely
as personal in expression as what has gone before. It leads at last to the
Prince's reaction in which, for the first of many occasions, denigration
of his character exacts the response of a fixed, firm intensity of purpose.
'I will redeem all this on Percy's head,' he replies, and goes on to paint
a picture of himself as a ruthless warrior which will be repeated in due
course, and in terms not altogether dissimilar, by Henry V at the gates
of Harfleur:[9]

> I will wear a garment all of blood
> And stain my favours in a bloody mask,
> Which, wash'd away, shall scour my shame with it . . .
>
> .   .   .   .
>
> Percy is but my factor, good my lord,
> To engross up glorious deeds on my behalf;
> And I will call him to so strict account,
> That he shall render every glory up,
> Yea, even the slightest worship of his time,
> Or I will tear the reckoning from his heart.
> This, in the name of God, I promise here . . .
>
> (III. ii)

The total effect of this speech is not easily to be described. The reformation of the private dissolute into the public figure is, without doubt,
essential to the conception; the Prince is vowing himself to duty, and
from this time his behaviour will never again be what it was in the irresponsible earlier scenes. Yet there are other aspects of this dedication
which need equally to be considered. Among them is the emphasis on
'I,' a cold determination which the speech also shows and which is, at
least in part, a reaction against the galling superiority attributed to his
rival; for behind the phrase 'your unthought-of Harry,' bitter resentment
exists side by side with filial concern. It is a rigid war-machine as well
as a prince finding his true nature that is being evoked here, and the
culminating dedication to 'God' needs to be seen simultaneously under
both aspects if the full value of the scene is to be realized. 'I will tear the
reckoning from his heart': from this moment on, an iron fatality has
been set in motion which will assert itself on the field at Shrewsbury
and—finally—at Harfleur and at Agincourt.

The following scene (III. iii), carrying on the device by which the

[9] See p. 152 below.

'serious' action and its comic parallel are alternately developed, reveals
a certain change in spirit. We are, in fact, leaving the free, irresponsible
world of tavern incident and moving towards another which will finally
lead, in this play, to the resolution of battle. In this new world Falstaff,
though he maintains his comic energies, will no longer stand supreme.
His first words take us back to the 'action' on Gadshill and its comic
sequel at Eastcheap, but in a changed and in some sense a chastened
spirit: 'Bardolph, am I not fallen away vilely since this last action? do
I not bate? do I not dwindle?' Falstaff can still look upon himself with
comic detachment, as when he says that 'my skin hangs about me like
an old lady's loose gown,' or compares his 'withered' state to that of an
'old apple-john'; but the emphasis on age and exhaustion, though hu-
mourously conceived, is new, and the elements of the following comedy
equally indicate a change of attitude. Immediately after these first indications, the comic phrases turn upon conceptions of repentance and
amendment, already used by Falstaff when, in the first tavern scene, he
had spoken of 'giving over this life';[10] but whereas repentance had there
been made light of, in a spirit of comic inversion, the new utterance is
perceptibly more sombre in tone:

Well, I'll repent, and that suddenly, while I am in some liking; I shall be
out of heart shortly, and then I shall have no strength to repent.

No doubt the element of religious parody is still present here, but Shakespeare, as he approaches his maturity, has a way of combining various
purposes in a single phrase, and the change of spirit at this point, confirmed as it is by what follows, is a clear sign that the discomfiture of
'misrule' is already acting as a limiting factor on the free expansion of
the comic spirit.

The dialogue which follows relates this shift of feeling to other facets,
equally traditional in derivation, of the character. When Bardolph comically falls in with his feigned spirit of repentance by saying 'you cannot
live long,' Falstaff replies by taking up the other, the 'fleshly' and dis-
orderly side of his nature: 'Come, sing me a bawdy song; make me
merry.' This continual capacity to move from one aspect of his presentation to another, balancing contrary impressions in a single complex
effect, is of the essence of the complete conception. At this point it turns
into a satire upon gentility. 'I was as virtuously given as a gentleman
need to be,' Falstaff begins, weighing comedy with a certain mock nos-

[10] *1 Henry IV*, I. ii.

talgia implied in his backward glance to a lost past. As a 'gentleman,' Falstaff was 'virtuous,' but mildly so, 'virtuous *enough*'; and the following phrases balance virtue with its opposite in humourous antithesis:

. . . swore *little*; diced not above *seven times a week*; went to a bawdy-house *not above once in a quarter—of an hour*; paid money that I borrowed, *three or four times.*

The whole is a satire on the life lived 'in good compass.' At the end of it, Falstaff falls back on yet another of his traditional aspects, that which he derives from the Vice, the incarnation of disorder and the refusal to accept 'rule'; for, in his own words, which characteristically combine his moral with his physical qualities, 'now I live out of all order, out of all compass.' Bardolph, in taking up this last phrase, stresses the purely physical aspect of thus living 'out of compass'; but the physical is, of course, a reflection of the spiritual reality, and Falstaff, in asserting his freedom, is in fact, and beneath the comic spirit of his references to age and repentance, limiting it, relating it to a spiritual tradition which the play in its moments of greatest depth at once accepts and balances against a profound if anarchic vitality.

The interchange with Bardolph, inserted here and turning apparently on nothing more serious than broadly farcical references to the colour of the old drunkard's nose, further illustrates this extension of the comic conception. There is in Falstaff a true and rare combination of the warm and alert humanity which in him modifies the condemnation of 'riot' with a background, rebelled against but persistently present, of inherited Christian tradition. This element, not less than the contrary aspects just mentioned, is further associated with the memory of the devices of the mediæval religious theatre. Falstaff's utterances are steeped in tradition, at once religious and theatrical, and upon the variety of his reaction to tradition depends a good deal of the force of his presentation. He shares with his audience a whole world of imagery, a common inheritance which gives him reality more especially by contrast with the orators and politicians of the 'serious' action. The ease with which the theatrical passes into the religious reference is clearly seen in his comment on Bardolph's nose, to which he refers as 'a death's head or a memento mori'—'I never see thy face but I think upon hell-fire and Dives that lived in purple.' In such phrases we feel what the strength of a still living popular tradition could offer to the dramatist. Assimilated into Falstaff's utterances as their natural background, it enables him to bring to his criticism of the political action a realism that is, in its profounder moments, neither self-regarding nor cynical, but derived from a balanced view, still accessible to the author for dramatic purposes, of man's nature and destiny. The recognition of the presence of this view, modifying the viciousness of Falstaff in the very presentation of it, is essential to a proper understanding of his function in the play.

The reverse side of the picture is stressed, almost immediately, with the entry of the Hostess. This brings out the predatory Falstaff, ready to live on unpaid debts, to borrow mercilessly, and to accuse his companions of having stolen his possessions. His attitude to the Hostess is marked by a persistent emphasis upon the flesh, less comic than sombrely realistic in tone: an emphasis unredeemed by the spirit of comedy and intended to stress the sordid manifestations of appetite in an aging cynic:

There's no more faith in thee than in a stewed prune; nor no more truth in thee than in a drawn fox; and for womanhood, Maid Marian may be the deputy's wife of the ward to thee.

There is no need to be sentimental over the Hostess, or, indeed, over those with whom she associates. This is the common language of the brothel in which passion is indulged without illusion and the reality behind it revealed as a compound of ambiguity and promiscuous appetite:

FALSTAFF: Why, she's neither fish nor flesh; a man knows not where to have her.

HOSTESS: Thou art an unjust man in saying so: thou or any man knows where to have me, thou knave, thou!

PRINCE: Thou sayest true, hostess; and he slanders thee most grossly.

The Prince himself, indeed, is more at home in this type of repartee, sharply and disillusionedly realistic, than in the freer comic world of Falstaff's earlier appearances. The change in spirit corresponds to the new temper which henceforward dominates the action.

Even at this point, however, the more serious elements behind Falstaff's conception make their presence felt. Faced by the unanswerable truth of the Prince's denunciation—'there's no room for faith, truth, nor honesty in this bosom of thine'—and the relation of it to his physical enormity—'it is all filled up with guts and midriff'—Falstaff can still balance this evocation of the life lived 'out of all compass' with a deeper, more tragic intuition which makes itself felt not less on account of the comic use to which it is put. At his most serious moments—for in him comedy repeatedly touches the serious—Falstaff, as he recognizes his faults, gives his comic utterances a taste of universality by relating them to the familiar drama of mankind worked out in the individual between birth and death, and in the race between the Creation and the Last Judgement: 'Thou knowest in the state of innocency Adam fell; and what should poor Jack Falstaff do in the days of villany? Thou seest I have more flesh than another man, and therefore more frailty.' To take this too seriously would be as misleading as it would be shortsighted to deny it all seriousness. Falstaff's tone is in part comic, mocking religious phraseology for ends of its own; but the reference to the flesh, so closely related to what has gone before, includes the spiritual meaning sanctioned by Christian tradition, and it is in his sense of the relationship between the two realities, a relationship covering dependence and separation in a single unity, that Falstaff acquires his full stature. We need not, should not, say that Falstaff simply accepts the Christian tradition. A great part of him, based upon unbridled fleshly instinct, clearly does not, and will finally be repudiated for its rejection by a serious political conception which will itself sacrifice humanity by the necessary exclusion; but the tradition is present, alive even in the utterances that express Falstaff's refusal to submit to it, and giving him, even in this refusal, this affirmation of anarchy, a complexity that enables him at his best to dominate an action whose internal logic drives it increasingly away from him. This, however, is an anticipation of things to come. For the moment, the spirit of comic independence reasserts itself in Falstaff's remark on rebellion: 'Well, God be thanked for these rebels, they offend none but the virtuous,' which at once confirms disorder and repudiates, in the act of inverting its own phraseology, the 'virtue' which will increasingly wear a political garb, cold and at times barely human, in the development of the series.

IV

In the last stages of _Henry IV_, Part I, the various threads of the action are drawn together till they meet at Shrewsbury. The disintegration increasingly apparent among the rebels is set against the growing clarity of aim which finds its point of concentration, not in the aging king, but in the figure of his son. Contact between the rival forces is first established in the parleys between the opposing leaders; and, after these have broken down, the battle itself culminates in the encounter between Hal and Hotspur, the new concept of political honour and its feudal counterpart. In the parallel exploits of Falstaff, honour itself is exposed to comic scrutiny at the same time as the exposure of the fat knight, the necessary prelude to his final rejection, is carried a step further by the indignity of his treatment of Hotspur's corpse. Over the entire action, thus exhibited on its various and mutually revealing levels, lies the shadow of 'fortune,' of the impersonal process of events provoking individual reactions which vary from vanity and impotent pathos to an assertion of purposes clearly willed but limited to the attainment of political ends.

The opening dialogue between the two men of action among the rebels, Hotspur and Douglas, shows them engaged in flattering exchanges which contrast notably with their self-styled character of plainspeaking men. Hotspur's first words,

> if speaking truth
> In this fine age were not thought flattery,

lead up to what is, in effect, self-conscious praise of the 'noble Scot,' his companion. The disclaimer 'I cannot flatter,' besides being contradicted by the general tenor of his words, produces from his fellow warrior the corresponding gesture of gratifying admiration: 'Thou art the king of honour.' There is about this verbal competition something at best naïve, touched with inadequacy. It is impossible not to feel behind it the satire intended on the old-fashioned concepts of feudal 'honour' which will be presented from various standpoints in the scenes to follow, as background to the type of active virtue which Prince Hal will embody in its qualities and limitations.

The news of Northumberland's 'political' infirmity indicates more directly the hollow nature of the confidence which these irreflexive warriors parade. As the moment of action approaches, fears and rivalries come to the surface, imposing division just as unity of purpose is supremely called for. Hotspur's first account of the contents of his father's letter is most revealing. Caught unawares, he admits the gravity of the blow dealt to the common cause:

> Sick now! droop now! this sickness does infect
> The very life-blood of our enterprise.

The pretexts offered by Northumberland fail, by their very multiplicity, to convince. As if the writer of the letter felt that his 'inward sickness' were not enough (and the 'inwardness' of the malady points to its moral as much as to its physical nature), the reference to it is broken off, replaced by a series of sketchy alternatives: the impossibility of gathering together his friends in time, the unwillingness to delegate responsibility, and so forth. All this is false, hollow; and the final incongruity emerges when, after thus revealing his own lack of decision, Northumberland concludes by enjoining upon others the boldness which he has himself declined to show:

> Yet doth he give us bold advertisement,
> That with our small conjunction we should on,
> To see how fortune is disposed to us.

The argument is rounded off with a supreme *non sequitur*, in which full admission is made of the true position. 'There is no quailing now,' Northumberland writes—in the very act of 'quailing' himself—

> Because the king is certainly possess'd
> Of all our purposes.

It would be hard to conceive a clearer exposure of the spirit of indecision and recognized impotence on which this enterprise rests. The rebel cause, desperately committed by its own supporters to the arbitration of a 'fortune' which they know to be definitely adverse to their purposes, is already shadowed by its inevitable ruin.

The rest of the scene consists of efforts made by these same leaders to evade the bitter truths they have by implication admitted. Hotspur and Douglas meet the news of Northumberland's defection with a specious show of confidence, based on the false exercise of reason and on the readiness to see things as they are not:

> DOUGLAS: A comfort of retirement lives in this.
> HOTSPUR: A rendezvous, a home to fly unto,
> If that the devil and mischance look big
> Upon the maidenhead of our affairs.

Worcester, however, with his steadier insight both into political processes and into the nature of the cause to which he stands committed, expresses himself to his colleagues in words which strike at the roots of the pretensions on which their common enterprise is based. In Worcester, as we have already seen, Shakespeare studied the type of the political courtier whose success, such as it is, is founded on the very limitations of his outlook. Persuasiveness and 'reason,' born of cunning and experience, are his gods, so much so that we have already seen him restraining his nephew's impetuosity with the very appeal to expediency that Henry himself has put before his son; for such impatience, he tells Hotspur, 'loseth men's hearts'[11] and compromises their chances of success. Yet Worcester, for all his devotion to reason and moderation, is a rebel and, as such, driven to exclude the operations of true reason as fatal to his own projects. For reason, according to the conception presupposed in these plays, is necessarily on the side of order, of established authority, and rebellion owes its origins to the promptings of a form of passion against rational restraint. Worcester admits this flaw when he tells his associates:

[11] *1 Henry IV*, III. i.

> For well you know we of the offering side
> Must keep aloof from strict arbitrement,
> And stop all sight-holes, every loop from whence
> The eye of reason may pry in upon us.

Once more we are conscious of an action dominated by 'fortune,' of human wills exposed to a temporal fatality which they know, in their hearts, to be adverse, but which they can neither dominate nor evade.

Worcester's reaction to the empty confidence of Hotspur and Douglas is, indeed, typically double in its implications. In stressing the need for unity and common dedication to the end in view,

> The quality and hair of our attempt
> Brooks no division,

it corresponds to an undeniable realism of vision and points to a principal cause of the disaster which will in due course overtake him and his companions; but—and here it amounts, in spite of itself, to a confession of weakness—in admitting that, for a rebel, this unity must be based on an exclusion of the rational, it touches upon a flaw which will prove, in the long run, fatal to his cause. The fruits of rebellion are, like its origins, disunity and chaos; this truth illustrates a fatality of which Worcester is dimly aware, which he strives to exclude, but which is seen at this moment in the process of overtaking the enterprise to which greed and the desire for power originally committed him.

Hotspur's rejoinder, not less typically, tries to give a rational disguise to unreasonable impulses. The absence of Northumberland, he insists, will lend 'a larger dare to our great enterprise.' The emphasis on daring is associated with the conception of 'honour' which is, with all its deficiencies, his most admirable quality. In the tendency, however, to seek in this emotional reaction a ground for reason to build on, we can feel the intimate causes of Hotspur's coming downfall:

> men must think,
> If we without his help can make a head
> To push against a kingdom, with his help
> We shall o'erturn it topsy-turvy down.

Not for the first time, Hotspur is confusing reasonable confidence with the will to believe. The flaw in his argument, related to the irresponsible gesture with which he declares his readiness to contemplate disorder as the end of his efforts, to endorse the 'topsy-turvy' view of things, is obvious: so much so that the self-heartening conclusion, 'Yet all goes well, yet all our joints are whole,' can only strike us as the absurdity it is.

Faced by the very different resolution of his rival, Hotspur will shortly pay for this absurdity with his death.

The end of the scene, with the intervention of Vernon, introduces in deliberate contrast a conception of chivalry which—whatever the human shortcomings it may ultimately conceal—is, by comparison, superior in power and consistency. This conception is brought home, poetically speaking, in the account of Prince Hal, now transformed into a figure of power imaginatively conceived:

> I saw young Harry, with his beaver on,
> His cuisses on his thighs, gallantly arm'd,
> Rise from the ground like feather'd Mercury,
> And vaulted with such ease into his seat,
> As if an angel dropp'd down from the clouds,
> To turn and wind a fiery Pegasus,
> And witch the world with noble horsemanship.
>
> (IV. i)

A reader used to the complexities of Shakespeare's mature judgements—and this play already reveals a considerable degree of maturity—will not give to this description either more or less value than can properly be attached to it. Already we have been presented with enough material to form a realistic, and in some respects a limiting judgement of the type of humanity which Hal has inherited from his family and which he will later elevate to a supreme political virtue. The limitations, however, belong to the human rather than to the political order, and are compatible with supreme value in action. This value is here caught in its first public revelation. Henry is here embarked on the process of development which will finally lead him to the triumph of Agincourt, a triumph which his very shortcomings will enable him to attain more securely by excluding all the complexities which might have undermined the self-confidence necessary to the patriotic function.

Certainly, by the side of this resplendent martial confidence, the rhetoric of Hotspur strikes us as hollow, without conviction, in a relevant sense as *dated*:

> No more, no more: worse than the sun in March,
> This praise doth nourish agues. Let them come;
> They come like sacrifices in their trim,
> And to the fire-eyed maid of smoky war
> All hot and bleeding will we offer them:
> The mailed Mars shall on his altar sit
> Up to the ears in blood.
>
> (IV. i)

The emphasis on 'blood,' the adolescent insensibility turned into verbal ruthlessness, strike a note which will be familiar in Shakespeare's Roman plays, and it is significant that they should be associated with the Roman war-god. They point, by contrast with the preceding picture of Hal's martial regeneration, to an essential emptiness. The Hotspur here revealed is connected with the object of the Prince's previous satire on his rival's domestic behaviour.[12] He appears as a man who has failed to mature, whose 'honour'—overtaken by the changing times—is in the last analysis an empty rhetorical device, and who will shortly be eliminated from a world in which he has resolved to play a part without, like Coriolanus after him though on a simpler level, understanding the true nature of the issues in which his fate, and the manoeuvres of the politicians around him, have involved him.

It is no accident that Hotspur's last words in this scene concentrate rhetorically on the idea of death: 'Doomsday is near; die all, die merrily.' The background of this rhetoric has been provided throughout by reports of desertion and approaching menace. After Northumberland's defection, the news comes of Westmoreland's approach. It is accepted—'No harm: what more'—and followed by that of the king's own preparation which is also faced in a spirit of defiance: 'He shall be welcome too.' The repudiation given by events to his contemptuous reference to Prince Henry strikes Hotspur more closely to the quick:

> No more, no more: worse than the sun in March,
> This praise doth nourish agues.

At this moment at least, the shadow of his approaching fate lies ominously across the speaker's path. His words of ill omen are followed by the confirmation of Glendower's withdrawal, which Douglas and Worcester agree to be a blow and to which Hotspur's own reaction is a harebrained defiance which can only lead to ruin:

> HOTSPUR: What may the king's whole battle reach unto?
> VERNON: To thirty thousand.
> HOTSPUR: Forty let it be.

As the final references, already quoted, to 'death' and 'doomsday' show this is less an affirmation of true confidence than an anticipation of disaster. It would be hard to imagine a more adequate exposure of the confidence which Hotspur himself has been striving to impose upon his growing sense of futility.

[12] *1 Henry IV*, II. iv. See pp. 68–69.

The reappearance of Falstaff (IV. ii) shows the approaching climax from yet another point of view. Falstaff, having left behind him the comic tavern world, has finally embarked on the course which will lead to his assertion of anarchy on the field of battle. As always, he appears in his double capacity as an independent figure of comic commentary and as supreme incarnation of disorder. Both aspects inspire his attitude towards the men under his command. Naturally, he has no illusions about his human material, the 'cankers,' as he describes them, 'of a calm world and a long peace.' Indeed, since he is himself exploiting this material, after allowing his original recruits to buy themselves out of service, this is no matter for surprise; but his account of them, in the same breath, as 'discarded unjust serving-men, younger sons to younger brothers, revolted tapsters, and ostlers trade-fallen' implies an awareness of social conditions echoed by no other character in the play. This awareness proceeds in turn from his outstanding human quality, the capacity for sympathetic participation which marks him out—rogue and dissolute as he is—in a world of calculation and inspires the irony implied in his reply to the Prince when the latter sums up the contingent under his eyes as so many 'pitiful rascals': 'Tut, tut; good enough to toss; food for powder, food for powder; they'll fill a pit as well as better: tush, man, mortal men, mortal men.' Once again, we shall avoid a simple reaction to the spirit of this utterance. Falstaff himself will shortly lead these same men into battle in the expectation that they will be killed to his own advantage. He is, in this sense, a predatory and sinister figure, subdued to the worst aspects of the world upon which he offers his comic commentary; and yet, his words equally clearly contain a parody of the insensibility of military commanders, and so indicate a deeper content. For the Prince, as for all the political leaders round him, soldiers are still primarily pawns, instruments valued for their possible efficiency in the tasks imposed upon them by their betters; for Falstaff alone, and because, in spite of his own calculations, he can share their outlook imaginatively, they are victims, 'mortal men,' and worthy as such, after detached and unsentimental scrutiny, of a certain respect. Once more, Falstaff's comedy is conveyed in a whole world of images which he shares with his audience, which is drawn upon when he describes his troops as 'slaves as ragged as Lazarus in the painted cloth, where the glutton's dogs licked his sores,' and which is capable of rising, when the occasion calls for it, to a sober sense of mortality. Seen in this way, the realism behind the comedy has a contribution of its own to make to the serious purposes of the play.

The first part of the next scene (IV. iii), returning to the rebel camp,

turns on one of those discussions of tactics which so abound in Shakespeare's plays at this period.[13] The rashness of Hotspur and Douglas and
Worcester's contrasted caution fail equally to meet the situation before
them. The main content of the scene, however, is introduced by the
entry of Sir Walter Blunt with Henry's offer of peace. Hotspur's reply,
couched for him in unusually politic terms, brings out well the common
weaknesses in which both sides are involved by their past acts. His first
words emphasize the mutual distrust which so dominates this unnecessary war:

> The king is kind; and well we know the king
> Knows at what time to promise, when to pay.

The rebels' distrust of Henry follows from their participation in his
crime; for, as Hotspur recalls, it was 'my father and my uncle and myself'
who gave him 'that same royalty he wears.' In this association lies the
root of endless recrimination. Hotspur, remembering Henry as 'a poor
unminded outlaw sneaking home,' recalls the humility of his first approaches and represents his father as moved by 'kind heart and pity,'
supposing an act of condescension which bred, in due course, Lancaster's
assertion of power:

> He presently, as greatness knows itself,
> Steps me a little higher than his vow.

From this moment follow, in Hotspur's view, the acts of barefaced ambition which brought the usurper finally to the throne. The scene ends,
on a balance of peace and war, with the king anxious to restore harmony
and the rebels afraid either to accept his offer or to commit themselves
to a conflict in which they have little real hope of success.

The opening of the decisive clash is heralded, at the outset of the
last act, by a characteristic piece of 'atmospheric' writing, after which the
king is brought face to face with Worcester (v. i). If desire for power
prompted both Henry's original usurpation and the rebellion which was
its natural rejoinder, it is now mutual fear, itself a consequence of crime,
that makes the clash inevitable. Both parties are less agents than victims
of an overriding fatality implicit in their respective pasts. Henry, aware
that his position was criminally obtained, cannot but suspect that those
who once followed their own interest in helping to dethrone a king may
seek to do so again; and the rebels (or the more reflective of them) understand that the king must think in this way and that they themselves

---

[13] Compare, most notably, *Julius Caesar,* IV. iii.

can therefore never be safe. The result is an endless mistrust, the consequences of which fatally conclude, in a way which neither party finally
desires, at Shrewsbury.

The preliminaries of the battle, thus regarded, are full of meaning.
Both sides at heart desire peace—the rebels because they know they are
not strong enough to win, the king because unity is the substance of the
royal vocation and because experience has taught him that the divisions
in his kingdom are not such as battle, even victorious, can resolve. Reason
and the royal function both demand peace and unity, and to the extent
that he stands for these, it is Henry—and not his enemies—who is finally
justified; but the consequences of his original crime against order, and
so against nature, are still present and must work themselves out in
blood. The king makes Worcester and Vernon a generous offer, in
which he sees the hope of a restoration of natural order based on the free
recognition of just and beneficent authority. His action in so doing is
proper to a king. He uses the familiar image of the planets to illustrate
the contrast between selfish anarchy and ordered peace:

> will you again unknit
> The churlish knot of all-abhorred war?
> And move in that obedient orb again
> Where you did give a fair and natural light,
> And be no more an exhaled meteor,
> A prodigy of fear, and a portent
> Of broached mischief to the unborn times?

(v. i)

Henry speaks here as he had spoken, at the outset, of his crusade. His
is the voice of a king, still seeking to fulfil his vocation but less than
fully confident of his ability to do so. Already an old man, who can refer
to his 'old limbs' crushed in 'ungentle steel,' he calls for unity, using the
accepted imagery; but the origins of his power, which he would now
wish to forget, make their endless consequences felt to frustrate his lawful intentions.

The rebels, however, can offer no proper answer to the royal plea.
When Worcester, equally at the 'lag-end' of his life, disclaims responsibility with his 'I have not sought the day of this dislike,' Falstaff is
allowed to slip in the brief but devastating observation: 'Rebellion lay
in his way, and he found it.' The following exposition of the rebel case
emphasizes still further the link in past responsibilities that binds Henry
to his foes; he is even described, tellingly, as 'that ungentle gull, the
cuckoo's bird,' who turns against the creatures in whose nest he has
grown to his present stature. If the observation be just, however, the

spirit in which it is made is unacceptable, an assertion of anarchy prompted by the desire for power; and the energy of Henry's reply, with its exposure of the devices used

> To face the garment of rebellion
> With some fine colour that may please the eye,

cuts across mere political consideration to guarantee the authentic quality of the argument. Here, at least, it is as king that Henry speaks; and if his past makes him an imperfect representative of the royal authority, it is not by such as Worcester that he can properly be rebuked.

The Prince's challenge to Hotspur, which here follows, takes us a step further in his chivalrous rehabilitation, and anticipates the central episode in the approaching battle. For the moment, however, neither it nor the modest confession of his past faults—'I have a truant been to chivalry'—are more than single strands in an effect more complex than themselves. The complete picture needs to include Falstaff's attitude to the coming clash, as expressed at the end of the scene, when he begins by turning his own bulk into comedy and ends, in his reflections upon 'honour,' by blending irresponsibility with a highly personal sense of human values. Precisely because he is so human in his irony he has no desire to die, to pay the debt of death 'before his day'; and because he can realize in others the strength of the desire to survive which he so strongly shares, he is aware that 'honour' in the mouths of politicians who have been brought to battle by a combination of past selfishness and present refusal to face their responsibilities is an empty word and a deception. If his attitude is, in its theatrical and popular origins, that of the cowardly braggart running away at the first sign of danger, it becomes, in the cool detachment of its utterance, a comment—relevant if not exhaustive—on the 'scutcheon' which is 'honour' as seen by Hotspur and transformed into the plaything of political intrigue by not a few of the political characters in this play. To hold these various themes together—loyalty and rebellion, chivalry and vanity, the desire to live and the acceptance of death—without seeing in any simple opposition the total effect intended, is to be very close to Shakespeare's conception; and, though Falstaff in no sense stands for all that is affirmative in that conception, his attitudes are such that the positive values of the action, if they are to be accepted, must be continuously weighed against them.

The next scene (v. ii) switches our attention once more to the rebel camp, and shows the reverse of the king's tired insistence on order in the preceding episode. Rebellion is still based on the exclusion of reason, though—as we have seen—it takes a rebel as rational as Worcester so to define it. Priding himself on his realism, Worcester is yet driven first to shut out reason and then to conceal the fact that peace has been offered and that the battle itself may therefore be unnecessary. His reasons are those given to Vernon:

> It is not possible, it cannot be,
> The king should keep his word in loving us;
> He will suspect us still and find a time
> To punish this offence in other faults
>
> .   .   .   .
>
> For treason is but trusted like the fox,
> Who, ne'er so tame, so cherish'd and lock'd up,
> Will have a wild trick of his ancestors.
>
> (v. ii)

Worcester's distrust, like Henry's tragedy, has its origins in the past. It owes its existence to the original crime by which, the bonds of freely accepted rule once broken, the seeds of disorder and suspicion were sown to work themselves out on either side in conflict. Both parties in this action are as much victims of 'fortune' as conscious agents of their respective purposes. Both evoke 'honour' and other lofty sanctions to confer dignity upon their cause; but, although their culpability can never be equal, it remains true that crime born on either side of self-interest is bearing fruit in unnecessary bloodshed.

Other issues, equally derived from the original conception, are relevant to the complete effect. Foremost among them is the opposition of Hal and Hotspur, now described by Vernon in terms which stress the new-found chivalrous modesty of the challenger:

> He gave you all the duties of a man;
> Trimm'd up your praises with a princely tongue,
> Spoke your deservings like a chronicle,
> Making you ever better than his praise
> By still dispraising praise valued with you;
> And, which became him like a prince indeed,
> He made a blushing cital of himself;
> And chid his truant youth with such a grace
> As if he master'd there a double spirit
> Of teaching and of learning instantly.
>
> (v. ii)

The emphasis on the Prince's chivalrous transformation belongs to the inherited conception; and, though we may hold that it has a certain external quality, reflected in rhythms that belong to an early stage in Shakespeare's development, it is certainly relevant to the whole. The spirit of the description needs to be set against the play's various attitudes to Hotspur, in whom we should not see, like the cynical Worcester, simply what is implied by the caustic phrase: 'A *hare-brain'd* Hotspur, governed by a spleen.' This, as we have amply shown, is part of the truth about the Prince's rival; but another would discover in him a manifestation, inadequate but sincere, of honourable chivalry. This type of chivalry can achieve the romantic quality of:

> I will embrace him with a soldier's arm,
> That he shall shrink under my courtesy,

lines which might have been uttered, towards the end of Shakespeare's career, by Coriolanus or his rival Aufidius.[14] As in the case of the Roman heroes, it combines an attractiveness of its own with an inadequacy which will be finally demonstrated in the warrior's own field of action. The chivalry which Hotspur represents falls before another conception, more self-conscious, more controlled, and, in the practical order, more efficient, than itself: before that, in short, implied in the descriptions, which abound at this point, of the Prince in his new maturity. Against that greater balance and resourcefulness, Hotspur's weaknesses are apparent in his self-confessed inarticulacy—'I, that have not well the gift of tongue'—but still more in the emotional glorification of 'honour' which, in its apparent but scarcely deep quality, gives the lie to his own affirmation of inexpressiveness.

More significant still, more closely related to the themes which dominate this part of the action, is Hotspur's assertion, as the scene ends, of the helplessness of human values against the action of time:

> O gentlemen, the time of life is short!
> To spend that shortness basely were too long,
> If life did ride upon a dial's point,
> Still ending at the arrival of an hour.
> An if we live, we live to tread on kings;
> If die, brave death, when princes die with us!
>
> (v. ii)

In this speech, Hotspur touches on something relevant not only to an understanding of his own nature but to the history as a whole. The

---

14 Compare Aufidius:

> Let me twine
> Mine arms about that body, where against
> My grained ash an hundred times hath broke,
> And scarr'd the moon with splinters.
>
> (*Coriolanus,* IV. v)

rhetorical flourish of his conclusion cannot conceal the fact that, as in so many of the sonnets which deal with similar themes, it is a sense of the precarious, the transitory qualities of the emotional impulses that appear to constitute life that dominates the speech. It makes Hotspur's affirmations of 'honour,' if not empty (for there is nothing dishonest about them), pathetic and ultimately invalid; and the sense of their inadequacy finally colours his true, but immature conception of chivalry. This immaturity, in which he participates in certain qualities common to many of the later tragic heroes—Othello, Antony, and Coriolanus, all warriors and all defeated, among them—is shortly confirmed by his own death at the hands of a more controlled and mature, if in some respects less personal, conception of duty associated with the growth of the ideal king.

Shakespeare's battle scenes, of which the two following episodes (v. iii and iv) are a fair example, show in their careful parallelisms a deliberate effort to turn the inadequacy of stage convention to dramatic effect. One has only to consider the treatment of material not altogether dissimilar in *Troilus and Cressida* and *Julius Caesar,* both written at dates not so much later, to realize that they turn upon a nice opposition between the conception of military 'honour' and a critical presentation of the heroism of war; as such, they offer, moreover, a first faint approximation to the characteristic Shakespearean attitude, involving a fine balance of contraries, to the tragic heroes of the mature masterpieces. Read in this way, the stage representation of the battle of Shrewsbury becomes something more than the rather perfunctory staging of action which we might otherwise be inclined to see in it. A truer estimate demands a certain suspension of judgement, in which neither the heroic nor the satirical element will predominate, but in which each will be seen as correcting its opposite to produce finally an impression where simplicity of evaluation has no place.

The opening presentation of the battle (v. iii) calls for a balanced reading of this kind. Sir Walter Blunt incarnates a simple conception of 'honour,' ready to assert itself in loyal service of his royal master; but the king for whom he is ready to die, and does so, is willing to use his loyalty for a stratagem which, without overstressing the case, can hardly be admired. Blunt, in fact, like so many others on this field, is something less than a master of his fate. After his death at the hands of Douglas, the double attitude to his sacrifice is brought out in the comments of his victor and of Hotspur. For Hotspur, to whom the simple idea of 'honour' has always been a sufficient guide to action, the dead Sir Walter was a 'gallant knight'; but his slayer, less committed to the heroic idea, and indeed a character drawn on lines altogether more barbarous, utters his epitaph in savage terms in which frustrated impatience and a certain contempt both play their part:

> A fool go with thy soul, whither it goes!
> A borrow'd title hast thou bought too dear.
>
> (v. iii)

Here again, though we need not overstress the casual scepticism implied in 'whither it goes,' the attitude fits well with the grotesque irony of the following reference to the royal disguises:

> I'll murder all his wardrobes, piece by piece,
> Until I meet the king.

A royalty that needs to disguise itself behind a 'wardrobe' is something less than truly royal; and both it and the callous, impatient brutality of this 'murderer' of wardrobes throw light on the spirit in which this part of the play is conceived.

As usual, something like the last word is left with Falstaff, whose part in the battle is not circumscribed to the mixture of self-interest and heroic values by which the main political actors are at once moved and limited. His first comment is a confession of fear—'I fear the shot here'— but a confession, as always, which implies a sense of the value of life, a protest—so to call it—against its sacrifice for motives finally obscure. As he glances down on Sir Walter's dead body, his point of view is uttered with greater force: 'Sir Walter Blunt: there's honour for you! here's no vanity!' To appreciate the comment we need to sense the touch of morality which here, as so often, underlies it. 'Vanity,' of course, offers a double sense, that of pride (which ends traditionally in death and is here associated, moreover, with the wearing of borrowed plumes) and that of nothingness, futility, itself related to death and to the sense of empty honour that has brought it upon the victim. To read such an utterance in its full complexity is to appreciate once more the baseless nature of the discussion as to Falstaff's 'cowardice' which reflects a fundamental misunderstanding of the dramatic function of the character. When Falstaff says, just below,

I have led my ragamuffins where they are peppered: there's not three of my hundred and fifty left alive; and they are for the town's end, to beg during life,

the question is not, finally, one of the speaker's bravery or its opposite. That Falstaff 'led' his men into battle is no more a proof of courage than his exclamation 'God keep lead out of me!' is an indication of its opposite. The essence of Falstaff lies in his standing, alone in this play and until the supremacy of the political theme of kingship finally asserts itself, outside the categories by which those round him are respectively defined and limited. We may agree, if we will, that he *is* a coward; the dramatic tradition (or part of it) behind the character accounts for this, but not for the fact that he can look with detachment on his own cowardice, present it as a normal human reaction, associate it with his clear conception of the nature of the 'ragamuffins' whom he shows, with a typical mixture of realistic contempt and understanding, as having deserted 'for the town's end, to beg during life.' Falstaff is, let us say, a coward who can contemplate his own cowardice with detachment; and, by so doing, he offers an estimate, not final indeed (for few Shakespearean judgements are final) but relevant, upon the heroic values which are themselves related to a positive interpretation of life, but which need the operation of this objective check to prevent them from degenerating into a verbose pose.

The concluding exchange with the Prince, now entirely dedicated to his political and chivalrous function, confirms this position. Hal, as befits his regenerated state, is concerned with the death of the 'noblemen' who lie

> stark and stiff
> Under the hoofs of vaunting enemies;

there is something limiting (which we need not, however, call insincere) about the rhetorical quality of the phrase which Falstaff is perfectly fitted to take up. He does so, indeed, first in his own parody of warlike boasting—'Turk Gregory never did such deeds in arms as I have done this day'—and then by giving Hal his 'pistol,' which turns out to be a bottle of sack. Once more, it is not cowardice or its opposite that is at stake, but rather the assertion of an independence that refuses to accept verbal values—however respectable and, in their own sphere, necessary they may be—at their own estimate, but plays upon them with a free judgement that expresses itself by converting humour and farce into a distinctive irony. Such is the spirit of the famous final comment on Blunt's sacrifice: 'I like not such grinning honour as Sir Walter hath: *give me life*: which if I can save, so; if not, honour comes unlooked for, and there's an end.' In the phrase 'give me life' may be found the key to this judgement in which once more we may detect, if we will, a foundation of fear, but in which this very 'cowardice,' if it exists, is transformed by self-awareness into something different; for this is a comment, human and finally dispassionate, on the waste implied (once again, among other things: the judgement is relevant, not final) in a battle so many of whose causes are suspect. Inspired by this spirit, Falstaff moves through the conflict without being subdued to its tone, viewing it, as he views himself, with characteristic frankness, and dominating it, when all the necessary reservations have been made, by the very force of his vitality.

The second and longer battle scene (v. iv) represents simultaneously the culmination of the 'honour' theme, as developed in the contrast between Prince Hal and Hotspur, and provides, in the customary way, a parallel comment through the fortunes of Falstaff. The earlier part of the scene, leading to the rescue of the king by his son and the discomfiture of Douglas, follows a familiar pattern and is expressed in rhetorical terms which culminate in Henry's recognition of his son's redemption on the field of battle:

> Thou hast redeem'd thy lost opinion,
> And show'd thou makest some tender of my life,
> In this fair rescue thou hast brought to me.

In the general conception of the play, this is a central moment. Hal, embarked on the path which will eventually lead him to the crown and to Agincourt, needed thus to be reconciled to his father as a result of his assumption of the values of chivalry. Yet, accepting this, we must also feel that the reconciliation is conventionally expressed, that—though it would be wrong to invest it with irony—it lacks the deeper feeling of other scenes in which the relationship between father and son is more intimately revealed. The Prince's reply is, as we may feel, a little too ready to take up the point which confirms his own justification:

> O God! they did me too much injury
> That ever said I hearken'd for your death.
> If it were so, I might have let alone
> The insulting hand of Douglas over you,
> Which would have been as speedy in your end
> As all the poisonous potions in the world
> And saved the treacherous labour of your son.
>
> (v. iv)

As a public justification, this is well enough; but as the attitude of a son to his father, who has just expressed his recovered faith in him, it is—to say the least—somewhat frigid. The truth is that King Henry IV and the Prince alike belong to the public rather than to the private sphere, and that such efforts as they make to move out of it are not always dramatically convincing. The relation between them is, at its most in-

teresting moments, of another kind, akin to tragedy, fraught with disturbing memories and laden with a sense of the burden, almost intolerable in its incidence and isolation, of authority. What is here expressed
belongs to the inherited conception on which the action is based, true
and necessary, but scarcely forming part of the deeper content of the
play.

With the entry of Hotspur, the central duel between rival conceptions
of 'honour' and their relation to the 'destiny' which overshadows them
is at last brought to a head. These conceptions are, indeed, mutually ex-
clusive; this is implied in the Prince's words 'Two stars keep not their
motion in one sphere,' and the type of 'glory' with which both are here
concerned is not of the kind that can be shared in life. The clash between them follows, and as a result of it Hotspur dies. His last speech
is important in its suggestion of a relationship between the speaker's
conception of 'honour,' now tragically affirmed in death, and certain
themes simultaneously growing to mature expression in Shakespeare's
work at this same period. Hotspur, dying, affirms the value of the
'proud titles' of glory above that of 'brittle life'; but in the adjective there
is a sense of hollowness, of disillusionment, which contrasts with the
content of the vaguely conceived 'titles' themselves and suggests, most
typically, that sense of tragic emptiness which Shakespeare, from this
time, comes increasingly to set in pathetic contrast to the heroic ideal.
The whole of Hotspur's final utterance is wrapped in a characteristic
pessimism:

> They wound my thoughts worse than thy sword my flesh:
> But thought's the slave of life, and life time's fool;
> And time, that takes survey of all the world,
> Must have a stop.
>
> (v. iv)

To interpret this speech adequately is to be aware of a conflict more
subtle than may immediately appear. It is, indeed, at once an attempted
excuse for inner emptiness, for chivalrous values seen at the decisive
moment to be void of true significance, and a pathetic affirmation of the
tragedy which the recognition of this emptiness implies. The sense of the
passage of time, unredeemed by a corresponding conception of 'value,'
is typical of many of the sonnets and of much of Shakespeare's work at
this period. Originally relatively abstract in expression, we see it now in
the process of acquiring a personal and pathetic quality which will
eventually affect the dramatist's attitude to his tragic heroes.

At this point, indeed, Hotspur is at once expressing disillusionment and, in expressing it, seeking a certain emotional compensation. His disillusionment, moreover, needs to be seen in relation to the action in which he has allowed his shallow, if true, generosity, to be involved. At Shrewsbury, he has fallen before a conception of 'honour' at once deeper and, as the future will confirm, more efficient than his own; but he has fallen also on behalf of the policies incarnated in Worcester, policies which his emotion has too readily accepted but which are less creditable than those which his own nature should have been capable of assimilating. Hotspur's death leaves us with an impression poised between the tragic and the ironic, adequately summed up in the self-conscious pathos of his reference to the 'earthy and cold hand of death' and in the contrast of attitudes contained in his conqueror's brief completion of his final 'food for—': 'For *worms, brave* Percy.' This is simply one aspect of the fatality that overshadows a battle in which the rebels fail to attain their end and in which it is foreseen that the king will equally be prevented from achieving the unity for which he is *now*, but too late, genuinely striving.

The Prince's oration over his dead rival is, as far as it goes, fitting and impressive; but it belongs, like so much in his nature, to the *public* rather than to the truly personal order. In calling Hotspur 'great heart' and 'so stout a gentleman' he affirms the values of courtesy which are to be a necessary part of his own developing royal virtues; but, even in so doing, in the lending of his 'favours' to cover his former enemy's 'mangled face' with 'rites of tenderness,' we feel a weight correspondingly laid on vanity:

> When that this body did contain a spirit,
> A kingdom for it was too small a bound;
> But now two paces of the vilest earth
> Is room enough.
>
> (v. iv)

Beneath the formal quality of this 'epitaph,' giving personal content to the conventional gesture, lies a preoccupation with 'ignominy' and with the 'vanity' upon which, as we have seen, Falstaff has already touched in irony; the modification of the chivalrous note by a qualifying sense of tragedy is full of meaning for the interpretation of the spirit of later plays.

It is no accident that Falstaff has been present as a spectator at this culminating moment in the duel of contrasted conceptions of 'honour.' Before the battle, his contact with the popular sphere represented a parallel, at once cynical and truly humourous, to the 'serious' action, and now his mock death at the hands of Douglas carries this parallel to a logical culmination; whilst the Prince, having delivered his chivalrous epitaph over Hotspur, turns to a comic shadow of it in his reflections over Falstaff's body:

> O, I should have a heavy miss of thee,
> If I were much in love with vanity!
> Death hath not struck so fat a deer to-day,
> Though many dearer, in this bloody fray.
>
> (v. iv)

The easy flow of rhyme offers a clear contrast to the preceding heroic seriousness in blank verse, and even the reference to 'vanity' rouses echoes from the past action. The Prince's own humour, with its self-conscious disclaimer 'If I were much in love with vanity,' is indeed in character, as is the spirit of the pun on 'deer' and 'dearer' which can be paralleled elsewhere in his utterances. Comic as the speech is in intention—lest we should be tempted to take Falstaff too seriously, a fault not always successfully avoided—its spirit is that of a commentary offered in character, a placing of what has gone before; nor is this mock death, and the Prince's equally mock farewell, at this moment in which he has decisively confirmed himself in his 'serious,' political function, entirely without significance for their future relationship.

Falstaff's following comment, after his 'resurrection,' contains as usual an assertion of life, of simple vitality, against the claims of verbal obligation: 'To die, is to be a counterfeit; for he is but the counterfeit of a man who hath not the life of a man: but to counterfeit dying, when a man thereby liveth, is to be no counterfeit, but the true and perfect image of life indeed.' In the light of this assertion, the speaker's 'cowardice' is seen to include a positive comic value, and even the final stabbing of Hotspur's dead body and the taking of the grotesque burden on to his back, though no doubt it is the final manifestation of the predatory tradition of the braggart soldier of theatrical convention, contains also an ironic reference to the serious, 'chivalrous' combat we have just witnessed. Equally, the very monstrous manner in which he claims his reward before the Prince—'I look to be either earl or duke, I can assure you'—is inspired not only by the hope of advancement but by an ironic attitude to the courtly dignities mentioned, in a similarly comic spirit, in his last words in this play: 'He that rewards me, God reward him! If I do grow great, I'll grow less; for I'll purge, and leave sack, and live cleanly as a nobleman should do.' The mock reference to emendation, the last of several in *Henry IV*, Part I, need not be taken solely, as some students of the play have taken it,[15] as an anticipation of the advances obtained by Falstaff as a result of his fictitious exploit. It is true that Falstaff will appear, in the following play, with a new range of monstrous social pretensions. To that extent, these concluding words look forward to what we shall see to be the changed spirit of Part II; but here its counterpart is the Prince's priggish (surely not 'generous,' as some have held it to be) and contemptuous comment:

> For my part, if a lie may do thee grace,
> I'll gild it with the happiest terms I have,

and its value is eminently satirical.

At this point, the last word of the play has really been spoken. The final scene (v. v) simply winds up the political action, justifies Henry—as far as may be, which is in terms of his desire to carry out his royal vocation—against the treachery of Worcester, and allows the Prince to express himself with proper generous 'chivalry' towards Douglas. The king's concluding reference to the future campaigns against the rebels in Wales and the North of England places us on the threshold of the play to follow.

---

[15] J. Dover Wilson, in *The Fortunes of Falstaff*, seems to me to argue one-sidedly on this point, and so to do less than justice to the full variety of Shakespeare's conception.

Chapter Four HENRY THE FOURTH, *PART II*

HENRY IV, Part II, although carrying on the design initiated in the preceding play,[1] differs in certain respects from its predecessor. Henry IV, whose struggle to assert his kingship against its dubious origins had provided a principal thread of action in Part I, has ceased in the sequel to exercise any positive influence over the course of events. As a result, the state of England—more extensively and realistically portrayed than before—is shown as given over to anarchy and corruption. Aged and cynical rebels, tragically involved in the consequences of their own past choices, share a sense of adverse fatality with the king whom they originally backed in his crime of usurpation; whilst in the popular sphere, a predatory and decaying Falstaff exercises his wits in drawing from misery, corruption, and impotence an uneasy and parasitic sustenance. The consequences of the crisis in authority initiated by Bolingbroke's murder of Richard cover the entire realm and threaten its vital unity with extinction.

Against this sombre background, the will to political action relinquished by the king is concentrated in the reaction, as legitimate as it is ruthlessly efficient, of a new generation in whom the doubts and divisions associated with Henry's exercise of authority have been finally eliminated. Rebellion, incapable of responding purposefully to the challenge of war, is defeated by a calculated stratagem which sums up the political spirit now abroad in England, and the Prince, having in the previous play asserted himself in chivalrous action, is engaged in the more arduous and sober pursuit of self-conquest, externally manifested in his submission to the Lord Chief-Justice. After the final reconciliation with his father, which confirms the subjection to rule of his wilder impulses, Hal is ready to assume the crown in a spirit in which intimate self-control and public devotion to duty are consciously combined in an image of political perfection.

[1] Professor J. Dover Wilson, in his studies already referred to, has argued forcibly that the two plays are to be regarded as forming a single dramatic unit. His arguments, however, have been strongly contested by other scholars.

I

The earlier political action of the play is concentrated, as though to emphasize the prevalence of disorder, upon the counsels of the rebel leaders. The spirit of these is anticipated, tentatively and imperfectly, in the Induction. The voice of Rumour, of course, links the events about to be presented with those of the preceding play by recalling the rebel defeat at Shrewsbury, Hotspur's death, and the fact that Northumberland is 'crafty-sick.' To that extent, it is eminently a practical device; but, in speaking of 'peace' whilst 'covert enmity'

> Under the smile of safety wounds the world,

this prologue conveys an impression of insecurity, of concealed menace, which the following action will amply confirm. The world, as it appears to the rebel chiefs, is full of deceptions, discrepancies between the apparent sense of events and their treacherous reality; for, as time will show,

> the big year, swoln with some other grief,
> Is thought with child by the stern tyrant war,
> And no such matter.

This is to be a play in which the external aspect of things frequently fails to correspond to their true nature, in which men, hoping to turn the course of history to their own purposes, are led to ignominy and disaster.

This, as the opening scene shows, is immediately true of Northumberland and his associates. The lengthy exchanges, which, by bringing home to them the certainty of irretrievable disaster, point the stages of their descent from facile confidence to the depths of despair, are marked by a rhetorical elaboration, a conscious literary artifice, which is barely compatible with true dramatic effect. There are moments, however, when a close study of commonplace and even confused lines will reveal the effort to create an instrument for the expression of new poetic purposes. Such is Morton's account of the part played by Hotspur in the recent battle:

> For from his metal was his party steel'd;
> Which once in him abated, all the rest
> Turn'd on themselves, like dull and heavy lead:
> And as the thing that's heavy in itself,
> Upon enforcement flies with greatest speed,
> So did our men, heavy in Hotspur's loss,
> Lend to this weight such lightness with their fear

> That arrows fled not swifter toward their aim
> Than did our soldiers, aiming at their safety,
> Fly from the field.   (1. i)

To read verse of this kind is to feel, as we feel continually in *Troilus and Cressida*, that two distinct intentions are, so to speak, superimposed upon one another and imperfectly unified. The first is purely formal, the development of an extended comparison to its logical conclusion; the second, springing apparently by chance from an idea contained in the simile, deviates the unfolding from its foreseen course. The passage opens with what must have been, for Shakespeare, a commonplace of quasi-scientific observation. The description of Hotspur's influence in terms of the 'steeling' power of his courage or 'metal' follows lines completely familiar until the reference, itself provoked by 'metal,' to 'dull and heavy lead' introduces a new line of thought: the word 'heavy,' caught up and repeated in the fourth line, brings in the general principle that 'enforcement,' physical compulsion, combined with weight produces a corresponding speed in motion. This speed is in turn associated with the rout of the rebel party after Hotspur's death. 'Heavy' in their loss, the 'weight' of their sorrow produces by a verbal paradox the lightness of fear, and this idea in turn brings us back to the notion with which the comparison opened. As arrows—impelled by their 'weight'—'fly' with light swiftness to the target at which they have been aimed (Morton, anticipating the rout of the rebel army, makes the arrows *flee* towards their goal, whilst the soldiers a little later *fly* from the field), so were the men of the rebel army, weighed down by the loss of their captain's inspiration, impelled to seek safety in the speed of flight.

The importance of similes of this kind, in which the play abounds, is not immediately apparent. It lies not in their poetic qualities—which are in most cases slight—but in the fact that they represent the creation by the dramatist of a poetic instrument adequate to the growing complexity of his intentions. A similar elaboration, more closely related to true dramatic ends, can be detected in the words spoken by Northumberland when the news of his party's defeat is finally brought home to him:

> In poison there is physic; and these news,
> Having been well, that would have made me sick,
> Being sick, have in some measure made me well:
> And as the wretch, whose fever-weaken'd joints,
> Like strengthless hinges, buckle under life,
> Impatient of his fit, breaks like a fire
> Out of his keeper's arms, even so my limbs,
> Weaken'd with grief, being now enraged with grief,
> Are thrice themselves.   (1. i)

The verse is, in ancestry, clearly that of the early Shakespeare. The use of neat antitheses, mathematically rather than emotionally opposed, is reminiscent of *Romeo and Juliet* and *Richard II*. The machinery is prominent to a degree that would never be tolerated in the greater plays; but there is a feeling, too, that the poet is reaching out through these devices to new complexities of experience. The speech aims, however obscurely, at a new effect, an attempt to carry the shifts and tensions of the speaker's consciousness in the strain of self-definition. In Northumberland's mind, health and sickness, action and renunciation, are inextricably intertwined. 'Poison' comes to him, or so he would like to think, in the form of 'physic'; the bad news, that in a state of health would have reduced him to sickness, has now, because he is 'sick,' created in him an illusion of health. The intention, indeed, is not simply to contrast age and weakness with the need for decisive action. It is to convey in the motion of the verse, the incidence of its intimate stresses, the tragic disharmony that exists in the old man himself and unites him to a history not less tragically conceived. The words 'well' and 'sick,' as he uses them, shift in their context, refer at different moments to his own condition and to the news which he has just received. It is the effect of perversity in rebellion to produce a state of rooted moral 'sickness,' of disillusionment, which the external action confirms and which, in the last analysis, Northumberland shares with the king he is striving to overthrow.

Northumberland, to put the matter in another way, is not, like the equally vacillating York in *Richard II*, simply a figure to be observed and analysed. From the beginning of this scene, his helplessness has been related to a sense of tragic circumstance. His first words, spoken to Lord Bardolph,

> The times are wild; contention, like a horse
> Full of high feeding, madly hath broke loose
> And bears down all before him,

have already conveyed a sense of impending disaster which, superbly embodied in the blind sensual power of the horse, looms with terrifying magnitude over the petty drama of senile indecision enacted, as it were, beneath its shadow. Now, as defeat is finally confirmed, the menace extends itself, finds issue in a vision of universal chaos:

> Let heaven kiss earth; now let not Nature's hand
> Keep the wild flood confined! let order die!
> And let this world no longer be a stage
> To feed contention in a lingering act;
> But let one spirit of the first-born Cain

> Reign in all bosoms, that, each heart being set
> On bloody courses, the rude scene may end,
> And darkness be the burier of the dead!   (I. i)

Here, if anywhere, individual rhetoric touches, through the broken and hysterical reaction of a defeated old man, upon the universal implications of sedition. The rebels of this play, although their divisions are related to those shown in Part I, are no longer primarily crafty politicians, realistically presented in the pursuit of their evil and irresponsible venture. The emphasis now is hardly upon responsibility at all. The dim figures who have survived the disaster of Shrewsbury are no longer, like Hotspur and Douglas, active and impetuous leaders; nor are they even particularly crafty, as Worcester had been, or, like Glendower, opinionated and vain. Their personal qualities, such as they are, have been relegated to the background; like Northumberland himself, though in varying degrees, they are old and disillusioned shadows, no longer in control of the flow of events which they have set in motion and which now pushes them on to conclusions only foreseen as disastrous.

Against a background vastly and menacingly chaotic, indeed, the political game is played out by these aging conspirators in frailty and impotence. Lord Bardolph and Morton, in their effort to restore Northumberland to a sense of reality, stress the need for unity and decision. Their argument, recalling the dependence of his followers on their leader's condition, is, in effect, an inversion of orthodox commonplace:

> The lives of all your loving complices
> Lean on your health;

and this dependence produces in turn, since that condition is unsound, an extended consciousness of disease. According to Morton, true leadership implies the control of passion by reason; for health is in this context a normal, rational state,

> the which, if you give o'er
> To stormy passion, must perforce decay.

From this condition, as Worcester has already recognized before Shrewsbury,[2] the rebel is excluded by the nature of his enterprise, which de-

---

[2] See *1 Henry IV*, IV. i:

> For well you know we of the offering side
> Must keep aloof from strict arbitrement,
> And stop all sight-holes, every loop from whence
> The eye of reason may pry in upon us.

mands unreason as the condition of its being. This unreason is supremely postulated, for these confused minds, in the lack of spiritual sanction which affects their cause. 'Rebellion,' we are told, led to division among the followers of Worcester and Hotspur at Shrewsbury, separating 'The action of their bodies from their souls,' so they that fought

> with queasiness, constrain'd,
> As men drink potions.[3]

The perversion of normal values implied by the rising is accordingly to be remedied by the entanglement of the spiritual power, personified by York, in secular intrigues. The remedy, however, partakes of the ambiguity which throughout vitiates the rebel cause. '*Supposed* sincere and holy,' York is in reality a political figure, engaged in turning 'insurrection to religion' and, above all, in covering the sinister intentions of his party with a condemnation, in itself just, of Richard's murder; in this last respect, at least, his accusations reflect the fatality which Henry's original crime has brought upon his rule. The justice of the Archbishop's denunciation, however, cannot cover the final perversity of the position which it seeks to justify. By the end of the scene, it is clear that these pusillanimous and self-seeking politicians have become involved, beyond the responsibilities which they so dubiously affirm, in an enterprise which tends by its own nature to chaos and which they can never hope to divert to purposeful ends.

The next episode (i. iii) in the political action shows the same leaders at closer grips with their situation. Their estimate of the future continues to be wrapped in the foreboding,

> Conjecture, expectation, and surmise
> Of aids incertain,

which their own arguments strive to conjure. Sedition, in the act of taking counsel, is being brought face to face with the shifting nature of its foundations. The rebel 'lines himself with hope, eating the air on promise of supply'; the beginnings of his venture lie in an illusory self-confidence and his end is only foreseen as an act of suicide. The lengthy piece of ratiocination by Lord Bardolph, to which these preliminary exchanges lead, is built on an elaboration of concepts which finally ex-

---

[3] I have discussed the function of this type of imagery, which is particularly common in *Troilus and Cressida* and other plays of the same period, in my book, *An Approach to Shakespeare* (Garden City, N.Y.: Doubleday & Company, Inc., 1956). See especially pp. 69–71 and 74–75.

cludes true purpose. His thesis has a speculative quality, detailed and
yet imperfectly lucid, which, in its anticipation of certain reflective
passages from *Troilus and Cressida*,[4] conveys a sense of argument turning, beneath the elaboration, into an effort at self-clarification. The
opening emphasis on the primary need for decision—the answer of
'*instant* action' to the challenge offered by 'the *present* quality' of war—
fades almost imperceptibly into a contrary stagnation. This development
answers to a natural process; for, as Bardolph himself immediately goes
on to recognize:

> a cause on foot
> Lives so in hope, as in an early spring
> We see the appearing buds; which to prove fruit,
> Hope gives not so much warrant as despair
> That frosts will bite them.[5]   (I. iii)

The image, like so many shared by the sonnets and plays of this period,
rests upon convention, but the contrast between 'spring' growth and the
lack of final fulfilment, between deceptive 'hope' and harsh reality, is very
close to the sense of frustration which dogs the rebel leaders in these
scenes and anticipates the tragedies to follow. This is already, in an elementary form, the problem with which Agamemnon and the Greek
leaders will so long and vainly wrestle under the walls of Troy.

As though to confirm the presence in his thought of this obscure
burden of impotence, Bardolph goes on to illustrate his argument by an
extended architectural parallel which we could readily imagine placed
in the mouth of Ulysses:

> When we mean to build,
> We first survey the plot, then draw the model;
> And when we see the figure of the house,
> Then must we rate the cost of the erection;
> Which if we find outweighs ability,
> What do we then but draw anew the model
> In fewer offices, or at last desist
> To build at all?

---

[4] The discussions between Agamemnon, Ulysses, and Nestor (I. iii) are notably similar
in conception.

[5] Compare, for the argument, Agamemnon's first speech in *Troilus and Cressida*:
> The ample proposition that hope makes
> In all designs begun on earth below
> Fails in the promised largeness: checks and disasters
> Grow in the veins of actions highest rear'd,
> As knots, by the conflux of meeting sap,
> Infect the sound pine and divert his grain
> Tortive and errant from his course of growth.   (I. iii)

Once more the promise of a businesslike return to first principles is strangely transformed as the speech proceeds. The argument, far from leading to the conclusion at which the constructive parallel aims, leaves us with a sense of indigence, a doubt whether we are witnessing the laying of 'Consent upon a sure foundation' or, in the nearest approach to a graphic image in the later stages, the recognition of rebellion as the 'part-created,' abortive reality it is. For, unless the projects which he now seeks to define are built on a true estimate of the situation in which he and his companions find themselves, Bardolph affirms that

> We fortify in paper and in figures,
> Using the names of men instead of men:
> Like one that draws the model of a house
> Beyond his power to build it; who, half through,
> Gives o'er and leaves his part-created cost
> A naked subject to the weeping clouds
> And waste for churlish winter's tyranny.   (I. iii)

In the distinction between men and their 'names' we come very close to the spirit of these scenes, in which politicians and those who follow their perverse designs are habitually the creatures rather than the creators of circumstance. The peculiar relation of the argument to the artifices of contemporary poetry is, not for the first time, revealing. The 'weeping clouds' and 'churlish' winter of Bardolph's comparison belong to the conventional language which is embedded in so much of the verse of this play; but the effort to place convention at the service of a deeper purpose is implied in Hastings' admission that his party's hopes—and here we return to the persistent theme of 'hope,' by which the rebels are alternately encouraged and deceived—may be 'still-born.' The show of resolution which ignores these premonitions, taking refuge in a fictitious self-reliance, is based less on rational confidence than on the impossibility of retreat; whilst the fact that the king himself is described, a little later, as 'unfirm' and his coffers as sounding 'With hollow poverty and emptiness' extends still further the sense of moral sickness and social decay which prevails throughout this part of the play.

The last important utterance in this scene is given to the Archbishop who, in his failure to lend a sense of spiritual fitness to his cause, contributes in his own way to the impression of political infirmity. 'The commonwealth is *sick* of its own choice,' he affirms, and goes on to ascribe its deplorable condition to a 'surfeit' of 'over-greedy love.' The fickleness of mob loyalty is characteristically denounced in terms of physical nausea:

being now trimm'd in thine own desires,
Thou, beastly feeder, art so full of him,
That thou provokest thyself to cast him up.
So, so, thou common dog, didst thou disgorge
Thy glutton bosom of the royal Richard;
And now thou wouldst eat thy dead vomit up,
And howlst to find it.   (I. iii)

The fact that these sentiments are given to a calculating rebel, who consistently misuses the power given by his spiritual office, should warn us against seeing in them no more than an expression of animosity to the mob. A more generalized disgust is being voiced, a universal distaste finding in bitterness its concentrated expression. The full meaning of such imagery will only be clear when we have seen, later in the play, that *both* sides are wrapped in the futility which their dubious past has imposed upon them, undermined by the consciousness of disease. This distaste, this rooted preoccupation with an infirmity which those who suffer from it are unwilling or unable to trace to its final causes, is further related by York to the operations of time and fatality. 'What trust is in these times?' and again: 'Past and to come seems best; things present, worst.' Guided by this spirit and deprived of belief in their own cause, the defeat of the rebels is inevitable. The nostalgia for Richard is in part—on such lips as these—false, in part a manifestation of the death of a better world. The one which has succeeded it is—whatever the positive values which may eventually emerge from it—certainly harsher, less immediately subject to human control. Hastings' last resigned words— 'We are time's subjects, and time bids be gone'—point to a spirit which will prove binding, as far as the elder generation is concerned, on both parties in the action thus sombrely conceived.

The last of these early political scenes (II. iii), stressing in more personal terms the contrast between past and present, confirms the death of virtue and its replacement by senile indecision in an age of policy. Northumberland is striving to maintain against his wife and Hotspur's widow the outward appearance of consistency and self-respect. It is his 'honour,' he argues, which is 'at pawn,' imposing upon him a course of action which he tacitly admits to be irrational. The word, so closely associated with her husband's memory, prompts Lady Percy to affirm the passing, in his person, of an order that died finally, as at once inadequate and incompatible with the spirit of the successful politicians of these plays, at Shrewsbury. Her answer to Northumberland's wavering appeal to 'honour' is clear and decisive; for when 'honour,' incarnated in Hotspur, was alive, he deserted it, leaving by his action 'two honours lost, yours and your son's.' Her outburst culminates in the celebration, as she poignantly recalls the person of her dead husband, of a chivalrous ideal at once compelling, endowed with a magnetism of its own, and irretrievably lost. Hotspur is remembered as the norm of aristocratic conduct, the inspiration by whose light

> Did all the chivalry of England move
> To do brave acts.

The inspiration, however, led only to public disaster and personal loss. The evocation of Hotspur's person, in which bereaved affection dwells on his physical features, his 'gait,' his manner of 'speaking thick,' his very defects, is also an elegy spoken over the mirror of a dead chivalry:

> in speech, in gait,
> In diet, in affections of delight,
> In military rules, humours of blood,
> He was the mark and glass, copy and book,
> That fashion'd others.[6]

Hotspur, however, is dead, 'food for worms.'[7] Those who have survived him in either party share between them a world of calculation, to which Northumberland, though without illusions, has already accommodated himself. The adjustment, dishonourable as it is, will not bring with it the safety for which he craves. He admits that, if he is to fight, it is as a victim caught in a web of circumstances from which there is no final escape:

> I must go and meet with danger there,
> Or it will seek me in another place
> And find me worse provided.

In the end, however, the instinct to temporize prevails, and the aged politician's last words confirm the uncertainty which derives from subjection to a temporal process which he, like his companions, knows to be beyond his control:

> 'Tis with my mind
> As with the tide swell'd up unto his height,
> That makes a still-stand, running neither way.

The inability to choose a course of action has already been indicated, in the portrayal of the rebel counsels, as a sign of the defeat to come. 'Time

[6] The association of 'diet' with 'humours of blood' is worth noting. It can be paralleled in *Troilus and Cressida* and elsewhere.

[7] See *1 Henry IV*, v. iv, and p. 105 above.

and vantage,' as evoked by Northumberland in his final phrase, are in charge of events, and no decision grasped at by his tortuous and infirm mind can turn aside the approaching execution of his fate.

II

The councils of the rebel leaders, which constitute—as we have seen—the 'serious' action in the first part of the new play are developed side by side with the realistic scenes of low life which form a fitting background for the Prince's affirmation of his vocation. The spirit of sombre realism which prevails in these scenes belongs to the new dramatic conception, and no attempt to explain it in terms of external models finally meets the case. No doubt, normal dramatic influences—notably that of Ben Jonson—may have been present; no doubt, too, the change of tone helps to alienate sympathy from Falstaff and to make his necessary rejection acceptable. The full sense of these episodes, however, lies in the relation which binds them, as parts of a consistently conceived dramatic world, to the main political action. If the political figures, loyal and rebel alike, are dominated by age and the sense of impotence, it is fitting that the comic scenes should undergo a similar change; it is, moreover, against this background of decay and vacillation that the Prince must make the choice upon which the political health of England will depend.

The first presentation of Falstaff, indeed, provides on its own level a parallel to the 'serious' episodes we have just considered. His own function is in part a continuation of, and in part a variation from, that performed in Part I. His words and actions still contain a commentary on political events, but the spirit of that commentary is notably changed. No longer felt to stand in some measure apart from the events in which he participates, he has been subdued to the tone of the life around him. The more realistic concentration on the grotesque, the deformed, and the dissolute answer to the graver infirmity of the social body which harbours him. If he feels his years as a burden, so do—almost without exception—the politicians who have accompanied, with approval or dissent, Henry's rise to power; and, if he is diseased, we have seen that disease is both the personal counterpart of rebellion and a sign of the disorder which it will be Hal's stern duty to extirpate from the imperilled body of his realm.

In the light of this general statement, it is worth noting that Falstaff's first words to the Page refer to the need to consult a physician. His 'water,' the boy reports the doctor as telling him, is 'a good healthy water,' but 'for the party that owed it, he might have more diseases than he knew for.' The statement is more than personal in its implications. It links the aging Falstaff to the infirm plottings of the rebel leaders and, beyond these, to the state of the English kingdom, infected—as will be progressively shown—by the dubious origins of its king's authority. It is true that Falstaff himself can still turn his circumstances to laughter, be not only 'witty' in himself, 'but the cause that wit is in other men'; but his jokes under the new circumstances deviate significantly from the best of those in Part I, are attuned to the world in which he finds himself. More especially, his phrases, deprived of their former expansiveness, turn habitually upon sombre details sharply and realistically conceived. Such is the quality of his first grotesque picture of himself as 'a sow that hath overwhelmed all her litter but one.' In this image, the self-consuming consequences of anarchy—comically incarnated in his own person—are emphasized in the act of reducing them to laughter; and the figure of the fat knight himself, 'attended' as a gentleman by his page, carries with it a satire on the claims to gentility which, since Shrewsbury, have occupied an increasing place in his thoughts. The comic reference next glances, in passing, upon the Prince himself, stressing his beardless youth and immaturity in ironic contrast to his claims to experience: 'Yet he'll be crowing as if he had writ man ever since his father was a bachelor.' This leads in turn to a first comic inversion of what will eventually be Falstaff's own rejection. 'He may keep his own grace, but he's almost out of mine, I can assure him.' The comic embodiment of 'riot' announces himself, in his growing presumption, as able to reject the master who will finally, in the culmination of the serious action, reject him.

The rest of the exchange with the Page confirms the play's new attitude to its comic matter. The Falstaff who is so concerned with the setting for his new cloak is committed to social pretensions in a way not previously imagined; and yet the lack of 'security' which accompanies these carries with it a comment, which this play will variously echo, on the acquisitive spirit abroad in society. In the eyes of this disillusioned comic figure, his own claim to 'gentility' and the avarice of the 'smooth-pates' who enrich themselves in a savagely competitive world are equally matter for satirical appraisal. The demand for 'security,' however, closely touches Falstaff himself, as his bitter comment shows: 'I had as lief they would put ratsbane in my mouth as offer to stop it with security.' This Falstaff, and he who revenges himself verbally by commenting on the 'lightness' of Master Dombledon's wife, is clearly conceived in a bitterness foreign to the earlier Sir John; but the tone of his utterances, sharp, disillusioned, and predatory in turn, reflects the state of the world around him. With his man 'bought in Paul's,' his horse at Smithfield, and his future companion 'in the stews,' Falstaff at once indicates the sombre end of 'riot' and passes an astringent comment, in the light of his aging experience, on the pretensions to gentility of a world in which avarice and corruption increasingly prevail.

These opening manifestations, however, are preliminary to the main purpose of the scene: the clash between Falstaff, in whom the spirit of anarchic self-assertion is embodied in the flesh, and the claims of control incarnated in the figure of the Lord Chief-Justice. The contrast is, at bottom, conceived in deadly seriousness. The need to impose moral discipline upon the world here presented is real, so real that satire upon that discipline is no longer in place; for the opposition between 'riot' and self-control, fleshly corruption and rigid principle, has penetrated, in the shadow of aging infirmity, the body of society itself. If this play is intended to confirm the Prince's growth into his royal vocation, the obligation to choose between these contrasted figures is inescapable, its result a foregone conclusion. The Prince, before assuming the crown, will have to submit to the justice which it will be his duty to administer, and this submission will carry with it the rejection of his former companion in the flesh; his own character, moreover, has been presented from the first as directed towards this choice. To recognize this, however, is not to side simply with the Lord Chief-Justice. He, like Falstaff, though to very different ends, is in some sense subdued to the prevailing spirit of the play. Respect for justice in this aging, crepuscular world has its partial reflection in dry legality, concentration on the letter rather than on the spirit of the statutes; and if Shakespeare, as he wrote this play, accepted the majesty of the law, he was also aware of the traditional attitude, in which satire and distaste play their part, to the lawyer. Falstaff, in seeking to evade the Chief-Justice—'I will not see him'—at once turns aside from just condemnation and embodies a certain reaction of life, even in age and corruption, against the frigid imposition of rule. As usual, to hold a balance between contrasted conceptions is to be true to the Shakespearean intention in this play.

The early part of the dialogue, with Falstaff assuming deafness and defending rebellion as an alternative to begging, comically asserts the claim of 'riot' to freedom from control. The new snarling tone in his repartee is apparent when he retorts to the Servant's 'You mistake me, sir,' with the bitter question: 'Why, sir, did I say you were an honest man?' and it is typical of the changed spirit of the play that the Servant has the better of the exchange. It is not, however, until the opening of the dialogue with the Lord Chief-Justice that the true sense of the scene begins to emerge. Falstaff begins by imputing to his reprover age and a suggestion of sickness:

I heard say your lordship was sick. . . . Your lordship, though not clean past your youth, hath yet some smack of age in you, some relish of the salt-ness of time;   (I. ii)

and he continues, in the same tone, by ascribing 'apoplexy' to the king, relating it, in terms comically fathered upon Galen, to 'a kind of leth-argy.' In such comments, the sense of disillusionment now characteristic of Falstaff's utterances spreads from him to become a part of the per-vading spirit of the play. The Lord Chief-Justice replies with stern propriety and ends by threatening Falstaff with punishment, pressing against him a charge for 'matters against you for your life'; to which his rival's retort is an assertion of his power to escape the consequences of his misdeeds which is, in its sober cynicism, nearer in spirit to the prose scenes of *Measure for Measure* than to anything in the previous play: 'it is the disease of not listening, the malady of not marking, that I am troubled withal,' and again: 'your lordship may minister the potion of imprisonment to me in respect of poverty; but how I should be your patient to follow your prescriptions, the wise may make some dram of a scruple, or indeed a scruple itself.' The reference to 'scruple' and the careful, hairsplitting distinction behind it, backed by the constant empha-sis on disease and the difficulty of cure, point to a new mood, akin to disenchantment and even, we may say, to cynicism, which now radiates from Falstaff and is his answer to the wintry austerity of a justice itself afflicted by age. His defence is of the kind that Pompey opposes to the strictures of Escalus[8] and, like it, based less on right or wrong than on a dispassionate and sombre reading of the moral possibilities of life in a society threatened with disintegration.

This part of the scene culminates in a direct clash of contraries, of order and anarchy, in a statement of irreconcilable positions:

C. JUSTICE: Well, the truth is, Sir John, you live in great infamy.
FALSTAFF: He that buckles him in my belt cannot live in less.
C. JUSTICE: Your means are very slender, and your waste is great.

---

[8] See *Measure for Measure,* II. i:
ESCALUS: How would you live, Pompey? by being a bawd? What do you think of the trade, Pompey? is it a lawful trade?
POMPEY: If the law would allow it, sir.
ESCALUS: But the law will not allow it, Pompey; nor it shall not be allowed in Vienna.
POMPEY: Does your worship mean to geld and splay all the youth of the city?

FALSTAFF: I would it were otherwise; I would my means were greater, and my waist slenderer.

C. JUSTICE: You have misled the youthful prince.

FALSTAFF: The young prince hath misled me: I am the fellow with the great belly, and he my dog.

(I.ii)

Beneath the play of verbal opposites lies a contrast close to the central conception. To the Chief-Justice's moral accusation, Falstaff, true to the traditional character of 'riot,' replies with an assertion of physical expansiveness, but, in accordance with the mood that increasingly prevails, physical freedom corresponds to profligacy, expansion becomes 'waste,' and finally, by a graphic twist of the comic vision, Falstaff turns his physical size to an evocation of penury and the Prince whom he is accused of leading astray into the 'dog' who leads the beggar in his helplessness. Falstaff's wit still imposes itself but its end is now, not the expression of a criticism of life, but an evasion of the claims of restraint, which will none the less in the long run prove inescapable for serious and comic, virtuous and profligate alike.

Hardly less important is the reference, a little below, to the 'unquiet time' in which Falstaff hopes to escape the punishment due to him. This is the natural reverse of his own claim that 'the laws of this land-service' have exempted him from respect for the law. Falstaff, in fact, is at once an adventurer and a figure with comic validity; but his freedom is now precarious and the change in spirit which is coming over the play can be felt in the Chief-Justice's grim warning: 'wake not a sleeping wolf,' countered only in part by Falstaff's cynical reply: 'To wake a wolf is as bad as to smell a fox.' This leads to the ruthless exposure implied in his accuser's final statement, 'you are as a candle, the better part burnt out,' which is rather evaded than answered, still in the spirit of 'riot,' by Falstaff's description of himself as 'a wassail candle, . . . all tallow,' and by the countering of the Chief-Justice's reference to 'gravity' with the fleshly, gluttonous assertion implied in 'gravy.' The ingredients of the conception are familiar, but the use made of them in juxtaposition is original; for 'gravity' is now the product of severity touched by age, whilst the opposite, for all its specious affirmation of independent life, is finally related to corruption and disease.

To the closing accusation that he is the Prince's 'ill angel' (and the monetary pun[9] responds, in passing, to the new spirit of the play) Falstaff replies, not with a bare denial, but with a declaration at once cynical and,

---

[9] This is taken up by Falstaff in his retort: 'Not so, my lord; your ill angel is light; but I hope he that looks upon me will take me without weighing.'

in its relation to the surrounding action, variously true. The sharpness of his phrasing stresses the transformation from the spirit of the earlier comedy:

Virtue is of so little regard in these costermonger times that true valour is turned bear-herd: pregnancy is made a tapster, and hath his quick wit wasted in giving reckonings: all the other gifts appertinent to man, as the malice of this age shapes them, are not worth a gooseberry.   (I. ii)

These are, indeed, 'costermonger times,' corresponding to an aging world in which 'virtue' is neglected and the figure of 'valour' has become that of the soldier returning broken from the wars and reduced to the miserable occupation of 'bear-herd.' The fruit of fleshly instinct has been relegated to the alehouse, and the vivacity in 'quick wit' which accompanied the earlier comedy has turned into sordid calculation; whilst the 'gifts appertinent to man,' which Hamlet in his famous apostrophe on the 'firmament' will, at a not distant date, at once exalt and reduce to the 'quintessence of dust,'[10] and which the comic spirit after its own fashion formerly defended, are debased by the proverbial 'malice' of the age and seen—with a final snapping cynicism of phrase—to be 'not worth a gooseberry.' It is true, of course, that these sentiments are given to Falstaff and are therefore not finally valid. Falstaff will be *rejected*, excluded from the final resolution of the political action; but the fact that his utterance here is less comic than realistic, and that it corresponds to much that is stressed in the behaviour of the political characters, gives it a relevance of its own in the complete effect.

The final exchanges answer to a similar spirit. The Lord Chief-Justice counters Falstaff's insolent reference to 'the capacities of us that are young' with a bitterly realistic catalogue of decay:

Have you not a moist eye? a dry hand? a yellow cheek? a white beard? a decreasing leg? an increasing belly? is not your voice broken? your wind short? your chin double? your wit single? and every part about you blasted with antiquity?

The Falstaff of Part I would never have been subjected to so merciless an exposure and would never have accepted it if he had;[11] but now his fictitious affirmation of perennial youth—'I was born about three of the clock in the afternoon with a white head and something a round belly'—

---

[10] See *Hamlet*, II. ii: 'What a piece of work is a man! . . .'

[11] Something like an approach to it is contained in the Prince's parody of his father (*1 Henry IV*, II. iv. See pp. 75–76 above); but Falstaff's reaction and the final disposition of sympathy are there very different.

and his satire on Puritan piety—'For my voice, I have lost it with hallo-ing and singing of anthems'—affect us chiefly as echoes of earlier, more carefree felicities. As always now, it is on the note of age and calculation that his reply ends: 'I am only old in judgement and understanding; and he that will caper with me for a thousand marks, let him lend me the money, and have at him!' Even in his final grotesque assertion of military prowess an anticipation, almost pathetic, of his own decline modifies the obvious comic intention: 'If ye will needs say I am an old man, you should give me rest. . . . I were better to be eaten to death with a rust than to be scoured to nothing with perpetual motion.'

The course of this scene, in short, confirms that we are moving in a new world and that, to play his part in it, the Falstaff of Part I has been prepared by a modification of his character. His wit—for he is still witty, and will remain so while he lives—relies on a new and almost uniformly sombre range of ideas which, moreover, reflect those in com-mon currency around him. Impecuniousness, in his final words, has become 'consumption of the purse,' an 'incurable' malady, whilst 'age' and 'covetousness' are seen as no less intimately connected than 'young limbs' and 'lechery'; but—as he goes on to say—'the gout galls the one, and the pox pinches the other,' so that the final effect is one in which comedy seems well on the way to the sardonic cynicism affected by Thersites in *Troilus and Cressida.* Falstaff, with the 'gout' or the 'pox' and affected by the 'incurable' disease of poverty which borrowing 'only lingers out;' ends by seeing in the supposed consequences of war no more than a means of putting off his inevitable discomfiture: 'A good wit will make use of any thing: I will turn diseases to commodity.' That the Prince will be amply justified in rejecting a Falstaff so conceived is not open to question; but the fact that the companion of his former tavern exploits so expresses himself is a sign, not only of his own decline in years and comic energy, but that of the world in which he and the Prince both move.

The next appearance of Falstaff (II. i) restores him to the tavern world which had been, in Part I, the scene of his most exuberant ex-ploits. Even here, however, the new spirit of the play pursues him in the 'action' entered against him by the Hostess. Those who see at this point no more than a further stage in the struggle between 'justice' and 'riot' for the Prince's soul may find it hard to explain why the minor ministers of the law—those whom the Hostess is pleased to call 'God's officers and the king's'—are given the graphic names of Fang and Snare. When the Lord Chief-Justice intervenes, however, Falstaff is unable to call his comic faculties to his aid, as he would certainly have done at an earlier stage. His defence takes the form of a series of cynical evasions, in which a new emphasis on sexuality, not present to the same degree in Part I, is associated with the hardening, in an aging ruffian, of the predatory instinct. Falstaff, in short, is engaged in evading the retribution which is closing in upon him; and this he endeavours to do by extending the area of ambiguity which now surrounds his decaying person. His efforts in this direction culminate in the jest, recorded by Mistress Quickly, which makes him liken the Prince's father by implication to a eunuch ('a singing-man of Windsor') and in the accusation, by which he counters this inconvenient revelation, that the Hostess herself has been relating 'up and down the town' that her eldest son bears the features of the Lord Chief-Justice himself.[12] To these evasions—for they are no more—his accuser justly opposes the 'level consideration' of his stern reproof:

Pay her the debt you owe her, and unpay the villany you have done her: the one you may do with sterling money, and the other with current repentance.

Repentance and restitution are proper concepts in a play which is rapidly changing in spirit from the comic to the severely moral, from the mood of *I Henry IV* to that—we may say—of *Measure for Measure*. Most of the comic action, as the time approaches for the Prince's final renunciation of 'riot,' is presented in a tone of sober realism and stresses the need for a ruling moral conception as well as the intractability of the material, time-conditioned and riddled with frailties, upon which that conception must impose itself.

Lest we should fail to relate this change in Falstaff to the surrounding action, the next scene (II. ii) introduces the Prince, almost equally subdued, to the general disenchantment. Hal has clearly, in view of his approaching choice, to be weaned from the influence of such as Poins, and no doubt the exchange which now takes place between them answers to this end. Hal is, in his own first words, 'exceeding weary,' and this weariness expresses itself in a self-conscious, plebeian tone which, if he repudiates it in his heart, he also regards as a necessary condition of his contact with the people, and so as a contribution to the success which he has set himself, from the moment of his soliloquy in Part I, as his goal.

---

[12] The entire complex of jests which, in this play, surrounds the Prince's origins, his beardless youth (see p. 119), and his relation to Poins (see, especially, pp. 126–27 below), is worthy of note.

His jests at the expense of Poins's linen are, indeed, parts of a larger effect. To this the observation, 'my appetite was not princely got,' offers a clue, implying a contrast between normal physical processes and the remoteness from common human considerations which his princely state seems to require of him. This remoteness, though Hal in his public, political character is called upon to accept it, none the less leads him to certain 'humble considerations' which make him 'out of love' with his greatness. The phrase, with its sense of an unexpressed burden lying close to the speaker's heart, is one which he will hardly utter again so clearly. The political vocation will shortly prevail in him, bringing together with success a certain detachment, a touch of necessary inhumanity which his exalted position will at times impose; but in the ambiguous tension of certain brief utterances, especially frequent at this point, the imminence of his father's death brings out a submerged note of reflection which anticipates, occasionally and incompletely, the future difficulties of Hamlet.

This note of mystery is emphasized when Hal, contemplating his father's illness, recognizes that his reputation has made it impossible for the sincerity of his grief to be accepted. Poins's routine reproof of his 'idleness,' uttered in self-defence, is countered by the enigmatic 'Shall I tell thee one thing, Poins?'—suggesting an earnestness which is at once balanced by the disillusioned tone of the remark which follows: 'It shall serve among wits of no higher breeding than thine.' Together, the two phrases touch on a central obscurity in Hal's nature, in which distaste for the company of such as Poins (a sign of his growing seriousness) seems to carry with it a certain tendency to disguise his innermost feelings by the use of irony, even to shrink from human contacts as such. The roots of this tendency are, in any case, deeply implanted in his situation; for the Prince goes on to say, with a true melancholy, born of his awareness that his sincerity will be called in question: 'albeit I could tell to thee, as to one it pleases me, for fault of a better, to call my friend, I could be sad, and sad indeed too.' The fluctuations of tone at this point recall, in their slighter way, some of Hamlet's self-revelations, such as those prompted by Rosencrantz and Guildenstern.[13] They convey a similar impression of being uttered by one who, even as he carries on a conversation which bears no intimate conviction for him, is engaged in a detached and somewhat melancholy self-scrutiny. 'I could tell to thee' (but would it serve any purpose?) as one whom 'it pleases me' (with a mixture of irony and condescension) to call 'friend' (the word may

[13] *Hamlet,* II. ii.

mean all that Horatio meant to Hamlet, but is here qualified by the disillusioned evaluation conveyed in 'for want of a better'), 'I *could* be sad' (*could*, but who would accept this sadness as genuine?) and 'sad indeed too'; the final emphasis stresses a true feeling, which, however, something in the speaker's make-up, and in his estimate of his situation, prevents him from turning to natural expression.

Poins's brief reply, the reflection—as the Prince well knows—of the world's reaction, shows him entirely incredulous. His scepticism, which confirms Hal's intimate mood, is met by an appeal to the future developments already foreseen in the present: 'let the end try the man.' The end will bring triumph, self-mastery, success; but even these desirable ends have their price, as is implied in the revived melancholy which peers through the conventional self-exculpation of the following phrase:

I tell thee, my heart bleeds inwardly that my father is so sick: and keeping such vile company as thou art hath in reason taken from me all ostentation of sorrow.   (II. ii)

It would be hard to find a better example of the way in which Shakespeare, following the traditional lines of his story, loads it with a complexity of feeling entirely his own. The 'vile company' which, in his first soliloquy, Hal accepted as a means to his political education, confident that he could discard it at will, has become a containing factor in his life. Poins, no longer merely the wayward companion of his leisure hours, now appears as an epitome of what the world thinks about him— 'never a man's thought in the world keeps the road-way better than thine'—and if the element of condescension, the belief that company can be assumed and discarded at will, like an old coat, is still present, there is also a new sense of confinement, of being caught in circumstances formerly accepted in levity which oblige him to keep his deepest emotions to himself, making them lie as an undivulged burden at his heart. For one brief moment, we see Hal as the victim of his own past choice, oppressed with emotions which he cannot, having chosen the path of public success, allow himself openly to express.

The comedy which follows on the entry of Bardolph and the Page adds little to the deeper content of the play, though the emphasis laid on the corruption of innocence in the boy, and Bardolph's grim reference to hanging is, perhaps, just worth noting as in tone with the prevailing mood. A little later, two remarks of Poins about Falstaff set the conception of 'riot,' graphically presented in the form of the 'martlemas,' the boar ready for the winter slaughter, in close contact with the sense of mortality, of moral retribution, which, though Falstaff refuses to recognize it, is in fact closing in upon him; for we are told that, though he is 'in bodily health,'

the immortal part needs a physician; but that moves not him: though that be sick, it dies not.

The Prince, in the meantime, as he remarks on Falstaff's outrageous letter, combines a certain displeasure at his own behaviour—'thus we play the fools with the time, and the spirits of the wise sit in the clouds and mock us'—with further contributions to the prevailing effect of disillusioned realism; for his comments on Mistress Quickly and Doll Tearsheet as 'pagans,' 'Ephesians of the old church,' combining the undertone of religious reference with the familiar jargon of the bawdy-house, leads to the sharply cynical account of the latter, in her relation to Falstaff, as 'even such kin as the parish heifers are to the town bull.' Such passages are true to the strain of self-conscious cynicism which Hal affects in combination with his other qualities; they also contribute to the bitter realism which is so frequently the vehicle of tragic feeling in this play. The Prince's last words, spoken in a tone of wry detachment, return to the sardonic condescension which seems to constitute at this stage his instinctive defence against thoughts which press too heavily upon him for complete recognition:

From a God to a bull? a heavy descension! it was Jove's case. From a prince to a prentice? a low transformation! that shall be mine; for in everything the purpose must weigh with the folly.

Once more a sentiment appropriate to the original conception is turned to uses more distinctively personal. The classical legend of the god's descent to animality fits well enough with the Prince's dispassionate and slightly frigid estimate of his youthful impulses: whilst the second, his own social transformation in this new tavern exploit, is conveyed with a touch of condescension which is true both to his past character and to his present situation. The concluding balance of 'purpose' against folly confirms, together with Hal's continued capacity to alter his status whilst leaving his more intimate feelings uncommitted, the sense of relativity which this very detachment imposes as part of the price of public success.

The great tavern scene which follows (II. iv) is deliberately designed to recall the Prince's former adventures at Eastcheap.[14] Once more Hal, subjected to Falstaff's ironic comments, discovers his identity and ex-

14 See *1 Henry IV*, II. iv, and pp. 67–77 above.

poses the distortions of fact upon which these rest; and once again Falstaff, asserting himself in the spirit of 'riot,' parodies the serious claims to valour of his aristocratic betters. The difference in mood, however, is more significant than these parallels. Falstaff, whose influence over the Prince is to all intents and purposes dead, is presented in conscious decline.[15] His victory over Pistol is a poor shadow of the exuberance which had formerly triumphed, in imaginative retrospect, over the 'men in buckram' and which is now reduced to mere evasions, to an effort—foreseen to be fruitless—to escape the imposition of fact. The spirit of comedy, modified to meet the approaching vindication of moral order, is blended with tragic pathos, burdened with a sense of the corruption of human values by time and ill living.

Behind these intimations of decay the scene stresses, through the relationship between Falstaff and Doll Tearsheet, the presence of a compensating humanity. This is accomplished with no undue concession to sentiment, no disguise of the corrupting effects of senile appetite. After the intensely realistic exhortations of the Hostess have prepared Doll to meet her grotesque lover, Falstaff's endearments play with rueful cynicism upon the corruption which overshadows his declining years: 'If the cook help to make the gluttony, you help to make the diseases, Doll; we catch of you, Doll, we catch of you; grant that, my poor virtue, grant that.' The combination of realism and decayed sentiment, ironic resignation and an echo of compassion ('my poor virtue') reflect a situation already charged with human complexity; and to it Doll, destined by necessity and the weakness of her sex to bear the 'huge full hogshead,' the monstrous weight of Falstaff's carnality, responds by clinging to his faded physical exuberance as to the shadow of life:

Come, I'll be friends with thee, Jack: thou art going to the wars; and whether I shall ever see thee again or no, there is nobody cares.

Throughout the scene, Doll's efforts to maintain her hold over Falstaff are accompanied by a sense, reflected here in the poignancy of 'nobody cares,' of tragic circumstance. This sense, whilst in no way invalidating it, necessarily colours the prevailing exposure of 'riot.' For Falstaff to inspire feeling of this kind, however absurd, however directed to ends of calculation, both his nature and his prospects have had to undergo a profound change. The fleshliness which, in Part I, had manifested itself in a spontaneous overflow of comic energy evading the limits of

15 The tone of his reflections, in which decline and a sense of leave-taking prevail, is anticipated by the Drawer's recording of his taking leave, in jest, of the 'six dry, round, old, withered knights' on the dish of apples set before him.

order, has become a burden which no echo of its former assertiveness can disguise. There could be no clearer intimation of the intricate human issues raised by his approaching, and necessary, separation from the Prince.

The clash with Pistol, an echo—under the new conditions—of Falstaff's former exploits, shows a similar change in spirit. Pistol is a 'swaggerer,' repudiated even by Dame Quickly in her concern for what she is pleased to call her good name. A creature in whom comedy rests on the striking of insubstantial attitudes, on the verbal inflation of his emptiness, he conforms perfectly to the prevailing tone, devoid of the normal expansiveness of humour, realistic and sharply disillusioned in spirit. For this very reason, Falstaff's 'victory' combines obvious irony with the scene's distinctive note of tragedy. Both, once again, are reflected in Doll's determined prosecution of sentiment. To her flushed imagination, Falstaff's moment of exertion presents itself as a heroic episode, to be celebrated in a grotesque parody of the bombastic rhetoric so prominent in Pistol's own utterances:

ah, rogue! i' faith, I love thee: thou art as valorous as Hector of Troy, worth five of Agamemnon, and ten times better than the Nine Worthies.

The effect here is purely comic; and in Falstaff's complacent appreciation of his own worth it is a similar absurdity, the contrast between his claim and its miserable object that counts. This incongruity, however, bears with it an intimation of decline which finally attaches itself to Doll's fuddled emotions. Thus moved, she takes up the image—already applied to Falstaff[16]—of the 'martlemas,' the boar destined for slaughter at the outset of winter, and invests it, beneath the obvious comedy, with a characteristic moral pathos:

Thou whoreson little tidy Bartholomew boar-pig, when wilt thou leave fighting o' days and foining o' nights, and begin to patch up thine old body for heaven?

At this point, the grotesque endearments of the prostitute, presented without abuse of sentiment, touch upon the scene's distinctive undertone of moral tragedy. If a sense of age and impotence now surrounds Falstaff's appearances, and if his behaviour, no longer fresh and freely personal, is concentrated on the sordid realities of brawling by day and lechery by night, the change carries with it an awareness, universal in its implications, of impending dissolution. A note of moral reflection

[16] In *2 Henry IV*, ii. ii. See p. 127 above.

colours, albeit unwillingly, the twilight of his relationship with Doll, and makes it the occasion for some of the deepest sentiments of the play.

Doll's expressions of affection, indeed, finally inspire the most un-equivocal of all Falstaff's intimations of decline: 'Peace, good Doll! do not speak like a death's-head: do not bid me remember mine end.' The phrase, in cutting right across the simplified effects of realistic comedy, responds to the sense of personal tragedy which dominates the scene. It also connects Falstaff with the dark feeling of the political action, a connection made still more explicit, a moment later, in Poins's ironic comment on his relations with Doll: 'Is it not strange that desire should so many years outlive performance?'[17] Once more, as in Part I—though to ends notably transformed—the 'low' episodes echo their aristocratic counterpart and Falstaff's burden of disease and concupiscence is presented as a reflection of the malady and disharmony shared by the senile rivals who, prior to the Prince's affirmation, divide between them the public life of England.

This change in Falstaff's situation does not prevent him from exercising his critical penetration, as occasion arises, upon his betters in the political sphere. His comments on the Prince, though coloured by his deepened cynicism, confirm the impression left by Hal's recent appearances. After describing him as 'a good *shallow* young fellow' and indicating his community with the lower orders he has always been so ready to patronize—'a' would have made a good pantler'—he stresses yet again the moral kinship that seems to bind him to Poins. Answering Doll's query on the nature of this strange relationship, Falstaff stresses comically the identity of interests and behaviour that links the pair as dissolute young men with pretensions to fashion. According to this view, the outward signs of this intimacy as revealed in Poins—the 'discretion,' the 'smooth' wearing of his boots, the swearing 'with a good grace'—reveal a more fundamental community of characters; for they show (in the lesser associate) 'a weak mind and an able body, for the which the prince admits him; for the prince himself is such another.' The evident malice which inspires this judgement should not obscure the presence behind it of a certain relation, however one-sided, to fact. If Hal's ability to share his experiences with the common man has involved from the first an element of calculation, a tendency to grade behaviour,

---

[17] This carries us forward, by its phrasing, to Troilus': 'This is the monstruosity in love, lady, that the will is infinite and the execution confined, that the desire is boundless and the act a slave to limit' (*Troilus and Cressida*, III. ii). The echo is striking testimony to the continuity of Shakespeare's thought in the plays of this period.

after the fashion of his family,[18] by its public effectiveness, it also appears, in the light of Falstaff's cynical comment, as a mark of the commonplace, of his final subjection to the limitations of the human material which it will be his destiny to rule.

It is, however, on a return to the scene's characteristic blend of sentiment and tragedy that the exchange with Doll ends. 'I am old, I am old,' Falstaff repeats, receiving in return another of those answers in which calculation and gross sentiment shade into an intimation of deeper feeling: 'I love thee better than I love e'er a scurvy young boy of them all.' This declaration inspires in turn the reply, 'Thou'lt forget me when I am gone,' in which the recognition by age of its own impotence is touched, at least for a moment, by the shadow of true emotion. The effect of these sombre intimations is greatly enhanced by their setting in the surrounding comedy, which leads finally to the renewed exposure of Falstaff. When the Prince and Poins reveal their true identity, he still has presence of mind enough to recover, to return to an echo of his former attacking mood; for the exclamation 'Ha! a bastard son of the king's? And art thou not Poins his brother?' shows him, as he strives to preserve the initiative, stressing the community between Hal and his associate to which these scenes so persistently revert. His gift for evasion, however, is now exercised under unfavourable conditions. The presence of moral reality which colours, however unwillingly, his thought makes itself felt almost immediately, when he crowns Doll's question to the Prince, 'What says your grace?' with the embittered pun 'His grace says that which his flesh rebels against.' The echoes which derive from this wry evocation of the conflict between body and spirit are indeed manifold. To link it with the reference, which immediately precedes it, to Lenten abstinence and the illegal eating of flesh, is to approach very closely the intimate spirit of this scene; and to see its further relation to the contrast between law and its evasion, moral rigour and unregulated appetite, setting the choice thus postulated against the background, also evoked at this point, of burning in hell-fire, is to respond to some of the sombre undercurrents which, associated with age, decay, and approaching retribution, amount to a profound transformation of the earlier comic effect.

The episode is finally broken up, as is fitting, by the pressure of outside events. The Prince meets the new emergency with an admission, still deliberately offhand, that his conscience pricks him. As he says,

---

[18] Compare the emphasis laid throughout on Bolingbroke's courting of popularity, especially in *1 Henry IV*, III. ii.

> I feel me much to blame,
> So idly to profane the precious time;

but the following reference to 'tempest of commotion,' appropriate though it is, belongs rather to convention than to true feeling. Falstaff is also called away, leaving 'the sweetest morsel of the night untasted' (unless Bardolph's final call to Doll is, as some have thought,[19] an indication that he has his way with her at the last), and the scene ends on a note of drunken sentiment from which, however, the sense of tragic circumstance is not entirely excluded.

III

By the end of the second act the internal strife and decay which threaten Henry IV's England with dissolution have been extensively portrayed. Both in the rebel counsels, destined by their perverse nature to disunity, and in the tavern world from which Prince Hal is now detaching himself, the shadow of age and impotence lies heavily over the action. The presentation of the king, from whose false position—false at least in its origins—this disorder springs, now marks a turning point in the entire history. After Henry's statement of moral abdication the course of events moves towards the assertion of a new political orthodoxy, supremely personified in his son. Before this can take place, however, the previous action, a compound of civil strife, move and countermove in the struggle for power initiated by Bolingbroke's act of usurpation, has to be wound up in a manner which befits the nature of the contending parties; and Bolingbroke himself, broken by the adverse fatality which he has brought upon his own head, has to die.

The achievement of his son, indeed, lies beyond doubt out of the aging king's reach. Henry IV, vastly changed from the active politician represented in *Richard II*, has lost most of his sense of vocation and with it the greater part of the practical attributes he formerly possessed. His old age is dominated by disappointment and by an obsessive preoccupation with infirmity which he shares with his rivals:

> Then you perceive the body of our kingdom
> How foul it is; what rank diseases grow,
> And with what danger, near the heart of it.[20]

The enterprises planned in the earlier part of the reign have all remained without fulfilment. Accepting this frustration as part of the

---

[19] Notably J. Dover Wilson, in *The Fortunes of Falstaff.*

[20] For similar reflections on sickness as a symptom of disorder in the body politic, see Northumberland's speech quoted on p. 110, and York's reflections in *2 Henry IV,* IV. i.

nature of things, Henry's strongest emotion has become a nostalgia for peace and sleep. This nostalgia is born less of immediate experience than of a sense of the meaningless procession of events beyond human control:

> O God! that one might read the book of fate,
> And see the revolution of the times
> Make mountains level, and the continent,
> Weary of solid firmness, melt itself
> Into the sea!   (III. i)

In these lines, steeped in emotion of a kind hitherto scarcely achieved by Shakespeare, there prevails what has now become Henry's chief desire, the wish to abandon the load of responsibility which weighs so heavily upon his disillusioned old age. To appreciate how closely this weariness with 'solid firmness,' this sense of the impersonality of the temporal process, are connected with the main development of the dramatist's work, we need only recall certain moments in *Hamlet*—'O, that this too too solid flesh would melt'[21]—and in the sonnets; many of these use similar language and turn upon related themes. There is, of course, a difference in *weight*, in personal content, for Hamlet bears within himself the burden of the flesh, whereas in Henry it is primarily an external situation, the load of a vocation imperfectly borne, that is in the process of giving life to conceptions themselves conventional. For the moment, it is enough to say that the spirit of these lines confirms the sense of organic sickness which now dominates both factions in this play. Loyalists and rebels, no longer merely acute political studies, have become complementary aspects of a dramatic unity conceived by the poet in terms of the rooted infirmity which threatens society with dissolution.

This stressed subjection to mutability, though its expression notably transcends all particular causes, derives none the less from the king's experience. As he considers his past career, he sees in it nothing but division proceeding (in great part by his own act) out of former concord:

> 'Tis not ten years gone
> Since Richard and Northumberland, great friends,
> Did feast together, and in two years after
> Were they at wars: it is but eight years since
> This Percy was the man nearest my soul,
> Who like a brother toil'd in my affairs
> And laid his love and life under my foot.   (III. i)

[21] *Hamlet*, I. ii.

The lesson of the past, indeed, comes home to him at the end of his career with the force of a universal law. Recalling Richard's original prophecy—

> The time will come, that foul sin, gathering head,
> Shall break into corruption[22]

—the king has come to read into his subsequent history a confirmation of the operations of fate; but it is his tragedy that, having accepted the reality of his position, he is no longer interested in any practical lesson to be drawn from the contemplation of it:

> O, if this were seen,
> The happiest youth, viewing his progress through,
> What perils past, what crosses to ensue,
> Would shut the book, and sit him down and die.
>
> (III. i)

An intuition of the weight of necessity, of an obscure fatality born of human error and bearing down upon individual helplessness, is the only lesson derived by Henry from the long chain of events which has brought him to exhaustion and his kingdom to the verge of dissolution.

To this necessity, however, men may react in different ways. Warwick, commenting on his master's reflections, finds behind the endless chain of disappointments which has inspired them a pattern or 'necessary form,' from a proper attention to which foreknowledge of the future may be derived;

> There is a history in all men's lives,
> Figuring the nature of the times deceased;
> The which observed, a man may prophesy
> With a near aim, of the main chance of things
> As yet not come to life, which in their seeds
> And weak beginnings lie intreasured.
> Such things become the hatch and brood of time.
>
> (III. i)

Like other plays of this period, *Henry IV,* Part II, stresses the problem of time in its relation to human endeavour, and this scene reflects two different attitudes to the 'necessity' which is generally agreed to emerge from the consideration of it. Whereas the king holds that the temporal process operates as a determined fatality so that all efforts to influence its course are destined to frustration, for Warwick the fact that the present pattern repeats that of the past implies that he who observes the

---

[22] See *Richard II,* v. i, and p. 44 above.

latter with understanding may anticipate (and so in some degree prevent) the misfortunes which the former imposes.

The 'form' of events, to put the matter in another way, is equally
'necessary' for both speakers, but the resolution which Henry finally
derives from an acceptance of this fact—

> Are these things then necessities?
> Then let us meet them like necessities

—is capable of more than one interpretation, each relevant for an understanding of the action to follow. Necessity, in one form or another,
is accepted by all the characters in this play, the young and successful to
whom the future belongs not less than the old and disillusioned elders
whose fruitless rivalries divide the past between them. *All* are 'time's
subjects': the principal difference, as Warwick here insinuates, is between those whom a recognition of this fact moves to inaction or despair, and those who are ready to accept the conditions imposed upon
them by reality to achieve the success which is both the end and the
limitation of political action as such. In the last analysis, this is a difference between two generations, between Henry and his son. The
latter will shortly assume the crown and proceed purposefully to the
triumphs which await a king in whose person true legality and dedicated clarity of intention are at last united; the condition of the former,
reflecting the sickness of his realm, is revealed by his weak harping on
the crusading purpose with which the scene ends:

> And were these inward wars once out of hand,
> We would, dear lords, unto the Holy Land.

The episode which immediately follows Henry's gesture of moral
abdication (III. ii) transfers the action to Falstaff's exploits in Gloucestershire. It may be said to underline the impression of 'necessity,' combined with aged helplessness, left by the previous scene; this it does in
the process of further extending the social range, the presentation of
England, which has been progressively developed through the series.
In his relations with Shallow and Silence, Falstaff is brought into touch
with the very embodiments of powerless old age. 'Mad Shallow,' 'lusty
Shallow,' shifting from the contemplation of mortality—'death, as the
Psalmist saith, is certain to all; all shall die'—and the memory of his
youth at the Inns of Court to matters of hard calculation—'How a good
yoke of bullocks at Stamford fair?'—is thoroughly in keeping with the
spirit of the play. The switch from tragic impotence to the hard bar-
gaining of the market place is various in its implications. It stresses,

indeed, the speaker's lack of sensibility, his senile tendency to turn, without any sense of incongruity, from universal tragedy to the petty routine of avarice; but equally the emphasis on the market place points in its own way to the continued processes of life, so clearly manifested in its agricultural forms, which individual decline cannot altogether obscure. Life goes on, in short, even under the shadow of death; its manifestations, grasping, absurd, and inadequate though they may be, are variously interwoven with the sense of mortality which the entire action at this stage confirms.[23]

Falstaff in turn responds to his new surroundings with a pitiless clarity of vision, from which, however, the comic energy formerly so triumphant in him is almost entirely excluded; for the new Falstaff, well aware of the nature of the world around him, is himself, in the clear-sighted scepticism which accompanies his decline, a part of it. He is, above all, entirely without illusions. Finding his companions among dotards far declined in years, he strips them mercilessly of their pretensions, penetrating with ruthless clarity to the reality beneath:

I do see the bottom of Justice Shallow. Lord, Lord, how subject we old men are to this vice of lying! . . . I do remember him at Clement's Inn like a man made after supper of a cheese-paring: when a' was naked, he was, for all the world, like a forked radish, with a head fantastically carved upon it with a knife: . . . a' was the very genius of famine; yet lecherous as a monkey, and the whores called him mandrake.   (III. ii)

This presentation of Shallow, indeed, the preceding dialogue has amply confirmed in its mixture of present helplessness and remembered, or coveted, lechery. The effect is one of realism incongruously mingled, through its relation to the universal human situation, with pathos. Shallow, as he looks back on his memories of Jane Nightwork, takes senile pleasure in thoughts which have long since been divorced from 'performance':[24]

SHALLOW: And is Jane Nightwork alive?
FALSTAFF: She lives, Master Shallow.
SHALLOW: She never could away with me.
FALSTAFF: Never, never; she would always say she could not abide Master Shallow.
SHALLOW: By the mass, I could anger her to the heart. She was then a bona-roba. Doth she hold her own well?

[23] E. M. W. Tillyard, in *Shakespeare's History Plays,* has written justly on this aspect of Shallow.
[24] See *2 Henry IV,* II. iv, and p. 130 above.

Thus far the emphasis is on a senile vanity which is grotesque, a proper object for Falstaff's pitiless comment; but the turn finally given to the exchange once more includes pathos, with the shadow of approaching death to modify the satiric intention:

FALSTAFF: Old, old, Master Shallow.
SHALLOW: Nay, she must be old; she cannot choose but be old; certain she's old; and had Robin Nightwork by old Nightwork before I came to Clement's Inn.
SILENCE: That's fifty five year ago.

The final effect, which embraces comedy, is more complex than mere comedy can suggest. It includes the absurdity which allows Shallow to remember, side by side with his own faded exploits, his 'bona-roba's' previous relation with 'old Nightwork'; but it includes them in a context, a set of moral and human references, which is not finally comic. Falstaff and Shallow, the cynical observer and his victim alike, are 'time's subjects.' 'We have heard the chimes at midnight, Master Shallow,' and the echoes which these chimes evoke touch life at numerous points. Falstaff's own vision is, like so much else in this play, the product of experience coloured by age. His previous repudiation of 'honour' is reinforced by a range of feelings which he no longer dominates, but which now, on the contrary, subdues him; these feelings are associated with and modify the exposure in his person of 'appetite' and amount, in their impact, to a tragic sense of the human situation.

The recruitment episodes, besides confirming the sardonic estimate already attached to the political action, support this interpretation. The 'food for powder' which Falstaff had formerly led to battle now speak through Feeble, who has also been pressed into a cause which has for him no meaning and who resigns himself to his probable fate in words that recall those once spoken by the Prince to Falstaff at Shrewsbury, 'a man can die but once: we owe God a death.'[25] The words are similar, but the attitude of Falstaff himself, confronted with all that they imply, has changed. Whereas at Shrewsbury, his reply to the Prince had been tinged, beneath its evident disrepute, with irony and wit and had implied an affirmation of the rights of life beyond the selfish calculations of politicians, the Falstaff of Part II, after allowing Mouldy and Bullcalf to buy their freedom, is content to accept his victim's submission to his fate; for such, and no other, is the nature of things, and in Glou-

---

[25] Compare, in *1 Henry IV*, the Prince's parting remark to Falstaff before the battle: 'Why, thou owest God a death' and Falstaff's comment: ' 'Tis not due yet; I would be loath to pay him before his day' (v. i).

cestershire, as in the counsels of kings and courtiers, *necessity* justifies all: 'if the young dace be a bait for the old pike, I see no reason, *in the law of nature*, but I may snap at him. *Let time shape*, and there an end.'

The scenes which follow lead to the final resolution of the political crisis. To the vacillation and disappointed hope stressed in the rebel leaders, Westmoreland first opposes for York's benefit a statement of what we may call the 'official' politics of the play. We should not be tempted to give his declaration of orthodox principle less than its true value. 'Rebellion' and 'damn'd commotion' are denounced, on the eve of their final and deserved discomfiture, as the ugly realities they are; and the contrast between the Archbishop's peaceful office and his 'ill translation'

> Into the harsh and boisterous tongue of war,

conveys a real rebuke. York's reply, however, besides confirming, by its weakness, the sense of organic failing and sickness which under-mines his cause, extends it to embrace the entire state:

> we are all diseased,
> And with our surfeiting and wanton hours
> Have brought ourselves into a burning fever,
> And we must bleed for it.   (IV. i)

The origins of this condition lie in a past shared by both parties alike; for of it, in the Archbishop's own words,

> Our late king, Richard, being infected, died,

and, in his manner of recalling this original crime, he simply echoes Henry's own references, not so far back,[26] to the 'rank diseases' which grow so near to the heart of his realm. The actions of the rebels are—in the words of their spokesman, which echo once more the prevailing line of imagery—conceived as efforts to

> diet rank minds sick of happiness
> And purge the obstructions which begin to stop
> Our very veins of life;

but the final impression is not one of personal responsibility. The Arch-bishop speaks throughout rather as excusing himself and his colleagues than in true conviction. The projects he defends are founded on a guess as to 'which way the stream of time doth run'; they have been elaborated

---

[26] *2 Henry IV*, III. i. Quoted on p. 133 above.

by associates who, far from acting as individuals to whom a free choice
has been granted, have been 'enforced' from their 'most quiet'

> By the rough torrent of occasion.

They respond, though in extreme and perverse form, to the spirit which
now embraces all those, not excluding the king himself, who originally
participated in Richard's overthrow and the affirmation of Bolingbroke.
From disease and the age-stricken impotence of Northumberland to the
weary fatalism expressed by Henry is an easy step, and so the infirmity
of which rebellion is the external symptom is connected at every point
with the disharmony between man and circumstance, the contrast between action and stagnation, which dominates the unfolding of events.

Westmoreland's reply to York's uneasy accusations emphasizes by
contrast the birth of a new resolution. In itself, it is a statement, relatively impersonal, of political orthodoxy. He accuses his rival of having
closed with 'a seal divine' the

> lawless bloody book
> Of forged rebellion;

but, though the argument is valid, we must feel that it covers less than
the true complexities which the expression elsewhere reveals. Westmoreland's advice to Mowbray, indeed, confirms indirectly that orthodoxy shares the prevailing sense of subjection to necessity:

> Construe the times to their necessities,
> And you shall say indeed, it is the time,
> And not the king, that doth you injuries.

Mowbray alone, at this point, makes an effort to repudiate this fatalism
by asserting that, had not Richard intervened at Coventry,[27] his father
would have overcome Bolingbroke in equal combat and so turned the
course of the tragedies to follow; but it is noteworthy that his evocation
of the two rival lords in conflict,

> Being mounted and both roused in their seats,
> Their neighing coursers daring of the spur,
> Their armed staves in charge, their beavers down,
> Their eyes of fire sparkling through sights of steel
> And the loud trumpet blowing them together,

reads like a self-conscious throwback to the spirit of *Richard II*, the
recalling of a vanished feudal order in which warriors still had confi-

---

[27] See *Richard II*, I. iii.

dence in their personal prowess, but which has no relation to the more complex realities of present conduct.

To Westmoreland, indeed, Mowbray's rhetoric appears as a digression. The reality before him is that of rebellion, which he represents—in accordance with orthodox ideas—as the supreme crime, and the interruption is brushed aside with a typical use of religious phrases—'prayers and love,' 'bless'd,' and 'graced'—to describe the popular appeal of the youthful Hereford. Mowbray, who (like Worcester[28] before him) knows that his cause brooks no inspection 'by the eye of reason,' seeks to refuse an offer of parley which proceeds, as he realizes, 'from policy, not love.' The wording of his refusal in certain respects anticipates *Troilus and Cressida*:

> every idle, nice, and wanton reason
> Shall to the king taste of this action;
> That, were our royal faiths martyrs in love,
> We shall be winnow'd with so rough a wind
> That even our corn shall seem as light as chaff
> And good from bad find no partition.   (IV. i)

As so often occurs in this play, the use of metaphor is at once intricate and in some sense confused. The image of 'taste' in the first two lines is followed by that implied in 'martyrs in love,' which is replaced in turn by the 'winnowing' of the grain by the 'rough wind' of hostile intention. The metaphor overlays the 'official' rhetoric with a sense of confusion, of meanings incompletely achieved in their expression; but it is the kind of confusion that, in answering to the dramatic intention, foreshadows an extension of the possibilities of poetic speech and anticipates effects later to be characteristic of the tragedies.

The Archbishop, meanwhile, voicing his own uncertainties in his reply, touches more closely upon the present spirit of the action:

> the king is weary
> Of dainty and such picking grievances;
> For he hath found, to end one doubt by death
> Revives two greater in the heirs of life.

He is not alone in this estimate of Henry's position. The king, indeed, even in the mind of his spokesman, has become himself a victim, engaged in an effort to separate the inseparable, to reduce to more manageable terms of external hostility a contradiction deeply rooted in his own nature and situation:

---

[28] For Worcester's attitude, see *1 Henry IV*, IV. i, and pp. 90–91 above.

> full well he knows
> He cannot so precisely weed this land
> As his misdoubts present occasion:
> His foes are so enrooted with his friends
> That, plucking to unfix an enemy,
> He doth unfasten so and shake a friend.   (IV. i)

The state of civil war as a reflection of internal disorder is rarely so clearly evoked. Henry is, in Hastings' following words, in a situation in which

> his power, like to a fangless lion,
> May offer, but not hold.

The fact that these are the sentiments of a rebel, and that circumstances will—as far as rebellion is concerned—qualify their validity, does not make them irrelevant. In truly estimating Henry's weakness, Hastings neither justifies his cause nor gives it true hope of success. Rebellion remains the supreme crime which these plays have always assumed it to be; as such, it calls for and meets condign punishment and merciless repression. The political vision, however, does not exhaust the whole truth, for another, more inscrutable in nature, overshadows it. A common subjection to 'necessity,' diversely reflected in the sphere of action, unites Bolingbroke's enemies to his supporters, the upholders of an established order itself originally built upon rebellious foundations to those who have followed their predecessors in invoking the true imperfections of that order to rebel against it in the pursuit of their own ambitions.

The political conception which animates this series of plays has reached, indeed, at this point a further decisive stage. The original presentation of monarchy as the necessary foundation of order in a world where human experience can still aspire to 'value' continues to be valid for *Henry IV*, Part II. It might even be said that its validity has been strengthened by the presence of deepening personal needs seeking expression through concentration upon the royal symbol. What has changed is the relation of this conception to the exigencies of political conduct. The responsibilities abdicated, to all intents and purposes, by Henry and shortly to be taken up by his son (who is not, however, prominent in this part of the play) are now concentrated upon Hal's more disagreeable echo, John of Lancaster. The attitude of father and sons, though founded on a common impression of 'necessity,' differs increasingly with the passage of time. What has been in Henry IV a tragic sense of adverse fatality becomes in his sons a practical grasp of human limitation. Having played no part in the crime which brought their father to the throne, the Prince and his brother are free to achieve in the political order all that he can no longer hope to attain. Yet—since the past after all lives on in their present circumstances—the achievement itself, positive and necessary as it is, loses some of its savour. The cool competence of Lancaster's handling of the rebels, his impeccable appeal to all the correct doctrines, lead up to the hollow victory at Gaultree, adequately summed up in his parsimonious ascription of it to divine collaboration: 'God, and not we, hath *safely* fought to-day.'[29] This confidence in the monopoly of the divine favour, soon to become so formidably familiar in Henry V, is typical of the new political generation. It is disturbingly linked in this play with a certain reversal of the qualities normally ascribed to human nature at different stages of life. Age, instead of producing insight and control, is associated with a peculiar feverishness and, sometimes, with a distasteful senile passion; whilst youth, far from showing itself generous and impulsive, is calculating, frigid, and inhuman in the pursuit of its ends. This inversion of normal human attributes, rooted in the past action, almost equally affects the future. It is accompanied, humanly speaking, by the loss of a moral dimension in the efficient young politicians of this play, a loss—we are to understand—without which their success could hardly have been obtained, but which is as characteristic as the petty and selfish futility which prevails in the rebel camp.

All this is admirably conveyed in the meeting between Lancaster and the rebel leaders which leads up to the final betrayal. To his efficient upbraiding of them, and in particular of York, as having invoked 'the counterfeited zeal of God' against 'his substitute, my father,' the rebels can only reply with a public disclaimer of responsibility which is finally an evasion of his denunciation:

> The time misorder'd doth, in common sense,
> Crowd us and crush us to this monstrous form;

the typical doubling of the verb to achieve emphasis, so common in this play, indicates that behind the speaker's obvious weakness we are to feel the pressure of adverse circumstances before which he is in reality helpless. Both this excuse and Hastings' more convincing prophecy Lancaster brushes aside with smooth sufficiency:

> You are too shallow, Hastings, much too shallow,
> To sound the bottom of the after-times.

[29] *2 Henry IV*, IV. ii.

The tone of the dismissal anticipates the spirit of the resolution to come. Perhaps we may think that although the competence, the mastery of events, is all on one side, shallowness, though of differing kind, is shared by all. Be that as it may, Lancaster, following purposes as yet concealed, admits that his father has erred and promises redress in no uncertain terms.

The pledging of his word, indeed, is stressed in a way that cannot, in the light of what follows, be accidental:

ARCHBISHOP: I take your princely word for these redresses.
LANCASTER: I give it you, and will maintain my word.

The rest of the scene, with its effective contrasts between York's complacent trust, the misgivings of Mowbray, and Westmoreland's calculated conviviality,[30] needs to be balanced against the ominous ambiguity of the latter's final promise:

> I pledge your grace; and, if you knew what pains
> I have bestow'd to breed this present peace,
> You would drink freely; but my love to ye
> Shall show itself more openly hereafter.

The exchange, a fine early example of Shakespeare's mastery of ironic contrast in his presentation of political discussion,[31] leads, after the dispersal of the rebel army, to the assured frigidity of Lancaster's final condemnation:

> I promised you redress of these same grievances
> Whereof you did complain: which, by mine honour,
> I will perform with a most Christian care.

The voice that speaks here is the voice of political sufficiency, condemning its enemies—justly—for their shallowness, in perfect mastery of the course of events. It bears with it, by implication, a clear and incisive judgement upon the inner contradictions, the combination of shallow optimism and powerless foreboding which have led the rebels to their merited doom; but—we must surely add—it is impossible to hear the

---

[30] MOWBRAY: You wish me health in very happy season;
  For I am, on the sudden, something ill.
ARCHBISHOP: Against ill chances men are ever merry;
  But heaviness foreruns the good event.
WESTMORELAND: Therefore be merry, coz; since sudden sorrow
  Serves to say thus: 'some good thing comes to-morrow.'
ARCHBISHOP: Believe me, I am passing light in spirit.

[31] Shakespeare's masterpiece in this kind is probably the reconciliation between Antony and Octavius in *Antony and Cleopatra,* II. ii.

phrase 'most Christian care' without sensing the irony that accompanies this assertion of all the correct virtues to compass, in all its necessary thoroughness, an act of political disinfection.

As usual, the final comment is left to Falstaff who, though in some ways the shadow of his former self, can still assert himself, occasionally and disreputably, against the prevailing tone of the action. The taking of Colevile after the rebel surrender reflects, though in a slighter way than the stabbing of the dead Hotspur at Shrewsbury,[32] upon the spirit of the episode we have just witnessed. This spirit is burlesqued by Falstaff when he says he will have his deed recorded 'in a particular ballad else, with mine own picture on the top on't, Colevile kissing my foot.'[33] Colevile himself speaks bitterly of the 'betters' who have led him to his fate; and both he and Falstaff are in turn commented upon, flatly and coldly, by the presiding genius of this most unsavoury action. For Falstaff, Lancaster has a level-toned rebuke, the theme of which has been often anticipated by Prince Hal himself in the tavern:

> These tardy tricks of yours will, on my life,
> One time or other break some gallows' back;

and for Colevile, 'famous rebel,' he decrees 'present execution.' In the political sphere the triumph of loyal efficiency is as complete and ruthless as it is salutory; yet even here, before the scene ends, we are allowed a glimpse of Falstaff's considered judgement on Lancaster and, through him, on so much in this play. He describes Prince John as 'a young, sober-blooded boy,' one of those who 'when they marry, get wenches.' The rich flexibility of the prose, as it flows in a succession of phrases like 'apprehensive, quick, forgetive, full of nimble fiery and delectable shapes,' emphasizes by contrast the coldness, almost the perversion, of normal human values which has inspired the successful princes and leaders in their vindication of the principle of authority. The phrasing, indeed, is in itself a product of 'inflammation,' and Falstaff has no illusions about his own pretensions to heroism. 'Some of us,' he comments, would also be 'fools and cowards,' were it not for the artificial heightening of the emotions; but emotion of any kind, after the action we have just witnessed, comes as a natural relief.

IV

The two scenes which follow, vitally placed in the main political conception, take us back to the infirm king, now about to die with the

---

[32] *1 Henry IV,* v. iv.
[33] *2 Henry IV,* iv. iii.

weight of his past acts lying heavily upon his conscience. His death, which necessarily precedes the restoration incarnated in his son, manifests the deep-seated malady of his realm, which the frigid triumph we have just witnessed has conjured in the external form of revolt but cannot, while he lives, serve as a foundation for the restoration of normal health. The crusading project, the craving for 'higher fields' and 'sanctified swords' is still uppermost in Henry's mind, countered, however, to the end by the lack of 'a little personal strength': in that simple phrase, pathos and a rooted impotence join to stress the vanity which throughout these plays has dogged his aspirations.

Not, however, until Henry turns to Clarence and admonishes him to cherish his brother's affection do we touch closely upon the intimate tragedy at his heart. The account of Prince Hal, observed by one who, besides being his father, has devoted his life to estimating the political value of men, offers further insight into the family character:

> For he is gracious, if he be observed:
> He hath a tear for pity and a hand
> Open as day for melting charity:
> Yet notwithstanding, being incensed, he's flint,
> As humorous as winter, and as sudden
> As flaws congealed in the spring of day.   (IV. iv)

Each point in this portrayal will be amply confirmed in *Henry V*. This is the Prince whose capacity, as king, to win the devotion of his soldiers is balanced by his readiness, when righteously 'incensed,' to put Harfleur to the sack and order his prisoners' throats to be cut at Agincourt: a prince, in other words, who stands normally in firm control over the passionate elements in his nature—the reference to 'winter' and the use of the word 'congealed' suggest the presence of a certain element of constraint in this impressive mastery—but whose anger can reveal itself, when stirred by opposition, in 'flinty,' inhuman feature. The force thus precariously held in leash needs, as Henry knows, to be 'well observed' by those who would exercise a restraining, positive influence upon his son; the motions of his 'blood' must be carefully studied, so that advice may reach him when his passions are inclined to 'mirth' without cutting across the impetuous self-will which, once directed to the end it has chosen, can only be left 'like a whale on ground,' to 'confound' itself 'with working.' Only by observing these practical hints, the legacy of one who has from the first seen even family relationships in terms of 'policy,' can the authority needed to check the disunity which the 'venom of suggestion' is always ready to insinuate in high places be confirmed, the necessary dedication of the realm to its glorious destiny be gathered in the 'united vessel' of common devotion to the royal purpose.

These renewed reflections on political unity serve as a background to Henry's final meditation upon the tragedy which overshadows his old age. As he recalls Hal's past behaviour, his bitterness expresses itself in the imagery of corruption which plays so large a part in the Sonnets. 'Most subject is the fattest soil to weeds,' and in the story of his own son the dying king sees closely reflected the process of his own decline from hope; for

> he, the noble image of my youth,
> Is overspread with them.

This disappointment imposes upon Henry a grief that 'Stretches itself beyond the hour of death,' leading him to anticipate for his kingdom a time of anarchy in which his cherished purposes will be replaced by ruin and unleashed appetite:

> For when his headstrong riot hath no curb,
> When rage and hot blood are his counsellors,
> When means and lavish manners meet together,
> O, with what wings shall his affections fly
> Towards fronting peril and opposed decay!

To this evocation of the disorder which will follow on Hal's dedication to 'riot,' Warwick replies with a justification rather political than moral, an echo, in fact, of the calculated public content of Hal's own first soliloquy.[34] The Prince, we are told, 'studies' his companions like a foreign tongue in which even 'the most immodest word' needs to be mastered:

> which once attain'd,
> Your highness knows, comes to no further use
> But to be known and hated.

Once he has learnt from them everything that is to his purpose, the Prince will 'in the perfectness of time' cast off his followers, who will be like 'gross terms,' only remembered for the experience which has been gained from his contact with them:

> their memory
> Shall as a pattern or a measure live,
> By which his grace must mete the lives of others,
> Turning past evils to advantages.   (IV. iv)

[34] *1 Henry IV*, I. ii.

Whatever may be said of this—and clearly no simple judgement would be appropriate—a political rather than a human justification is being advanced. The growing exclusiveness of the two orders is, indeed, a feature of the play, both its chosen end and—in so far as political success implies the setting aside of normal instincts and partialities—its problem. To appreciate the fact of this separation without failing to weigh the claims of either reality is to keep close to the spirit which animates the entire series.

Henry IV, indeed, remains to the last poised between expediency and conscience, bound by his own past choice and yet aware of a broken aspiration to escape from its consequences to a purer order of reality. His comment on Warwick's defence of the Prince is, accordingly, one in which scepticism and bitterness prevail:

> 'Tis seldom when the bee doth leave her comb
> In the dead carrion;

and, a little later, he receives the news of the triumph of his arms in a mood that recalls the contradictions of the aged Northumberland:[35]

> And wherefore should these good news make me sick?
> Will Fortune never come with both hands full,
> But write her fair words still in foulest letters?
> She either gives a stomach and no food;
> Such are the poor, in health; or else a feast
> And takes away the stomach; such are the rich,
> That have abundance and enjoy it not.

It is—as we have seen—no accident that the king and his former accomplice, now his defeated enemy, are thus bound together by age and the sense of a lack of solid achievement. Both belong to a world in which sickness and decline prevail, and are mirrors of inner tragedy. Both are victims rather than agents, once at least their respective selfish choices have been made; and both stand, without the prospect of entering it, upon the threshold of a world in which the criterion of effective success, necessary in the political sphere, will be married to a simple and positive set of moral judgements.

The end of the scene, balancing the news of victory against the king's collapse, shows anticipations of Shakespeare's use of stylistic variations to point his dramatic ends. The 'public,' rhetorical style so much in evidence in these plays is here overladen with images that, beyond their

---

[35] See p. 110 above.

obvious purpose, hint at the approach of a turning point in the action.
The king, as we have seen, meets the news of success with a relapse into
infirmity:

> O Westmoreland, thou art a summer bird,
> Which ever in the haunch of winter sings
> The lifting up of day.

Corruption (the bee in the 'dead carrion') and 'winter' correspond to
his condition, though the coming 'summer,' in which his son's rule will
lead to the final elimination of rebellious faction, is already foreseen.
His collapse, the physical reflection of a moral breakdown, produces
from Clarence an impressive image of the spirit undermining the 'mure'
of the body with the 'incessant care and labour' of the mind, until it becomes

> So thin that life looks through and will break out.

The scene ends with an accumulation of adverse omens that recalls, in
a slighter form, devices which will be used to greater effect in *Macbeth*.[36]
The people, according to Gloucester, are disturbed by

> Unfather'd heirs and loathly births of nature,

and the order of the seasons is unnaturally reversed; 'the river hath thrice
flow'd, no ebb between' and the 'old folk,' repositories of tradition and
experience, relate these unnatural events to the approaching death of the
king. Henry's closing words, as he momentarily recovers, and his final
'softly, pray,' clearly indicate the imminence of his end.

The scene we have just considered leads, in its successor (IV. v), to
an event long anticipated both by this play and by its predecessor: the
final reconciliation of the Prince to his dying father and the acceptance
by him, in all its glory and burden, of the exalted vocation which his
birth has imposed upon him. Not for the first time we may feel, as we
follow the sombre formality of the speeches, that the dramatic action
moves upon two planes of emotion not entirely to be squared one with
another. On the one hand, we have the inherited theme of the Prince's
'conversion,' his final setting aside of 'riot' on the threshold of his new
responsibilities: on the other, beneath the grave resonance of the public
theme, anticipating the return, under his rule, of order and purpose to
the English realm, which has so long been deprived of both, we detect

---

[36] More especially in the scene between Ross and the Old Man, which follows the discovery of Duncan's murder (*Macbeth*, II. iv).

also a more intimate sense of the burden which his vocation imposes upon the monarch, and of the cost, in personal terms, of achieved success.

Left alone with his sleeping father, the Prince's first words dwell upon the weighty cares of office, traditionally symbolized, together with their splendour, in the golden circle of the crown:

> O polish'd perturbation! golden care!
> That keep'st the ports of slumber open wide
> To many a watchful night!

The paradoxical nature of power that,

> Like a rich armour worn in heat of day,

'scalds with safety,' imprisons even as it seems to confer freedom, provides a sombre background to the Prince's determination to assume responsibilities not of his own making, but from which he cannot, even if he would, honourably escape. It leads him to a statement of his position in which the personal and the political elements are each precisely defined. 'Thy due from me,' he says, addressing his father, 'is tears and heavy sorrows of the blood.' These are prompted by 'nature, love, and filial tenderness': but once this debt has been paid, there remains, handed from the king to his successor, a corresponding inheritance of public duty:

> My due from thee is this imperial crown.

The distinction between the two spheres, and the firmness with which it is drawn, at once confirms the public, 'official' attitude to monarchy which prevails throughout these plays, and provides a further key to the Prince's character. He is at this point, though projected against a traditionally sombre view of the implications of power, the embodiment of authority, and it is typical of him that his speech should end with an assertion of control that is not less weighty in its impact for being stated in terms of sober simplicity:

> Lo, here it sits,
> Which God shall guard: and put the world's whole strength
> Into one giant arm, it shall not force
> This lineal honour from me: this from thee
> Will I to mine leave, as 'tis left to me.   (IV. v)

The affirmation of will in power, the determination to maintain the principle of lineage so doubtfully derived from his usurping father, is characteristic of Henry: from this time on, he who speaks is no longer primarily Prince Hal, a wayward son seeking reconciliation with his father, but, openly and directly, the future Henry V.

Shortly after the Prince leaves, with the crown, Henry awakes to find both gone. His son's absence provokes him to a further outburst of pessimism, in the form of a meditation upon the traditional cares of 'gold,' which serves as a prelude to the final expression of the bitterness that has separated father from son throughout the series:

> This part of his conjoins with my disease,
> And helps to end me. See, sons, what things you are!
> How quickly nature falls into revolt
> When gold becomes her object!

Power, as achieved by Henry in the past, has become a factor that disrupts 'nature.' Associated with the corrupting influence of 'gold,' the supreme traditional symbol of material wealth, it is a source of care and endless preoccupation. This perturbation is expressed, in the lines which follow, through a wrought and artificial complexity, in the convolutions of which we may detect—as so often in this play—the presence of a deeper feeling striving for expression. 'For this,' Henry bitterly reflects, fathers in the uneasy possession of authority

> have engross'd and piled up
> The canker'd heaps of strange-achieved gold,

only to be faced, at the end of their labours, with a tragic deprivation expressed through the image of the bee to which Shakespeare, in varying forms, has recourse both here and in *Henry V*:

> When, like the bee, culling from every flower
> The virtuous sweets,
> Our thighs pack'd with wax, our mouths with honey,
> We bring it to the hive, and, like the bees,
> Are murdered for our pains.

The direct brutality of the conclusion, the expression of the 'bitter taste' which almost entirely prevails at this moment in the dying king's reflections, cuts across the careful elaboration of the expression with tragic immediacy. The presence of both these elements, conventional and personal, inherited conceptions of monarchy and an intimate sense of tragedy, are close to the central inspiration of the play.

After Warwick, in a brief speech, has affirmed the reality of the son's grief, father and son are left at last alone for a decisive confrontation.

The fateful decision, to which the whole action has been tending, is now expressed in two speeches. In the first, the king, conscious of the approach of death, gathers up his sense of vanity in one complete evocation of the rule of 'riot' which, as he foresees, will fall upon England when his son rules. Hal, he begins by asserting, seeks for himself the greatness that will in due course 'overwhelm' him; and in so doing he shows, as he has shown throughout his life, that he is a stranger to his father's heart. Beyond the vanity of death, Henry sees another, still more bitter vanity: the dissolution of everything for which he has striven into the chaos of 'misrule':

> Harry the Fifth is crown'd; up, vanity!
> Down, royal state! all you sage counsellors, hence!
> And to the English court assemble now,
> From every region, apes of idleness!
>
> .   .   .   .
>
> For the fifth Harry from curb'd license plucks
> The muzzle of restraint, and the wild dog
> Shall flesh his tooth on every innocent.
> O my poor kingdom, sick with civil blows!
> When that my care could not withhold thy riots,
> What wilt thou do when riot is thy care?
> O, thou wilt be a wilderness again,
> Peopled with wolves, thy old inhabitants!   (IV. v)

In this speech, the emotions provoked by imminent death give added force to the expression of a public, political care. Henry is affected personally, tragically, if we will, by the foreseen ruin of the structure to which he has so painfully devoted his life; for his son's assumption of the crown will, he foresees, lead to the destitution of his officers and the abandonment of his decrees. In the culminating part of the speech, the whole 'public,' as distinct from the human significance of the Falstaff scenes is summed up in a bitter apprehension of chaos. 'Form,' by which alone the fragile political structure can be maintained through allegiance to its royal keystone, will be mocked and 'vanity' rule to the dissolution of civilized customs. The gold recently evoked, through the crown, as the emblem of kingship will 'gild' the shame of misrule, and the result will be endless disorder, symbolized here by the 'wild dog' and the 'wolves' which it has been the vocation of monarchy to hold so uneasily in check. In a word, the rule of 'riot,' deprived of its mask of conviviality, will assume its true visage of predatory ruthlessness, leading to the dissolution of the national community and of all civilized life.

To this bitter reproach, the Prince replies with an expression of filial reverence that brings him at last to reconciliation with his father. His kneeling is an exterior expression of obedience, the sign of a 'most inward true and duteous spirit'; and it leads to an affirmation of the conversion which has been from the time of his first appearance anticipated and is now at last an achieved reality:

> If I do feign,
> O, let me in my present wildness die
> And never live to show the incredulous world
> The noble change that I have purposed!

It is noteworthy, however, and typical of the spirit of the scene, that this 'conversion' is still essentially a *public* matter, a question of showing the 'incredulous world' to what extent it had misjudged the future king. Here we are in the presence of a factor which needs to be properly weighed if we are to understand the spirit of the political action. We need not, should not, affirm that the Prince is insincere because he stresses the external effect of his transformation; for he is essentially a public figure, and his emotions are of necessity publicly, politically conceived. If this play contains deep personal feeling, this lies precisely in the gap which is felt at certain moments to exist between public and private emotion; where the one is triumphant in the necessary assertion of authority, the other sees in the exercise of the royal power a burden of responsibility almost intolerable to be borne, a constricting framework enclosing life and making the king's office barely human in its implications. This latter sense the Prince expresses, when he sums up the content of his meditations on the crown:

> thou, most fine, most honour'd, most renown'd,
> Hast eat thy bearer up.

The incidence here of intense private sentiment is communicated, after the careful antitheses of the preceding lines ('thou best of gold art worst of gold: Other, less fine in carat, is more precious'), in words which point equally to the presence of inherited, traditional feeling. For this play shows emotion of a tragic kind making itself felt, in its attitude to the royal office, partly through traditional conceptions and partly in contrast to them; and in the shifting relationship between these two strains lies the explanation of some of the deepest effects which it is capable of producing.

At the end of his speech, the Prince, responding to his father's situa-

tion, asserts his own attitude to the crown in a spirit which combines
sober resolution with a necessary touch of pessimism:

> Thus, my most royal liege,
> Accusing it, I put it on my head,
> To try with it, as with an enemy
> That had before my face murder'd my father,
> The quarrel of a true inheritor.
> But if it did infect my blood with joy,
> Or swell my thoughts to any strain of pride;
> If any rebel or vain spirit of mine
> Did with the least affection of a welcome
> Give entertainment to the might of it,
> Let God for ever keep it from my head,
> And make me as the poorest vassal is,
> That doth with awe and terror kneel to it!   (IV. v)

The sense of the crown as an 'enemy' is close indeed to the deeper personal feeling of the play, and cuts across the confidence required by the
'public' action in a way that we can only call tragic. As a public figure,
Hal has justly asserted his determination to maintain the royal power
which God has conferred upon him; but here, in the face of his father's
disillusionment, he speaks of the crown itself as a 'murderer' and ab-
jures the very 'strain of pride' which his own words, not so long before,
seem to have reflected. His vocation is a severe and sombre one, and to
rejoice in it at this moment, in the presence of his father who has, indeed, been 'murdered' by the weight of it, would be to show a 'rebel
spirit,' an 'infection' of the blood. On the threshold of his assumption of
the power he is vowing to maintain, the Prince shows himself aware of
a need for moral vigilance, for keeping in check the temptations which
accompany the exercise of authority; in this sense of a tension between
control and the assertion of self-will lies, as we shall see, the key to certain elements in the nature of Henry V.

The father's reply is poised to the last between contradictory emotions. He is happy to hear this rehabilitation of his son's 'public' character and filial devotion to his own person; but, in his 'latest counsel,' his
meditations turn back to the 'by-paths and indirect crook'd ways' by
which he achieved the crown. His hope is that with his death the
shadow of his crime against Richard will disappear, enabling his son's
authority to unite his realm as he himself has desired in vain to do:

> For all the soil of the achievement goes
> With me into the earth.

As he looks back upon his reign, he sees it as showing the response of anarchy to the anarchy which his own actions first set loose:

> For all my reign hath been but as a scene
> Acting that argument;

and even though his death 'changes the mode,' so that what in him was vile 'purchase' is translated 'in a more fairer sort,' it is noteworthy that his last advice is still pessimistically conceived:

> all my friends, which thou must make thy friends,
> Have but their stings and teeth newly ta'en out.

Surely in this use of the word 'friends,' we may detect the presence of a deep tragic irony. These were the associates by whose 'fell working' the speaker had been first advanced, and by whose power he has since feared 'to be again displaced.' This fear, allied to the possession of power, formerly bred in him a necessary ruthlessness towards these same 'friends,' as a result of which he 'cut them off': and the speech, expressing Henry's last advice to his son, ends on a typical note of policy, for he had, he says,

> a purpose now,
> To lead out many to the Holy Land,
> Lest rest and lying still might make them look
> Too near unto my state.

The purpose of Henry's crusade is to the last political, a device, in his own phrase,

> to busy giddy minds
> With foreign quarrels; that action, hence borne out,
> May waste the memory of the former days.

The best comment on this intention appears at the end of the scene, when the Jerusalem of the king's living thoughts is transferred from the Holy Land to the Westminister chamber in which he is destined to die. It confers upon his life, as he takes leave of it, a sense of ironic fatality against which even his son's determined practical affirmation seems strangely limited:

> My gracious liege,
> You won it, wore it, kept it, gave it me;
> Then plain and right must my possession be:
> Which I with more than with a common pain
> 'Gainst all the world will rightfully maintain.   (IV. v)

The words 'right' and 'rightfully,' 'plain' as their sense is to the speaker, show already the virtues and limitations of the future Henry V. It is no part of the Prince's nature to look too closely at the origins of his power, with which his father has been so closely concerned. By refraining from so doing, by regarding his inheritance of the crown as a sufficient reason for affirming the justice of his holding of it, he lays the foundations for his future success and for the precious unity of his kingdom; but, amply justified though he is in the political order, and though confidence in his own right is a proper attribute of kingship, we cannot but sense that 'public' necessity has triumphed over the personal theme, and that from now on individual feeling will have no primary part to play in the political action. Its exclusion, together with that of anarchy, 'riot' and indulgence, will be confirmed in the last meeting with Falstaff.

V

The last scenes, indeed, lead each in its own way to the final rejection. The first, as though to anticipate the return of the Lord Chief-Justice, shows us something of the local application of the law as opposed to the grandeur of the abstract principle upon which royalty itself is to rest, admitting the necessity of its restraining power. The Gloucestershire of Justice Shallow, indeed, has been conceived from the first as a reflection, a kind of petty microcosm of the surrounding world. As in England itself, authority, placed in the enfeebled hands of its age-stricken representative, totters on the brink of impotence and becomes—not less than the royal office in its more extensive sphere—the prey to conflicting intrigues, pursued in the first place by his own servants and supremely, with a greater and more consistent self-awareness, by Falstaff.

Justice, in fact, as Shallow exercises it, is close, narrow and mean in the defence of petty interests—as in the decision to 'stop . . . William's wages, about the sack he lost the other day at Hinckley fair'—ungenerous in its treatment of those below and aware, in its senility, of the need to propitiate 'appetite,' when it is believed that 'appetite,' in the person of Falstaff, has the ear of authority: 'I will use him well: a friend i' the court is better than a penny in purse.' Davy, Shallow's servant, is in turn a hanger-on of the local power, which he seeks to use for his own ends. To further these, he asks his master to 'countenance' William Visor against Clement Perkes 'of the hill,' in spite of his admitted roguery. The grounds of his plea for the 'knave' amount, on their own petty level, to an inversion of the impartiality of justice:

An honest man, sir, is able to speak for himself, when a knave is not. I have served your worship truly, sir, this eight years; and if I cannot once or twice in a quarter bear out a knave against an honest man, I have but a very little credit with your worship. The knave is mine honest friend, sir.

(v. i)

Once more, the last word is left, in a spirit now openly cynical, to Falstaff. Between Shallow and his men there is, he says, a 'semblable coherence'; for

they, by observing of him, do bear themselves like foolish justices; he, by conversing with them, is turned into a justice-like serving-man: their spirits are so married in conjunction with the participation of society that they flock together in consent, like so many wild-geese.   (v. i)

This, observed by one outside all forms and restraints of society, is the picture of an England which this play consistently represents as old and corrupt, where power and 'appetite' reign unchecked, and where the naked reality of each is only partly transformed respectively in the forms of royal authority and free human energy. The Falstaff of this play is shrewd enough to see things as they are, and not as convention would have them be; but, having so seen them, he is ready to ascribe to them a propensity to evil, invincible in man—'It is certain that either wise bearing or ignorant carriage is caught, as men take diseases, one of another'—and, beyond this, to turn them into jest: 'I will devise matter enough out of this Shallow to keep Prince Harry in continual laughter the wearing out of six fashions, which is four terms.' Here, however, he overreaches himself. The Henry whom he will soon meet for the last time is no longer in a mood to be kept in 'continual laughter' by those who formerly amused him. Believing fundamentally in nothing, except perhaps in the comic energy which is now failing him, Falstaff is confident enough to suppose that his wit can impose itself indefinitely, dominating society in the light of his own nihilism and to his own advantage; and this pride, which has long outlived any validity which his former vital energy may have conferred upon it, is the prelude to his fall.

The following scene at last brings Henry, now about to be crowned, face to face with the personal embodiment of the justice upon which his power will rest. It returns, in other words, to the *public* issues, in which Falstaff has no part and which he has throughout repudiated. After the opening expressions of foreboding by the Lord Chief-Justice and the younger princes, Henry appears 'attended,' no longer Prince Hal, as we have hitherto known him, in some sense now less a man than a symbol of the majesty of power demanding the reverence by which alone—it seems—anarchy can be avoided. His first speech, for all the deliberate intent to set his hearers at ease—

> Not Amurath an Amurath succeeds,
> But Harry Harry

—confirms this new situation. From now on, Henry is a public figure, consecrated to the royalty he has assumed; and even natural grief has become for him a garment to be worn, not, indeed, in insincerity, but in the light of a vocation in terms of which no emotion can be purely private or personal:

> Sorrow so royally in you appears
> That I will deeply *put the fashion on*
> And wear it in my heart.

This heart, though capable no doubt of true feeling, is now a 'public' heart, dedicated to the austere necessities of a great office; and, as the spirit of the assertion balances true emotion—'deeply'—against its proper external manifestation—'fashion'—so the final reassurance, rather than resting on personal sentiment alone, looks forward to the exercise of the royal vocation:

> weep that Harry's dead; and so will I;
> But Harry lives, that shall convert these tears
> By number into hours of happiness.

Henry, as king, can say what might, in Harry the son, have appeared presumptuous; for the man is now being assumed into the monarch, the private into the public figure, and the father's desire to conciliate his rivals is from now on assumed into the son's determination to lead his country in unity and concord.

The two central speeches of the scene convey a second public 'conversion' to correspond to the first, already revealed in his reconciliation to his father. They have, without doubt, their value, indispensable to the political conception; but, when due weight has been given to this, it is hard to feel that the dramatist's principal interest lies here, or that the Lord Chief-Justice occupies a central place in this series of plays, or can be described as a sufficient counterpart to the 'riot' incarnated in Falstaff. In accordance with the inherited theme, the Lord Chief-Justice stresses his position as the 'image' of the royal power, and insists upon the dependence of rule itself on a proper respect for the sanctions he embodies. The argument is a weighty one, for behind it lies the fear of chaos so close to the Elizabethan mind (and not least to Shakespeare's own), the repudiation of an 'appetite' that, once allowed free play, would

> spurn at your most royal image
> And mock your workings in a second body.

Weighty as it is, however, it is a *political* argument, and as such its advocate advances it. Personal considerations have little room for expression here and indeed, when the Lord Chief-Justice calls on Henry to imagine himself as king confronted, like his father before him, with a rebellious son, there is a deliberate frigidity about his assertion of the judicial function from which we may feel that personal feeling has been excluded:

> Behold yourself so by a son disdain'd;
> And then imagine me taking your part
> And in your power soft silencing your son:
> After this cold considerance, sentence me.   (v. ii)

The appeal is to the king in his public function, in which 'cold' consideration is needed, not to the presumptive father in his affection; and in the exercise of just power, 'soft silencing' the rebellion of his own blood, the emphasis is on impersonal severity rather than upon human bonds of unity. The Chief-Justice, in other words, though he belongs beyond doubt to the political framework on which this play, and its predecessors, rest, is barely touched by the currents of more intimate feeling that animate its finest episodes; and in this division between public theme and private emotion, politics and humanity, we may sense the presence of some of the deepest inspiration of these plays.

The king, in his reply, assumes the impersonal function required of him. His obeisance, confirming the renunciation of his past, is to the 'bold, just and impartial spirit' with which justice needs to be exercised if it is to raise itself above faction and civil strife. Once again, the emphasis is on the 'public' essence of the royal function. *Publicly*, Henry announces his determination to 'stoop and humble' his intents to 'your well-practised wise directions,' to what is, in effect, less a moral conception than one of policy and practical wisdom; though in saying this one does not assert the presence of deceit, but rather of a necessary Machiavellism, as essential to the conception. The gesture of acceptance having been made, as befits a king who is renouncing not only his unruly past, but, in some sense, his free impulses, the speech rises to a firm affirmation of self-control, as impressive as it is curiously strained, emptied of normal feeling:

> The tide of blood in me
> Hath proudly flow'd in vanity till now:
> Now doth it turn and ebb back to the sea,
> Where it shall mingle with the state of floods
> And flow henceforth in formal majesty.   (v. ii)

This is an assertion of moral power rather than of human understanding. Behind the image of the tide so impressively evoked, there is a sense of the various resources of man turned, harnessed to an end, which is the end of 'formal majesty.' This conception prepares us, once Falstaff has been finally rejected, for the spirit of Henry V.

Before the rejection, however, the background, at once comic and sombre, of the real England of this play returns in two short, but telling scenes (v. iii and iv). The first shows Falstaff at a pretence of merry-making with Shallow and his companions in Gloucestershire: Falstaff flattering the victim whose senility he hopes to turn to profit—it is now ' 'Fore God, you have here a goodly dwelling and a rich'—and Shallow accepting the flattery and yet turning it, with the disillusionment that goes with age, to a sense of vanity: 'Barren, barren, barren: beggars all, beggars all, Sir John.' The opposition of emotional motives—Silence's senile effort at mildly dissolute songs in memory of his lost youth, Falstaff's ironic comment, 'I did not think Master Silence had been a man of this mettle,' the last faint echo of 'riot' which is itself a sign of its approaching death—is already typical of Shakespeare at his mature best. It belongs to the spirit of conscious decline in which the human spirit of the play is now plunged, a decline which Henry's firm affirmation of purpose, though supported by the symbol of justice, cannot altogether conjure: and it leads directly to the return of Pistol, hollow and flamboyant as ever, a singularly appropriate messenger, with his news of the Prince's accession.

On that news, the scene quickly breaks up. Before the 'Helicons,' the 'Africa and golden joys' of Pistol's absurd enthusiasm, the dead become 'dunghill curs' to be set aside in the last and most presumptuous adventure of 'appetite.' The old king, pitifully enough beneath the ridiculous callousness of the phrase, is dead 'as nail in door,' and in the light of his passing Falstaff, strangely quiet up to this moment, comes to sinister life:

Away, Bardolph! saddle my horse. Master Robert Shallow, choose what office thou wilt in the land, 'tis thine. . . . I know the young king is sick

for me. Let us take any man's horses; the laws of England are at my com-
mandment. Blessed are they that have been my friends; and woe to my lord
chief-justice.   (v. iii)

In the light of this, all sentimental approbation of Falstaff is placed
finally out of court. This is the voice of 'appetite,' approaching its prey
in the prospect of anarchy: rapacious, cruel—as in Pistol's echoing comment on the Chief-Justice: 'Let vultures vile seize on his lungs also!—
and blown out, no longer merely with good living, but with the arro-
gant self-confidence that anticipates in reality nothing but its own ruin.
The 'pleasant days' of Pistol's final dream will be confronted with reality
in the icy wind of righteous authority that will blow at Westminster;
but, inhuman as the wind may seem and to some extent be, the corruption it blows away will, at least in the political order, justify it.

One further glimpse of the world of 'riot' is afforded us before the
final confrontation of authority and misrule, sober order and overween-
ing anarchy, takes place. The weight of justice—not the abstract principle, but its ruthless application—falls first on the subsidiary creatures
of Falstaff's tavern realm, those on whom he has consistently preyed and
who are now swept away into a grim underworld where feeling, even
corrupt and degenerate, can have no place. The realism is of a kind that
will be repeated and extended in later plays. The writer who conceived
the sombre little episode of Doll Tearsheet's arrest and the cruel clarity
of Mistress Quickly's comment, 'I pray God the fruit of her womb mis-
carry,' was also the creator of the low scenes of *Measure for Measure*;
in each case, and allowing for the difference in scale, the intention is
intensely serious, uncompromisingly moral. On each occasion, a fundamental evil, which in this play Falstaff supremely incarnates, is firmly
taken up, delivered to the 'whipping-cheer' which is the real embodiment, at this level, of the stern proprieties uttered by the Lord Chief-
Justice. Its discomfiture, the correction of a state of disease in which
physical reflects moral malady, is necessary, and Henry's own treatment
of Falstaff is about to confirm it; yet even here we are not allowed to
forget that human reactions are at stake, that not all can be gain in the
imposition even of a just order. The final words of Doll and the Hostess,
as they are dragged to correction, stress once more the wintry conception
of justice which prevails throughout:

> DOLL: Come, you rogue, come; bring me to a justice.
> HOSTESS: Ay, come, you starved blood-hound.
> DOLL: Goodman death, goodman bones!
> HOSTESS: Thou atomy, thou!

Part of this, necessary and normal as the treatment is by Elizabethan standards, represents a certain reaction of life against the age, frigidity, and indifference which have from the first shadowed the operations of justice in this play; and, in the last resort, the impersonality of the Beadle's final 'Very well' confirms the effect.

These considerations throw light, in turn, upon the famous crux which rounds off the play — the rejection of Falstaff by the newly crowned king as he assumes his responsibilities. Falstaff comes to West-minster full of his new and sinister confidence. He will 'leer' upon the king to attract his favour, he will assume 'earnestness of affection,' 'devotion,' associating a feeling which may once have possessed a certain sincerity with his newly stressed spirit of conscious calculation. The crowning moment is reached when Pistol, having almost pathetically evoked Doll's imprisonment (almost, because the burlesque intention of his exaltation of her as 'Helen of thy noble thoughts' also belongs to the complete effect), prompts the pretentious confidence of his reply— 'I will deliver her'—and utters the final phrase 'There roar'd the sea, and trumpet-clangor sounds,' in which poetry and base rhetoric are so richly combined. The moment of settling accounts has at last come and it will show, among other things, that Doll is far beyond Falstaff's power to redeem.

The scene, indeed, balances the contrasted themes of the play to remarkable effect. The breaking of the wave of Falstaff's enthusiasm against the fixity of the royal purpose is admirably conveyed in dramatic terms. 'God save thy grace, King Hal! my royal Hal!' Falstaff cries, transported by the prospect of his coming prosperity, and after Pistol has echoed him—'The heavens thee guard and keep, most royal imp of fame!'—he further adds, 'God save thee, my sweet boy!' only to find this transport checked by the cold austerity of Henry's indirect rejoinder: 'My lord chief-justice, speak to that vain man.' This in turn leads him to express—this time in terms of true pathos—his unbelief in what he has heard: 'I speak to thee, my heart,' deliberately ignoring the Lord Chief-Justice's reproof: 'Have you your wits? Know you what 'tis you speak?' before he receives finally, from the king's own mouth, the decisive, unanswerable rejoinder: 'I know thee not, old man.' The whole exchange is, in its brevity, marvellously varied, charged with the con-trasted motives that go to make up the play. From this moment, the full content of the scene is, to a discerning attention, apparent.

Shakespeare, indeed, not only accepted the artistic difficulty involved in the rejection, which the nature of his material and his own earlier presentation of Falstaff imposed upon him, but wove it into his own conception; it is a most revealing example of the subjugation of plot to the growing necessities of expression. For the cleavage between Falstaff and Hal is a projection of one between unbridled impulse, which degenerates into swollen disease, and the cold spirit of successful control, which inevitably becomes inhuman. There is no doubt that the change noted in the presentation of Falstaff in this play aims, among other things, at making the rejection at once feasible and necessary. The Falstaff of Part I would never have allowed himself to be turned off without visible reaction, an aged, broken shadow, beneath his cynicism, of his former self. It is not accidental that he has been given a new burden of age, lechery, and disease, which fits in with the changed spirit of the play even as it justifies, and not only in political terms, his treatment at the hands of his former friend. Here, as so often in Shakespeare, we should not simplify the issues. When Henry denounces Falstaff as

> So surfeit-swell'd, so old and so profane,

he is responding to the traditional content of his theme, which called for the young king to reject 'riot' on the threshold of his new responsibilities. He makes, in other words, a true criticism which an Elizabethan audience would not have found excessive and which follows inevitably from his changed situation; and the criticism so made is backed with the austerity of a great religious tradition when he adds:

> Make less thy body hence, and more thy grace.

From the *public* standpoint, which also carries with it in its own sphere a moral implication, this judgement represents a culminating point in the entire action. Henry, as king, cannot but make it, and by making it he lays the foundation of political and moral salvation for his kingdom.

Yet there is, equally, another side to the picture. Though the king's words must be taken at their proper value, the same applies to Falstaff's repeated criticisms of the royal family, which have run as an accompaniment through the preceding action and are no less part of the truth: in much the same way we can accept Isabella's virtue in *Measure for Measure* without closing our eyes to a certain partiality of vision which goes with it. This balancing of the issues, in fact, which should not be confused with indifference and unwillingness to assert judgement, is especially characteristic of the plays of this period. The contrasted characters of Falstaff and Prince Hal, Angelo and Isabella, occupy no more than a part of the whole field of reality which conditions their dramatic being; they are complementary aspects of a creation whose principle of unity lies not solely in the vision of any one of them, but in the author's integration of the various standpoints which constitute his material as a whole. Like Isabella's judgements, though in another degree, those of Henry—valid as they are—suffer from being too easily made. Never is this more so than at this moment, in which he assumes the dignity and impersonality of his vocation. The denial of past friendship involved in 'I know thee not, old man,' the tight-lipped implication of disgust in his advice to 'leave gormandizing,' the studied gesture to the gallery, so appropriate in one whose life is to be lived from now on as a public function: 'Presume not that I am the thing I was'—all these are as revealing as the afterthought by which Falstaff, banished scarcely five minutes before, is arrested and thrown into prison by the returning ministers of the royal justice. This final severity has been variously interpreted by those who wish it to fit in with their conception of the new king's character: but surely, however we may choose to connect it with Henry's own transformed nature, its final meaning is related also to the blow that it strikes at Falstaff's halfhearted attempt to revive his confidence—'I shall be sent for soon at night'—and with the dissipation of the hopes, themselves connected with his recent exploitation of Shallow, to which he clings. This interplay of intimate motives, all relevant and none final, we should by now have learnt to see as a characteristic manifestation of Shakespeare's genius.

The final condemnation of Falstaff is accompanied, typically, by Lancaster's flat and unpleasing comment:

> I like this fair proceeding of the king's:
> He hath intent his wonted followers
> Shall all be very well provided for.

The concluding provision for Falstaff, though it clearly corresponds to an effort to justify the royal action in public terms, is only on the public plane satisfactory:

> For competence of life I will allow you,
> That lack of means enforce you not to evil:
> And, as we hear you do reform yourselves,
> We will, according to your strengths and qualities,
> Give you advancement.   (v. v)

Though perhaps a sufficient justification of the king, it does not help us to form a kinder estimate of the man. The comment surely needs to be read in the light of Falstaff's death as announced in Henry V. Far from being an afterthought, or—as some have held—a practical device to dispose of a character whom Shakespeare himself, having created him, could neither repeat indefinitely nor allow to dominate his political conception, Falstaff's death is surely the logical conclusion of this action and has been prepared for by the change in sentiment that has been increasingly evident in *Henry IV*, Part II. Death and mortality are of the essence of this play, and if the political development is dominated by these realities, so that only the frigid imposition of the will to govern, exercised in the common good, can obtain some measure of triumph over it, it is logical that the humanity which that will cannot compass, having undergone a corruption of its own, should finally die. Fair provision by the grace of the new order is no destiny for the creature that Falstaff has been. Even in his old age, his spirit is nearer to the related decay and tenderness of the exchange with Doll Tearsheet: and since neither tenderness nor decay has henceforth any real part in the new king's character, his death, and not merely his exposure as a symbol of 'riot,' is inevitable.

There is no need, in the last analysis, to be sentimental on behalf of either the Prince or Falstaff. The 'unpleasantness' in their relationship is a necessary part of the play. It springs from all that is most individual in its conception; it translates yet again into dramatic terms of personal opposition the 'disease' which we have found hanging over the English state, and it relates all the divisions between age and youth, action and inaction, anarchic folly and cold calculation which embody that disease to a developing split in the dramatist's conception of the world as his plays reveal it. The precise meaning, in terms of the sensibility here revealed, of this bitter contrast between aged dissolution and the controlled frigidity so unnaturally ascribed to youth, needs to be defined in relation to certain of the Sonnets, to *Troilus and Cressida,* and to *Measure for Measure. Henry IV,* Part II, provides, in a word, through the presentation of a society in which the normal attributes of life are subject to a peculiar and disquieting inversion, a fruitful approach to the issues more completely handled by Shakespeare in the first plays of his maturity.

Chapter Five HENRY THE FIFTH

THE NATIONAL unity aimed at by Henry IV is finally achieved, in the last play of the series, by his son. The principal theme of *Henry V*, already approached in its predecessors, is the establishment in England of an order based on consecrated authority and crowned successfully by action against France. The conditions of this order are, again in accordance with the main conception, moral as well as political. The crime of regicide which had stood between Bolingbroke and the attainment of peace no longer hangs over Henry V—unless as a disturbing memory—and the crusading purpose which had run as an unfulfilled aspiration through the father's life is replaced by the reality, at once brilliant and ruthless, of the son's victorious campaign.

This, as critics have not always realized, is less a conclusion than a point of departure for the understanding of *Henry V*. It was the conditions of kingship, as much as its results, that interested Shakespeare in these plays; and these conditions are viewed, by the time the last of them came to be conceived, in a light definitely akin to the tragic. The problem of political unity and that of personal order have been brought in the course of these historical studies into the closest relationship. Just as the state, already in *Henry IV*, Part II, is regarded in its divisions as a diseased body ravaged by a consuming fever, so is the individual seen increasingly as torn between the violence of his passions and the direction of reason; and just as the remedy to political anarchy lies in unquestioned allegiance to an authority divinely constituted, so does personal coherence depend upon the submission to reason of our uncontrolled desires. The link between the two states, political and personal, is provided in these plays by concentration upon the figure of the king. The problem of the state becomes, in a very real sense, that of the individual at its head. The king, who rightly demands unquestioning allegiance from his subjects, is first called upon to show, through the perfection of his self-control, a complete and selfless devotion to his office. The personal implications, as well as the military triumphs, which that devotion brings with it, are considered in *Henry V*.

I

The simplicity of structure which is one of the most obvious impressions left by *Henry V* is by no means incompatible with effects of a less direct and heroic kind. It is significant that the play, in taking up almost at once the theme of Henry's 'miraculous' transformation from dissolute prince to accomplished monarch, gives it a setting of political intrigue which barely conceals the presence of a subsistent irony. The opening scene is, in this respect, full of meaning. A bill is to be passed, as prelude to the new reign, which will deprive the Church of 'the better half' of her temporal possessions; and the bishops of Canterbury and Ely, with pondered and diplomatic cunning, are debating how to avoid a measure which would 'drink deep,' would indeed 'drink the cup and all.' The remedy lies, to Canterbury's mind, through the spiritual virtues of the king, who is 'full of grace and fair regard' and, moreover, 'a true lover of the holy church.' In words which underline the incredible, the unmotivated nature of the change wrought in Henry, Canterbury proceeds to describe these virtues:

> Never was such a sudden scholar made;
> Never came reformation in a flood,
> With such a heady currance, scouring faults;
> Nor never Hydra-headed wilfulness
> So soon did lose his seat, and all at once
> As in this king.

Never, indeed; and there is something unreal, more than a hint of exaggeration, in the studied phrases with which the Archbishop proceeds to particularize the royal gifts:

> Turn him to any cause of policy,
> The Gordian knot of it he will unloose,
> Familiar as his garter: that, when he speaks,
> The air, a charter'd libertine, is still,
> And the mute wonder lurketh in men's ears,
> To steal his sweet and honey'd sentences.   (I. i)

The evident servility of the prelate ends by casting an indefinable reservation on the very reformation he is describing. That Henry should be able suddenly to undo 'the Gordian knot' of policy may pass, but that he should do it negligently, 'familiar as his garter,' passes belief: and the suggestion of cloying persuasiveness behind the reference to 'his sweet and honey'd sentences' leads us, not only to question the speaker's sincerity, but to reflect upon the intricate and deceptive nature of the background against which the moral choices of the new king are projected. The thing, to be true, must be a miracle; and 'miracles,' as Canterbury himself points out in an oddly skeptical conclusion, 'are ceased.'

The words of the bishops should not, of course, be applied directly to Henry's own situation. Their speeches illustrate primarily their own outlook, which is that of spiritual leaders almost exclusively concerned to maintain their temporal advantages; and, if their attitude is related to the political climate in which Henry moves, it does not necessarily imply an evaluation of his own motives. The nature of his transformation is more closely indicated by Ely when, giving an individual turn to a conventional expression, he relates the change in Henry to the mysterious processes of growth to maturity. As the 'strawberry,' he says, 'grows underneath the nettle,' so did the Prince 'obscure' his capacity for contemplation 'under the veil of wildness'; and, thus disguised, the same capacity

> Grew like the summer grass, fastest by night,
> Unseen, yet crescive in his faculty.

It is, however, in a slightly earlier speech by Canterbury that the theme of moral growth is most explicitly related to a spiritual conception which transcends the ironic spirit of so much of this opening and will in due course be echoed in Henry's own utterances:

> The breath no sooner left his father's body,
> But that his wildness, mortified in him,
> Seem'd to die too; yea, at that very moment
> Consideration, like an angel, came
> And whipp'd the offending Adam out of him,
> Leaving his body as a paradise,
> To envelope and contain celestial spirits.   (1. i)

The difficult processes of moral growth are here related, in complete seriousness, to a conception of control acquired through mortification, through the death of the 'offending Adam' and the transformation of the body into an 'envelope' for 'celestial spirits.' The gaining of maturity through consciously accepted mortification is thus stated from the first as a necessary feature of Henry's royal nature.

It is a necessity, indeed, closely related to the absolute measure of self-domination demanded by his office of the king. Called upon to exercise justice and shape policies for the common good, Henry can allow no trace of selfishness or frailty to affect his decisions. He must continually examine his motives, subdue them in the light of reason; and this means that he is engaged in a continual struggle against his share of human weakness. This struggle, as Canterbury's speech on mortification already implies, is presented in terms of one between passion and the controlling 'reason.' The mastery of passion, and its relation to action, are themes which *Henry V* shares with most of the plays written by Shakespeare at this time. Such control, essential in a king, is yet infinitely dangerous in its possible consequences. It turns easily, almost inevitably, to cruelty and selfishness. Sonnet XCIV is decisive on this point:

> They that have power to hurt and will do none,
> That will not do the thing they most do show,
> Who, moving others, are themselves as stone,
> Unmoved, cold, and to temptation slow:
> They rightly do inherit heaven's graces.

These lines can be variously and crucially related to the plays of this period. The gap, so momentous and yet so slight, between Hamlet's rather abstract longing for the man 'that is not passion's slave,'[1] and Angelo, who sets out by emphasizing his incorruptible self-control and ends by an abject surrender to 'blood,' is here clearly stated. The virtuous man is he who, without exercising it, has 'power to hurt,' the man who is cold, impassive as stone before the claims of his own humanity. He seems, and indeed is, in full possession of his impulses, but his control is only separated by a continual and conscious effort from cruelty and the satisfaction of desires which long denial has set increasingly on edge. The similarity of the king's position is obvious. He too has 'power to hurt' and may easily abuse it; he too, whilst moving others to action, must keep the firmest check upon his impulses and watch sleeplessly over his judgement. And he too—we may add—can easily fall from his position of vigilance into an unrestrained and savage indulgence. If these are the problems of the just man, in short, Henry V is fairly representative of him.

The circumstances of Henry's first appearance before his court make this clear. The subject under discussion is the action shortly to be taken by the freshly united kingdom against France. The idea of war has already been obviously accepted. Henry does not, in reality, look for advice, but for a public statement of the justice of his cause. He prompts the subservient Archbishop at each step to the required action:

> My learned lord, we pray you to proceed
> And justly and religiously unfold
> Why the law Salique that they have in France
> Or should, or should not, bar us in our claim. (I. ii)

[1] *Hamlet*, III. ii.

When the matter has been expounded to his satisfaction, he further
prompts his adviser to the expected conclusion:

> May I with right and conscience make this claim?

The king's mind, in short, is already made up, and his decision only
awaits public confirmation. The perfunctory flatness of Canterbury's
long exposition, which no one could possibly hear without indifference,
contrasts most forcibly with the rhetoric with which he and his fellow
courtiers underline the foregone conclusion:

> Gracious lord,
> Stand for your own; unwind your bloody flag;
> Look back into your mighty ancestors.

For the first time in this series of plays, a king and his subjects are embarking upon action in full unity of purpose. The distant crusading aspirations of the father are about to bear fruit in the son's decisive, if more
limited, project of national affirmation.

Already, however, a theme of deeper significance has made itself felt
in Henry's utterances: the theme of the horrors of war and, by implication, of the responsibility which weighs upon the king who would em-
bark upon it:

> Therefore take heed how you impawn our person,
> How you awake our sleeping sword of war:
> We charge you, in the name of God, take heed;
> For never two such kingdoms did contend
> Without much fall of blood; whose guiltless drops
> Are every one a woe, a sore complaint
> 'Gainst him whose wrongs give edge unto the swords
> That make such waste in brief mortality.   (i. ii)

Much of Shakespeare's conception of his hero is already implied in this
speech. Throughout the play, Henry is not deaf to the voice of conscience. It pursues him, as we shall see, with almost superstitious insistence to the very eve of Agincourt, where the memory of his father's
crime is still present in his mind.[2] Bolingbroke's original transgression
is now only a memory, but here, at the outset of Henry's proposed enterprise in France, a misgiving not altogether dissimilar is already present.
The awareness that his future victories will be bought at a terrible price
remains with him throughout the play; but—and here is the flaw essen-

---

[2] See *Henry V*, iv. i, and p. 190 below.

tial to the character—so does his willingness to shift the responsibility upon others, to use their connivance to obtain the justification which he continually, insistently requires. Take heed, he warns the prelate, 'how *you* impawn our person,' 'how *you* awake our sleeping sword of war,'

> For we will hear, note and believe in heart
> That what you speak is in *your* conscience wash'd
> As pure as sin with baptism.

Henry's political success is definitely associated, at such moments, with the ability to direct his conscience into convenient channels. Once Canterbury has spoken, once the dutiful moral echo has been obtained, the very ruthlessness which had so disturbed him at the opening of the scene enters into his own rhetorical utterance:

> Now are we well resolved; and, by God's help,
> And yours, the noble sinews of our power,
> France being ours, we'll bend it to our awe,
> Or break it all to pieces.

The reference to conscience, the inevitable preface to each of Henry's statements of decision, remains in the propitiatory aside 'by God's help,' and it would be forcing a balanced interpretation of the character to give it less than its proper weight; but, once it has been spoken, the sense of power implied in 'sinews' joined to the verbs 'bend' and 'break' takes possession of the speech. This overriding—for in the last analysis it is nothing else—of private feeling by the will to power is a process which constantly repeats itself in Henry's utterances.

The relationship between conscience and political necessity sketched in this scene, and amply confirmed elsewhere in the play, is not, of course, the whole truth about Henry, or about the conception of kingship in him represented. *Henry V* combines acute analysis of motive in its hero with a conception of the royal office which has been carefully built up from the beginning of the series and against which the personal issues need to be continually balanced. If Henry, as a man, is subject to the stresses which the exercise of power brings out in human frailty, he is also, as king, the guarantor of a necessary order: an order, moreover, which finds in active patriotic affirmation its proper expression. Both aspects, the personal and the political, need to be held in a continual balance, and, if we should not neglect the frailty which emerges from Henry's attempts to clarify his motives, it is equally true that his actions must be considered in relation to the conception of order which his office implies. Exeter's speech, reacting against the suggested threat from Scotland, is in this respect important:

> For government, though high and low and lower,
> Put into parts, doth keep in one consent,
> Congreeing in a full and natural close,
> Like music.

Canterbury's further comments, with their elaborate and dignified comparison of the human state to that of the beehive, point in the same direction, stressing unity in divergence of function as the distinctive mark of a healthy polity:

> As many arrows, loosed several ways,
> Come to one mark; as many ways meet in one town;
> As many fresh streams meet in one salt sea;
> As many lines close in the dial's centre;
> So may a thousand actions, once afoot,
> End in one purpose, and be all well borne
> Without defeat.   (I. ii)

The opulence of the preceding description of the hero, the rich reference to the 'tent royal' of the emperor bee, and to the constructive effort of the 'singing masons building roofs of gold,' is sufficient proof that this conception of 'degree' needs to be accepted as a principal and positive element in the play. It must neither be allowed to overshadow the effect of the psychological analysis, producing a conception of *Henry V* as a mere repetition of traditional ideas, nor be obscured by it; for it is the interplay between the two ideas, the concept of a necessary order based on kingship and the stress laid on the individual by the inhuman nature of the vocation thus confided to him, that gives the play its living interest.

For it is beyond question that Shakespeare's interpretation of the hero's character, as the scene goes on to present it, involves a subtlety of analysis which no simple response can entirely cover. As the action proceeds, we become increasingly aware that there is in Henry an uneasy balance between unbridled passion and cold self-control. The latter element has been present in him from the first. Prince Hal shows it, as we noted when considering *Henry IV*, Part I, in his first soliloquy,[3] when he announces his utilitarian attitude to the company he is keeping, and it is strongly felt, of course, in the rejection of Falstaff. Such control is an essential part of his political capacity, a natural consequence of the very scope and responsibility of his vocation. Without it, Henry would

[3] *1 Henry IV*, I. ii. See pp. 57–58 above.

not be a true king at all; but it has behind it the unmistakable sense of constraint which makes itself felt, for instance, in his opening greeting to the French ambassador:

> We are no tyrant, but a Christian king;
> Unto whose grace our passion is as subject
> As are our wretches fetter'd in our prisons.   (1. ii)

Here, we may reasonably feel, the consequences of the process of mortification stressed in the Archbishop's account of the way in which Henry, through 'consideration,' 'whipped the offending Adam' out of himself, are being stated in terms of human motive and behaviour; and the results, we must surely feel, are a little disquieting. The harshness of the comparison is, to say the least of it, remarkable. Such self-control is necessarily precarious; the passions, held in subjection, 'fettered,' treated with a disdain similar to that which, as Prince Hal, the speaker has already displayed to normal feeling when his success depended on the renunciation of his past, may be expected to break out in forms not altogether to his credit.

Almost at once, in fact, they do so. The French ambassadors, in fulfilling their mission by presenting him with the Dauphin's tennis balls, touch on one of Henry's most noticeable weaknesses; they expose him to ridicule and, worst of all, they refer—by the observation that 'You cannot revel into dukedoms there'—to the abjured, but not forgotten past. Henry's reaction, in spite of the opening affirmation of his self-control, takes the form of one of those outbursts which are habitual with him whenever his will is crossed. As when France was to be 'bent' or 'broken,' his rhetoric, measured and even cold on the surface, is full of accumulated passion:

> When we have match'd our rackets to these balls,
> We will, in France, by God's grace, play a set
> Shall strike his father's crown into the hazard.

The reference to 'God's grace,' rarely omitted from Henry's official utterances, clearly befits a Christian king, and we need not deny its propriety; but from the personal point of view, which the play is also concerned to stress, the note of resentment which rises through the speech is equally significant. It rankles at this point until the real motive becomes at last explicit:

> we understand him well,
> How he comes o'er us with our wilder days,
> Not measuring what use we made of them.

The personal offense once mentioned, the considerations of conscience previously expressed are brushed aside, at least for so long as the new emotion is in command. The horrors of war, the slaughter and misery attendant upon it, are once again mentioned, but only—as so often in Henry—that he may disclaim responsibility for them. The tone of the utterance, following the swell of emotion, rises to one of ruthless and triumphant egoism:

> But *I* will rise there with so full a glory
> That *I* will dazzle all the eyes of France,
> Yea, strike the Dauphin blind to look on us.
> And tell the pleasant prince this mock of his
> Hath turn'd his balls to gun-stones; and his soul
> Shall stand sore charged for the wasteful vengeance
> That shall fly with them: for many a thousand widows
> Shall this his mock mock out of their dear husbands;
> Mock mothers from their sons, mock castles down;
> And some are yet ungotten and unborn
> That shall have cause to curse the Dauphin's scorn.
>
> (I. ii)

'*I* will rise there': '*I* will dazzle all the eyes of France.' The Dauphin's gibe has set free Henry's fettered passions and these express themselves forcibly in a cumulative vision of destruction. The tone of the utterance—the impact of 'strike,' the harsh reference to the balls which have been turned to 'gun-*stones*,' the sense of irresistible, ruinous force behind 'mock castles down'—reflects the new feeling and anticipates the later, more masterly picture of Coriolanus in action.[4] The sense of power, inhuman and destructive beneath the surface of righteous anger, is at last unleashed in the king. The responsibility for coming events, already assumed by the Archbishop, has now been further fastened upon the Dauphin, and Henry is in a position to wind up the picture of his coming descent upon France (which had been decided upon, in point of fact, before the ambassadors appeared) with a phrase that incorporates into his new vehemence the convenient certainty that his cause is just:

> But this lies all within the will of God,
> To whom I do appeal.

No doubt the conviction is, as far as it goes, sincere; for the will of God and the will of Henry, now fused in the passion released by the Dauphin's jest, have become identical.

---

[4] Compare *Coriolanus*, II. ii, and especially the feeling behind such a phrase as:

> with a sudden re-enforcement struck
> Corioli like a planet.

II

After the dismissal of the ambassadors the structure of *Henry V* expands to take in further aspects of its theme. It embraces in succession a presentation of the popular material which Henry will take with him to his wars (II. i), the presence around him of a treachery which further deepens the sense of tragedy implicit in the nature of his office (II. ii), a reminder, also tragic, of the former life which he has renounced as incompatible with his vocation and which now significantly dies (II. iii), and, finally, a first indication of the attitude of those against whom he is leading his kingdom in arms. Each of these new developments is, in some degree, an extension of the original simplicity of the chronicle conception; each contributes to expanding the simple patriotic theme (which, of course, continues to exist as the principal unifying factor in the whole) by relating it to a more personal and universal reading of life.

The first of these scenes turns from the court to the street, from the political action to its counterpart in popular life. The spirit of these popular scenes, however, has undergone since *Henry IV* an important change of which the exclusion and death of Falstaff will be, as it were, a symbol. There is in *Henry V* little room for the distinctive note of comedy. The delineation of character in the scenes of popular life is as clear-cut as ever, and the dialogue abundantly if discreetly flavoured with the sense of humanity; but there is about this first introduction, in their London setting, of characters who in former plays had derived a certain reflected life from the abundant energy of Falstaff a desiccated flatness that contrasts sharply with the earlier exuberance. We may detect, if we will, an increasing interest in Ben Jonson's handling of 'humours' to fit a new kind of moral purpose;[5] but in that case we must add that the new spirit is no mere imitation, but the reflection of an intention that is neither comic nor simply patriotic, but loaded to an increasing degree with some at least of the attributes of tragedy.

Read in this light, it is possible to extract some meaning from the otherwise disappointing scene (II. i) which first shifts our attention from Henry's court to the streets of London. Pistol, Nym, and the others, whether new characters or survivors in a world no longer enlivened by contact with Falstaff, are presented quarrelling like curs. Their jokes turn largely upon the bawdyhouses from which they come, and which will swallow them up on their return to England at the end of Henry's campaign, and—in anticipation of the behaviour of some of them—upon the

---

[5] Some such purpose, as we have already noted, is certainly reflected in the prose scenes of 2 *Henry IV*.

cutting of throats: 'men may sleep, and they may have their throats about them at that time; and some say knives have edges.' Nym's remark, itself dark and enigmatic, is prefaced by a fatalistic 'things must be as they may,' which modifies the speaker's comic sententiousness and implies a certain resigned acceptance of the ordering of things. The humourous conception of the character, in short, is toned down to fit in with a spirit no longer essentially comic; and this applies not only to Nym, but to his future companions in arms. Fluellen and the new characters, who represent—on the popular level—the instruments of the royal purposes in France, belong to a new and entirely different generation of comic personages from Bardolph and Pistol, who are here introduced as survivors from another order of things, less respectable and—now that they are deprived of contact with Falstaff—less comically alive than they had formerly been. Fluellen and Gower, Williams and Bates, are distinguished, not by comic vitality nor primarily by the penetration of their comments on events, but by the qualities of common sense which underlie their stressed idiosyncracies and by a tough sense of loyalty and dedication to the work in hand; and it is by their devotion to the strictly practical virtues—which they so notably share with their king—and by the definition of their national peculiarities that they live.

The scene, indeed, stresses that this is no longer the world of Henry IV. Falstaff himself, out of place in this new order, is remembered only in his illness, serving, if we will, as a kind of measure to emphasize Shakespeare's changing vision of humanity. His condition—it is worth noting—is ascribed directly to the king, who has 'killed his heart'; and Nym, repeating that phrase of resignation which conveys so much more than we may hold him to realize of the spirit of his environment, relates Henry's treatment of his former companion to an obscure fatality: 'The king is a good king: but it must be as it may; he passes some humours and careers.' In a play where the touchstone of conduct is political success, and in which humanity has to accommodate itself to the claims of expediency, there is no place for Falstaff. Shakespeare had already recognized this and prepared for the necessary adjustment in the rejection which had brought the previous play to a close; and now, in *Henry V*, his death, the relation of which almost immediately follows (ii. iii), affects us tragically as the last glimpse of another and less sombre world. His companions who remain must now accommodate themselves to the times. They do so—and this is significant in defining one aspect of Shakespeare's attitude to the patriotic war—by abandoning domestic differences to follow their king to France. War and its prospects of plunder are for them no more and no less than a means of livelihood and an alternative to preying upon one another. As Bardolph puts it (II. i): 'We must to France together: why the devil should we keep knives to cut one another's throats?'

The complexities that surround the dedicated austerity of the king, making it appear at once more necessary and more inhuman, are more directly approached in his exposure of the treason that has bred at his court (II. ii). This scene would be sufficient to prove, were proof necessary, that it would be wrong to suppose that Shakespeare, in portraying Henry, intends to stress the note of hypocrisy. Its effect is rather to bring out certain contradictions, moral and human, inherent in the notion of a successful king. As the play proceeds, Henry seems to be increasingly, at least in a moral sense, the victim of his position. The cunning calculations of the ecclesiastics, with which the play opened, have already given us a hint of the world in which he moves and which, as king, he has to mould to his own purposes: and the treasonable activities of Cambridge, Grey, and Scroop are further indications of the duplicity with which monarchs are fated by their position to deal. Henry's treatment of the conspirators is, like everything he does, firm, just, and decisive; but, as he reflects upon the betrayal, a tragic note makes itself felt which is an indication of the later development of the character.

The complexity of the situation explains the curiously equivocal tone of the references to loyalty in the early part of the scene. It seems strange that Exeter should say that the king has 'dull'd and cloy'd' his followers with his favours; and the political instability which Henry has inherited from his father is implied in the dubious tone, combining acidity and sweetness, of Grey's statement that

> those that were your father's enemies
> Have steep'd their galls in honey.[6]

There are numerous parallels for this imagery of the palate, this sensibility to contrasted tastes, in *Troilus and Cressida*, parallels which—in plays of the same period—certainly point to a transformation of spirit. Somewhere at the heart of this court, as in the heroic world of Troy, there is a flaw which, although it does not yet affect Henry's belief in his vocation or his capacity to act in accordance with it, must constantly be allowed for by a successful king. In Henry's long speech of denuncia-

---

[6] Compare, for the tone, the dying Bolingbroke's reference to his 'friends' in *2 Henry IV*, IV. v:

> all my friends, which thou must make thy friends,
> Have but their stings and teeth newly ta'en out.

tion, which follows on his unmasking of the conspirators, a note of reflection, a universalizing of the individual fault until it becomes a general aspect of the human situation, makes itself felt. The first signs of
it are in the charged linguistic content of the denunciation of Scroop,
'Ingrateful, savage and inhuman creature,' and of the treachery of which
he has been proved guilty. 'Treason and murder' are described as

> two yoke-devils sworn to either's purpose,
> Working so *grossly* in a natural cause,
> That admiration did not *hoop* at them,

where the diction is unusual enough to stress the incidence of deep personal emotion beyond the needs of the chronicled action; and the same
can be said of the use of reinforced pairs of direct, vernacular words—
'*botch* and *bungle up* damnation'

> With *patches, colours,* and with forms being *fetch'd*
> From glistering semblances of piety.

As he contemplates the gap that separates appearance from reality, inner
duplicity from the outer show of loyalty, Henry's words convey a sense
of disillusionment, of intimate tragedy, that is less political than human
in its implications. These are the faults, it seems, against which a king
has to arm himself, preserving the barely human purity of his motives
against the presence of universal weakness.

The speech finally leads, indeed, to a climax directly related, in the
religious tone of its expression, to the need for constant mortification
stressed by the ecclesiastics in the opening scene.[7] Scroop's betrayal appears to Henry deep-rooted enough to be associated with the original
fall of man:

> seem they religious?
> Why, so didst thou: or are they spare in diet,
> Free from gross passion or of mirth or anger,
> Constant in spirit, not swerving with the blood,
> Garnish'd and deck'd in modest complement,
> Not working with the eye without the ear,
> And but in purged judgement trusting neither?
> Such and so finely bolted didst thou seem:
> And thus thy fall hath left a kind of blot,
> To mark the full-fraught man and best indued
> With some suspicion. I will weep for thee;
> For this revolt of thine, methinks, is like
> Another fall of man.   (ii. ii)

[7] See p. 168 above.

It is remarkable that Henry, as he meditates upon this betrayal, should return once more to that theme of control, of freedom from passion, which is so prominent in his own nature. Much in the expression—notably the references to 'diet' and purging and the presence of adjectives like 'garnish'd' and 'bolted' drawn from material processes to express a moral content—anticipates the 'problem' plays which were soon to follow. There is the same tendency to load the versification with added stresses of meaning, the same effort to convey through a difficult concentration of imagery a spiritual condition that obstinately refuses to clarify in the expression. By concentrating on the functioning of the body, and on the sense of divergence between eye, ear, and judgement in the difficult balance of the personality, the speech sets spiritual control in contrast with a sense of anarchy that proceeds, most typically, from the contemplation of physical processes. '*Gross* passion'—the adjective is significant—is associated with the irrational 'swerving' of the 'blood,' and the judgement which controls it needs to be 'purged' by fasting ('spare in diet') before it can attain a scarcely human freedom from 'mirth or anger.' By thus emphasizing the difficult and even unnatural nature of such control, the speech casts some measure of doubt, at least by implication, on the possibility of Henry himself consistently maintaining it; but it is also necessary, inescapable from his office. The administration of justice, upon which depend order within the realm and success in its foreign wars, demands in the monarch a detachment which is almost inhuman and borders on the tragic in its implications. The state must be purged of 'treason lurking in its way' before it can be led, with a single-minded purpose, to the victorious enterprise in France.

Having thus expressed, perhaps more deeply than he knows, his innermost feeling, the control and self-dedication which are the outward signs of Henry's character once more gain the upper hand. Speaking as king, and deliberately abjuring personal resentment, he delivers his enemies to the law:

> Get you therefore hence,
> Poor miserable wretches, to your death;

and, having discharged his duty, turns to the purpose which he has principally in hand:

> Now, lords, for France; the enterprise whereof
> Shall be to you, as us, like glorious.

The moment of tragic doubt safely overcome, the king returns to the unity of thought and purpose which action requires; the discovery of treason becomes, not a cause for inner searching, but a sign of the divine approval, and the 'puissance' of the realm, delivered 'into the hand of God,' sets forth on the enterprise in which its unity is finally to be confirmed.

The following scene (II. ii) is mainly taken up with the Hostess' account of the death of Falstaff: an account which perhaps contains the most direct and human feeling in this otherwise rather coldly conceived play, and the spirit of which, in relation to the 'comic' action, we have already considered. Falstaff still exercises his influence, but as *dead*; and it is significant that Pistol, in the act of turning away towards France, stresses the predatory impulses which will henceforth play so large a part in the 'lower' action:

> Yoke-fellows in arms,
> Let us to France; like horse-leeches, my boys,
> To suck, to suck, the very blood to suck!   (II. iii)

The parody of the rhetorical line of melodrama, never far from Pistol's utterances, is here subdued to the mood of prevailing realism. The following scene (II. iv), introducing the French court, and bringing a little closer the ruthlessness of Henry's approach, is mainly remarkable for the words in which Exeter, echoing his master's determination, anticipates the spirit of the scenes to come:

> if you hide the crown
> Even in your hearts, there will he rake for it;
> Therefore in fierce tempest is he coming,
> In thunder and in earthquake, like a Jove,
> That, if requiring fail, he will compel.   (II. iv)

Like the following references to the horrors of war, which only submission to the invader's will can avert, the iron quality of these threats will be amply confirmed on the fields of France.

III

It is not, indeed, until the opening of the third act, which coincides with the first stage in the French campaign, that the characteristic qualities of Henry's utterances are translated into action. The poetry of war in this play deserves careful attention. Much of it, corresponding to the spirit of the patriotic chronicle, is full of life and vigour; such is the elaborate description in the Prologue to this same act of the 'fleet majestical' which bears the English forces to Harfleur. The king 'embarks his royalty' on a 'brave fleet,' adorned and lighted by the dawn:

> behold the threaden sails,
> Borne with the invisible and creeping wind,
> Draw the huge bottoms through the furrow'd sea,
> Breasting the lofty surge: O, do but think
> You stand upon the rivage and behold
> A city on the inconstant billows dancing;
> For so appears this fleet majestical.   (III. Prologue)

This imagery, splendidly and consciously laden for its effect, is a contribution to the spirit of the play. It may be that some of its deeper notes are not included in it, but the effect of a pageant, of the confident display of might in beauty, is undoubtedly part of Shakespeare's debt to his story which, whilst balancing it against other elements, it was no part of his intention to forego. If, in much of this play, he qualifies the note of majesty with more sombre and reflective tones, the effect of these tones is in part gained by the contrast with the appeal of majesty itself.

Yet when, immediately after, Henry himself appears, much of his first utterance is unmistakably associated with the element of constraint already noted in his nature. The rhetoric with which he incites his followers to battle includes in itself a strong flavour of artificiality and strain. There is about his picture of the warrior in action something grotesque and exaggerated:

> Then imitate the action of the tiger;
> Stiffen the sinews, summon up the blood,
> Disguise fair nature with hard-favour'd rage;
> Then lend the eye a terrible aspect;
> Let it pry through the portage of the head
> Like the brass cannon; let the brow o'erwhelm it
> As fearfully as doth a galled rock
> O'erhang and jutty his confounded base,
> Swill'd with the wild and wasteful ocean.
> Now set the teeth and stretch the nostril wide,
> Hold hard the breath and bend up every spirit
> To his full height.   (III. i)

The spirit of much of this could no doubt be described in terms of the early Shakespeare somewhat painstakingly sticking to his chronicle purposes, rendering in self-conscious verse something of the effort and cruelty of war; and yet, as we read it carefully, we cannot but feel that these lines reflect also a note of detachment, an ability to *evaluate*, which is at least indicative of later developments. For there is about Henry's incitation something forced, incongruous, even (if we may risk taking the point a little too far) slightly absurd. The action of the warrior is, after all, an *imitation*, and an imitation of a wild beast at that, carried out by what Henry himself feels to be an exclusion of 'fair nature.' The blood is to be 'summoned up,' the sinews 'stiffened' to the necessary degree of artificial ruthlessness, whilst the involved rhetorical comparisons which follow the references to the 'brass cannon' and the 'galled rock' strengthen a certain impression of unreality. In stressing the note of inhumanity, the speech does not deny the poetry of war, which has already found expression in the Prologue; but here, as later in *Coriolanus*,[8] the author balances the conception of the warrior in his triumphant activity as 'a greyhound straining upon the start' against that, not less forcible, of a ruthless and inhuman engine of destruction. The mastery of phrase and rhythm is far less developed, the prevailing tone more immature than in the Roman tragedy; but the immaturity still reflected in the convolutions of the verse is not such that the critical purpose cannot make itself felt. The ruthlessness as well as the splendour of the warrior, will be given in *Coriolanus* an expression incomparably finer; but both are already present and fully conscious in the earlier play.

Henry's treatment of the Governor and citizens of Harfleur (III. iii), almost immediately after this apostrophe, relates this conception of the warrior to strains already apparent in his own character. Shakespeare, not for the first time, places the two scenes together in such a way that each throws a light of its own upon the other. The way in which Henry presents his ultimatum is full of that sense of conflict between control and passion which was so prominent in his first utterances. The grotesque inhumanity implicit in his attitude is balanced, indeed, by a suggestion of tragic destiny. Beneath his callousness is a sense that the horrors of war, once unloosed, once freed from the sternest control, are irresistible. His soldiers, he warns the Governor, are still held uneasily in check. 'The cool and temperate wind of grace,' whose control over passion has already been indicated by Henry himself as the distinctive mark of a Christian king, still exercises its authority; but 'licentious wickedness' and 'the filthy and contagious clouds' of '*heady* murder' threaten to break out at any moment. In his catalogue of the horrors of unbridled war stress is laid continually upon rape and the crimes of 'blood.' The 'fresh-fair virgins' of Harfleur will become the victims of the soldiery, whose atrocities are significantly referred to in terms of 'liberty':

> What rein can hold licentious wickedness
> When down the hill he holds his fierce career?

---

[8] See, for example, Cominius' account of Coriolanus before Corioli (*Coriolanus*, II. ii).

The process of evil, once unleashed, follows courses fatally determined; but Henry, as usual, having described them in words which lay every emphasis upon their horror, disclaims all responsibility for them, just as he had once disclaimed all responsibility for the outbreak of the war. The whole matter, thus taken out of his hands, becomes indifferent to him:

> What is it to me, *when you yourselves are cause,*
> If your pure maidens fall into the hand
> Of hot and forcing violation?

Yet this very assertion of indifference implies, at bottom, a sense of the tragedy of the royal position. Only this denial of responsibility, it would seem, only the exclusion of humanity and the acceptance of a complete dualism between controlling 'grace' and the promptings of irresponsible passion, can make possible that success in war which is, for the purposes of this play, the crown of kingship.

The scene between Henry's soldiers, sandwiched between the two chronicle episodes, serves, in accordance with a technique by now familiar, as a commentary upon them. Here, indeed, are the greyhounds straining at the leash, not the courtly warriors who may be held to correspond to all that is heroic or patriotic in the spirit which this play derives from its chronicle origins, but the basic human material which, besides being in a sense its instrument, offers a detached evaluation of it. The comic spirit, which would have inspired such a scene in the preceding plays, is indeed lacking, and the comment is not consciously made —as Falstaff would have made it, imparting some of his life to the cruder material around him—but more simply derived from the presentation of human realities. The behaviour of Nym, Bardolph, and Pistol before Harfleur (iii. ii) reads with double force after Henry's stress on breeding and the patriotic virtues. The general tone of these soldierly meditations is familiar enough and recalls Falstaff's observations at Shrewsbury. 'The knocks are too hot'—as Nym puts it—'and, for mine own part, I have not a case of lives'; whilst the Boy's comment—'I would give all my fame for a pot of ale and safety'—makes him the inheritor, at least for a moment, of the philosophy of his former master. The difference in spirit, however, is more important than the resemblance. The Boy, indeed, is a poor substitute for Falstaff, and if we accept him as such, we must consider that this play was written not so far in time from *The Merry Wives of Windsor*, where it seems clear that the great comic character was resurrected, for reasons of popularity, by an author no longer working on the lines which had originally led to his creation.

The tone of the scene is less one of comic commentary than of a conscientious and sober realism set in contrast to the patriotic utterances required by the chronicle theme.

We may, indeed, go a little further in interpreting the scene. The Shakespearean attitude to war in this play implies, beyond the evident appeal to common sense, an additional element scarcely suggested in *Henry IV*, Part I, though it is in process of development in the sequel to that play. The values towards which Shakespeare now seems to be feeling his way are, if anything, essentially moral and tragic. Even in Pistol's flamboyant bravado and evident cowardice, there is a new note of reflection, a serious reference to the wastage of human lives. 'Knocks go and come; God's vassals'—the phrase, for all its comic sententiousness, is not unaffected by a sense of religious seriousness—'drop and die.' Striking too, though in another direction, is the repeated emphasis upon stealing in the scenes which portray the invading army. These make their first appearance at this point, and will be developed shortly. Henry's Englishmen, the followers of the 'noblest English' who are a copy for 'men of grosser blood,' are the same who 'will steal anything, and call it purchase.' Once more the comment is related to those made by Falstaff upon his enforced levies before Shrewsbury; and once more, though a very different spirit prevails in the aristocratic action, we feel sufficient connection to exist for the spirit of the play to be affected. These soldiers will steal, moreover, not in the spirit of the earlier Falstaff defying 'the rusty curb of old father antic the law,'[9] but to keep body and soul together or in simple obedience to their innate cupidity; and, in the intervals of stealing, there will be abundant opportunity for the throat-cutting which plays so great a part in the military vocation. As Macmorris reminds his fellows, 'there is throats to be cut, and works to be done,' so that Henry's coming treatment of his prisoners in the hour of battle,[10] far from being an isolated incident, simply answers to the common reality of war.

The presence of these elements in his army imposes on the king certain necessities in the fulfilment of his responsibilities. Cupidity is balanced by uncompromising rigour in the maintenance of elementary moral law. Besides being ready to inflict suffering upon his enemies, Henry has to enforce good conduct upon his own men. In so doing, the claims of morality and those of political calculation are intertwined in a way highly typical of this play. When Bardolph, adding sacrilege to

[9] *1 Henry IV*, I. ii.
[10] *Henry V*, IV. vii.

theft, steals a pax from a French church on the march in Picardy, Henry has no hesitation in ordering him to be hanged; for discipline, as the faithful Fluellen observes, 'ought to be used,' and the offender should die, even if 'he were my brother.' In thus imposing discipline Henry makes the sacrifice called for by his office. Once more, justice requires authority to be ready, when necessary, to cut across human feeling; and we shall not be responding fully to the spirit of the most individual parts of the play unless we are continually ready to balance hard necessity against humanity, the impersonality required of the king in the persecution of his purposes against the sympathy which the terms of that pursuit often require him to ignore.

The final effect is complicated by the familiar presence, beneath Henry's necessary severity, of a note of expediency. Even the enforcement of honesty in this play is not without a certain basis in sober calculation. Henry, as he confirms the sentence passed on a thief who has been presented as the product and, in some sense the victim, of adverse social circumstances, leaves the last word not to justice but to diplomacy: 'for when lenity and cruelty play for a kingdom, the gentler gamester is the soonest winner.' Moral principle, coming into contact with political reality, translates itself—in its own despite—into a question of expediency; and it is expediency, the condition of successful leadership aiming at an end recognized to be desirable, which is the touchstone of Henry's conduct.

Two other scenes (III. v and vii), introduced as preludes to the climax of Agincourt, establish a contrast between the realistic sobriety of the English camp and the artificial pretentiousness of their French opponents. It would be perverse, of course, not to see primarily in these scenes a satiric purpose, a contribution to the patriotic chronicle being enacted; and yet the cleavage between the two sides, as it is expressed more particularly in terms of imagery, does have a certain relationship to the conflicting tendencies revealed in Henry's own nature. Shakespeare, in other words, differentiates between the English and French forces in a way which remotely anticipates the balance held in *Troilus and Cressida* between Greeks and Trojans; though it is true that here the unfavourable estimate of the English, which is scarcely compatible with the spirit of the story, is expressed only in the words of their enemies and finally recoils upon their own weaknesses. The English in *Henry V* are beyond doubt morally worthy of their victory, but the French account of them does to some degree indicate the possibility of criticism. The French, combining a touch of what later became the insubstantial chivalry of Troilus with a more than Trojan vanity are, like the Trojans, defeated; the English, represented by them as gross and dull-witted, are more undeniably successful than the Greeks.

In its treatment of the nobility of France, indeed, the play seems to be in the process of turning a popular satirical conception to fresh purposes. The Dauphin's description of his horse (III. vii), which is typical of many French utterances, combines a certain elemental lightness with a euphuistic hollowness of phrase: 'It is a beast for Perseus: he is pure air and fire; and the dull elements of earth and water never appear in him.' The contrast between the opposed elements is typical, but so is the reference just below to the conventional love poetry of the courts. For the Dauphin goes on to say that he once wrote in praise of his horse a sonnet beginning 'Wonder of nature,' to which Orleans retorts 'I have heard a sonnet begin so to one's mistress'; and the Dauphin, oblivious to the reversal of values involved, comments 'Then did they imitate that which I composed to my courser, for my horse is my mistress.'

The society from which such comments emerge is already, in embryo, that of the early scenes of *Troilus*: a society still far less seriously treated and with much less evidence of a dominating purpose, but clearly sceptical and revealing a fundamental moral carelessness, a tendency to view with cynicism the phrase-making of its own leaders. Equally significant are the slighting references of the French to the heavy wits and bodies of their adversaries, references which bear some similarity to Shakespeare's future treatment of the dull, brainless Ajax and Achilles his rival in ponderous inaction. At one point the criticism is enforced by a comparison between the qualities and effects of wine and water:

> Can sodden water,
> A drench for sur-rein'd jades, their barley-broth,
> Decoct their cold blood to such valiant heat?   (III. v)

The difference is described here—and this is the most interesting thing about a passage which might otherwise pass for nothing more than a piece of satire on national humours—in terms of 'blood.' Hot blood, sensual, frivolous and ineffective in its pretension to nobility meets the cold fixity of purpose which it affects to despise, and is hopelessly defeated. Without overstressing the importance of this passage, we may hold that there are elements in this picture which Shakespeare was soon to use with greater consistency and for more serious purposes. Meanwhile, Orleans contemptuously refers to the king of England and his 'fat-brain'd followers' as empty in the head—'for if their heads had any intellectual armour, they could never wear such heavy head-pieces'—and, according to the Constable, dependent for their courage on the fact that they have left 'their wits with their wives'; but, like the Greeks in *Troilus*—and more deservedly—they prevail. Shakespeare's handling of the battle will largely carry on this conception. The French, trusting to a thin and rhetorical belief in their own aristocratic superiority, rush hastily and incompetently to their deaths; the English, deriving their spirit from their king, win the day by perseverance and self-control.

IV

The scene which follows immediately on the elaborate set piece which constitutes the Prologue to the fourth act gathers up into an immediate form much of the truly personal feeling of this play. It will be clear by now that *Henry V* represents, however tentatively and partially and however mingled with other purposes related to the original chronicle conception, a step in the realization of themes only fully developed in the tragedies. Inheriting a conception of Henry as the victorious ruler, perfectly aware of his responsibilities and religiously devoted to the idea of duty, Shakespeare seems to emphasize the difficulties of the conception, the obstacles, both personal and political, which lie between it and fulfilment. These difficulties, however, never amount to a questioning of the royal judgement. Even in his decisive debate with Williams and Bates on the morning of Agincourt (IV. i), where the implications of his power are most searchingly discussed, the king's right to command obedience is never in question. The claims of authority, as fundamental to the Shakespearean conception of the body politic as are those of judgement and control to the moral idea, must still be advanced and accepted. Henry's soldiers, in spite of their pessimistic views of the military situation, accept them without reserve. For Bates the duty of a subject lies in loyal execution of the royal will, and the responsibility for wrong action, if wrong there be, rests beyond the simple soldier with the king: 'we know enough, if we know we are the king's subjects.' Williams is more sceptical, but his scepticism, far from sapping the will to action, as it might have done in the following 'problem' plays, reflects a sturdy and independent nature. Replying to Henry's assertion that the cause is just with a doubtful 'that's more than we know,' he never questions the postulate that the subject is bound to obey. On the contrary, he openly asserts that this is so. To disobey, as he puts it, 'were against all property of subjection,' and the emphasis is still upon the 'proportion' to be observed between king and subject, directing head and executing body, and upon the proper submission required for the successful military effort. Henry, of course, accepts this view of his position. Indeed, the temper of the play, still strongly orthodox in its politics, would not in any case permit him to do otherwise; but the manner of his acceptance, modified as it is by a consistently sombre estimate of human possibilities, is at this moment decidedly tragic in spirit.

For the arguments of his followers, though they do not—and cannot— lead Henry to question his own authority, correspond to his own mood, force him to reflect deeply upon the weaknesses which even kings cannot overcome. It is in the tone of these reflections that he approaches most closely the spirit of later plays. 'The king is but a man, as I am: the violet smells to him as it doth to me; . . . all his senses have but human conditions: his ceremonies laid by, in his nakedness he appears but a man; and though his affections are higher mounted than ours, yet when they stoop, they stoop with the like wing.' There is about the argument a universality which transcends the royal situation. Men, differentiated by a 'ceremony' ultimately vain, are united in their common 'weakness,' and the most notable feature of human behaviour seems to the speaker to be its domination by impulse, its helplessness before the universal stooping of the affections.[11] In this respect, at least, the king is one with his men; and just because he is so like them, because his senses too 'have but human conditions' and are continually liable to break through the guard of rigid self-control imposed upon him by his vocation, there is something precarious and disproportionate in his absolute claim upon the allegiance of his followers. Nowhere in this play are we closer to the spirit which, modifying the simplicity of the original conception, carries us forward in anticipation of the tragedies to follow.

The tragic spirit is expressed through the king's increasing awareness of his isolation. Williams underlines this when he points out the spiritual consequences of a conflict for which his master, as unquestioned head of his army, is alone responsible: 'For how can they [Henry's soldiers] charitably dispose of any thing, when blood is their argument? Now, if these men do not die well, it will be a black matter for the king that led them to it.' These words repeat once more, but with a greater urgency, the preoccupation with the horrors of war which Henry has already expressed, even if he succeeded in shaking off responsibility for them, to the French ambassadors and to the Governor of Harfleur. They repeat it, moreover, in terms of that friction between flesh and spirit, the

---

[11]. The reference to the violet and its smell in connection with corrupt sensuality can be paralleled in the words of Angelo in *Measure for Measure*, II. ii:

> it is I
> That, lying by the violet in the sun,
> Do as the carrion does, not as the flower,
> Corrupt with virtuous season.

presence of which is so persistently implied in the king himself. The words of Williams indicate, in fact, beyond the religious sense of responsibility which derives from the traditional conception of monarchy, a contrast—already familiar—between the Christian law of 'grace' or 'charity' and the 'blood'-spurred impulse to destruction that threatens it in the necessary acts of war with the consequences of unleashed brutality. The connection between this conflict of flesh and spirit and the tendency of human societies, states, and families alike to dissolve by the questioning of 'degree' into anarchy is not established in this play as it is in the tragedies which follow. But Hamlet himself might have reflected like Henry on the precarious basis of human pretensions, and Angelo defined in similar terms the catastrophic realization of it brought about by his fatal encounter with Isabella. Had Henry once followed his line of speculation far enough to doubt the validity of his motives for action, or—on the other hand—had he given free play to the sinister impulses he dimly recognizes in himself, the resemblance would have been complete; as it is, there is only a premonition, a first indication of possibilities brought more fully to light in later plays.

For the moment, Henry counters Williams' argument by pointing out that soldiers 'purpose not their death, when they purpose their services.' The latter's sombre view of human nature, however, imposes itself upon the king, attaches itself to his own meditations, and is profoundly echoed in his words. Connecting war with sin, and in particular with overriding passion, he repeats the tone of earlier statements: 'Besides, there is no king, be his cause never so spotless, if it come to the arbitrement of swords, can try it out with all unspotted soldiers: some peradventure have on them the guilt of premeditated and contrived murder; some, of beguiling virgins with the broken seals of perjury.' The result is, in part, a fresh emphasis on meticulous self-examination as a means of conserving spiritual health—'Therefore should every soldier in the wars do as every sick man in his bed, wash every mote out of his conscience'— and, in the verse soliloquy which closes the scene, one of those outbursts of nostalgic craving for release which have appeared already in *Henry IV*, Part II, and will be repeated with a new, more *physical* apprehension of existence in Hamlet's soliloquies and the Duke's incitations to Claudio in *Measure for Measure*:

> What infinite heart's-ease
> Must kings neglect, that private men enjoy!

The craving for 'heart's-ease' in this long speech is still, generally speaking, what it is in *Henry IV*—a desire to be freed from the burden of an office in which human purposes seem so often fatally divorced from human achievement. The development of the verse is still painstaking, leisurely in the expansion of its long periods, and a little rhetorical; but there are moments, generally traceable to characteristic touches of imagery, which anticipate the association in *Hamlet* of this familiar nostalgia with a desire to be free from the intolerable incumbrances, the 'fardels,' the 'things rank and gross in nature,' by which the flesh persistently seems to obstruct the unimpeded workings of the spirit. 'Greatness' is a 'fiery fever' which consumes its royal victim like a bodily disease, and the contrasted peace of the humble subject is described with a curious ambiguity of tone:

> Not all these, laid in bed majestical,
> Can sleep so soundly as the wretched slave,
> Who with a body fill'd and vacant mind
> Gets him to rest, cramm'd with distressful bread.
>
> (IV. i)

In the association of peace with bodily fulness and vacancy of mind, in the impression, harshly and directly physical, behind 'fill'd' and 'cramm'd,' there is a distinct suggestion of certain descriptions of satiated, idle contentment in plays as far apart as *Troilus and Cressida* and *Coriolanus*.[12] Here already such imagery represents a kind of residue standing, intractable and irradicable, in direct contrast to the king's increasing emphasis on the need for spiritual discipline. It is no more than a suggestion, unabsorbed as yet into the main imaginative design of the play; but, tentative as it is, it stands in a certain relationship to the clash of flesh and spirit—'passion' and 'grace'—which exacts continual vigilance from Henry, and which is slowly moving through these developments of imagery towards more open realization.

The tragic sense which dominates this episode is finally related, before it concludes, to a main argument of the entire series, the sense of the crime, still imperfectly expiated, by which Henry's father took possession of the crown, and which still lives at this moment of self-scrutiny in his own mind:

> Not to-day, O Lord,
> O, not to-day, think not upon the fault
> My father made in compassing the crown!   (IV. i)

---

[12] I have indicated the importance of imagery of the same type in both these plays in the sections devoted to them in my book *An Approach to Shakespeare* (Garden City, N.Y.: Doubleday & Company, Inc., 1956).

In this reflection, at least, the religious note which runs through Henry's utterances is associated with a sense of deeper feeling than elsewhere; and by the end of the same speech, after he has listed his efforts at reparation, the sense of being unable to escape the consequences of past actions emerges with an intensity that anticipates the presentation of some of the great tragic figures:

> More will I do;
> Though all that I can do is nothing worth,
> Since that my penitence comes after all,
> Imploring pardon. (iv. i)

The expression here, though not of course the speaker's situation, recalls that of Claudius in his vain attempts to pray.[13] The later Shakespearean villains—Claudius and Macbeth—seek to repent, but are unwilling to relinquish the fruits of their original crime. Henry's situation, it need hardly be said, is not the same as theirs. The most hostile interpretation could not make him in any sense a 'villain,' and the 'crime' committed to which he refers is not his but part of the burden planted upon him and carried to Agincourt; but in the expression, at least, there is sufficient similarity to indicate that one of the themes which were later to bear fuller tragic expression is here in the process of emerging from a play conceived originally in a very different spirit.

V

After this introduction, the scenes leading up to and including the battle of Agincourt strike us, in the main, as belonging rather to the chronicle material than to the more deeply personal conception of the play. The first two (iv. ii and iii) set forth once more the contrast between the spirit that animates respectively the French and English camps. The French are introduced (iv. ii) with the spurious lyricism that has throughout been characteristic of them. Orleans refers at the very start to the sun that gilds his armour, and he and the Dauphin go on to apostrophize, in French, the elements as indicative of their conquering spirit. The object of this presentation, however, is rather plain ridicule than any contribution to the spirit which prevails in the better scenes of the play; when the Constable goes on to speak in contrast of the 'starved band' of English as 'shales and husks of men,' his account is connected, poetically speaking, with the spirit of the Prologue to this same act and stresses, dramatically, the folly and vanity of the estimate so lightly delivered. The following account of the English put into the

[13] *Hamlet*, iii. iii.

mouth of Grandpré is still more clearly a piece of literary elaboration, laboured in its pictorial emphasis and charged with a weight of descriptive content that gives to such phrases as 'The gum down-roping from their pale-dead eyes' a sense of artificiality which fails to contribute, by mature Shakespearean standards, to any living effect. We may feel in these lines the effort of the literary craftsman to extend and define his style through recourse to a conscious artifice perhaps not entirely disconnected with the more elaborately wrought verse of certain parts of *Troilus and Cressida*, but less related to any discernible unity of spirit.

In contrast with this vacant and pretentious verbalism the English, regarded so mistakenly as 'lifeless' by the French (whose conception of 'life' has just been proved, rather heavily, to be so artificial and without content), are presented (IV. iii) in a scene in which the patriotic purpose of the original history prevails almost exclusively. A sober confidence and piety is the keynote to the scene, and from it the king's own set-piece of rhetoric, in the 'Crispin Crispian' speech, emerges naturally as the thing it is—an admirable piece of declamation based on values which the most mature part of Shakespeare's experience, in the very act of accepting them, was already subjecting to a disturbing contact with other, more complex ways of thinking. The Shakespeare who put into Henry's mouth the words,

> if it be a sin to covet honour,
> I am the most offending soul alive,

would appear, at first sight, not to be the one who had already, in Falstaff's repeated utterances, exposed to examination the same concept of 'honour' and arrived, on some occasions, at very different conclusions. He is clearly a less complex and, in some sense, a less interesting writer; and yet we should not understand the full achievement of the mature dramatist if we did not see that this too is an essential element that went to the making of it. If Falstaff, at his best moments, rejects a certain conception of 'honour,' he does so in the name of life, of a vitality that will not be constrained to the empty forms of rhetoric which interest manoeuvres for its own ends; and if the clash between this refusal and a positive attitude which is not less necessary for its deliberate dedication to the public, the political sphere, produces—in the later plays of the sequence—an outlook increasingly sombre, the simple acceptance of duty is still a possible, and indeed necessary attitude. Henry is never more attractive than at this moment of accepted decision, when his dedication to the responsibilities of office blossoms forth into a simple and deeply human comradeship.

Only at the end of the scene, when the French herald comes to demand ransom, does the king's anger express itself in something like the iron rigidity we have learnt to associate with him in earlier scenes. The reference to the 'dead bodies' of the coming battle—who are to be famous,

> for there the sun shall greet them,
> And draw their honours reeking up to heaven;
> Leaving their earthly parts to choke your clime,
> The smell whereof shall breed a plague in France
>
> (IV. iii)

—some critics will perhaps be content to relate to the spirit of the times; but the note struck is not dissimilar to one we have learnt to associate with Henry from the time of the attack on Harfleur. It belongs, indeed, to his nature, and—we may say, without overstressing the point—to the less admirable part of it, which always emerges when his will is crossed or his self-esteem insulted; and it is not until we return to the sober note of

> tell the constable
> We are but warriors for the working-day,

that the more positive conception again prevails.

The battle scenes which immediately follow scarcely add to the stature of the play, though one or two touches contribute to the complete conception. The first (IV. iv) could be regarded as a comic commentary, offered through the bragging of Pistol, upon the heroic conception of war; and yet its content forbids us to claim so much individuality for it. It is worth reflecting that the original titles advertising this play recommended Pistol as its chief comic attraction: worth remembering because that is in itself some comment on the change of mood since the rejection of Falstaff.[14] The chief quality of Pistol is *emptiness*, a bombastic show that wordily covers vacancy: as the Boy, whose remarks throughout are a kind of dim shadow of the comic perspicacity of his former master, puts it, 'I did never know so full a voice issue from so empty a heart.' Pistol is *empty*, indeed, both of sense and of the comedy that goes with it. The most significant phrases uttered by this camp follower, this scavenger of fortune, are those which turn upon the theme of throat-cutting, already anticipated by Nym[15] and to be echoed again in the scenes immediately following. The Boy, turning from him, contributes to the spirit of the whole when, after comparing Nym and Bardolph favourably to 'this roaring devil i' the old play,' he goes on to refer to them as *dead*, elimi-

---

14 Reference here is to the title page of the Quarto edition.
15 See pp. 175–76 above.

nated by the ruthless—and necessary—moral efficiency on which Henry's victory is to be built. 'They are both hanged': the times have changed indeed, and the empty brags of Pistol are hollow echoes of a comedy that has ceased, since Falstaff died, to illuminate events with its own distinctive life.

The short intervening scene (iv. v) in which the French, having failed in manliness and efficiency alike, rush to their fate, calls for no comment. The next (iv. vi) is only remarkable for the romantic deaths of Suffolk and York, steeped in gore and in the familiar imagery which, from the time of the earlier chronicle plays on the reign of Henry VI, associates love and death:

> over Suffolk's neck
> He threw his wounded arm and kiss'd his lips;
> And so espoused to death, with blood he seal'd
> A testament of noble-ending love.
> The *pretty* and *sweet* manner of it forced
> These waters from me which I would have stopp'd.

Poetic effects similar to these, deriving from Shakespeare's early manner, appear in his later work in connection with a firmer and more dramatic grasp of the realities of character; but here, as the final adjectives show, the romantic and decorative elements prevail in a thoroughly theatrical comradeship in death. The scene, ends, however, on a grimmer note in Henry's concluding command to 'every soldier' to kill his prisoners. The juxtaposition with the preceding heroics, though we need not go so far as to imply a condemnation foreign to the spirit of the times, cannot be altogether accidental.

The throat-cutting note, indeed, is carried on, in the next scene (iv. vii) to the end of the battle. It is a necessary part of Henry's triumph. Justified as it no doubt is in terms of military tactics, it is also related to the tougher strain of disillusioned realism that emerges from the play. The self-control which we have learnt to associate with the victorious king is, as we have repeatedly had occasion to see, not without a suggestion of harshness and inhumanity. His righteousness is of the kind that does not prevent him from inflicting merciless reprisals on his enemies, reprisals preceded by the characteristic rising of a passionate anger—

> I was not angry since I came to France
> Until this instant

—which the justice of its occasion does not make less typical of the speaker's nature. This anger, once it has taken possession of him, expresses itself in the cold purposeful determination that has always been part of his make-up:

> Besides, we'll cut the throats of those we have,
> And not a man of them that we shall take
> Shall taste our mercy. (IV. vii)

This is once more the Henry who can contemplate suffering from which his normal, peaceful humanity would recoil, but of which he feels himself, in war, not to be the cause. It is, moreover, an action for which much in the so-called comic action has prepared us,[16] and which leads us to find something sardonic in Gower's comment that 'the king, *most worthily*, hath caused every soldier to cut his prisoner's throat. O 'tis a gallant king!' By such excellence, Shakespeare would seem to say, must wars be won.

The rest of this episode adds little of interest to the play. The final count of the dead on either side, and Henry's dedication of his 'miraculous' victory to the will of God, related though they are to his character as consistently developed, belong to the spirit of the original chronicle; and the comic business between Williams and Fluellen, arising out of the king's earlier discussion with the former, reflects not the spirit of comedy associated with the prose scenes of the preceding plays, but the sense of tough loyalty which is closer to the new conception and belongs— in its better moments—to the ultimately tragic tendency which the play reveals. The best of this scene is contained in Fluellen's expression of devotion to his king: 'I will confess it to all the 'orld: I need not to be ashamed of your majesty, praised be God, *so long as your majesty is an honest man*.'[17] Should we need a word to describe the best positive values of this play, that which distinguishes it from mere patriotic rhetoric on the one side and sardonic pessimism on the other (and both moods are constituent parts of it), it would be the word 'honesty' as here used; honesty which can offer loyalty whilst maintaining independence of judgement, and which is brought out, as much as the cruelty which balances it, by the sombre circumstances of war which no merely patriotic show of rhetoric or romantic comradeship in death can conceal. This 'honesty,' expressed also by Williams in his robust self-defence before Henry—'you appeared to me but as a comman man; . . . and what your highness suffered under that shape, I beseech you to take it for your own fault and not mine'—is characteristic, in its directness, of the play. These soldiers, revering the necessary form of monarchy upon which all

---

[16] See the relevant phrases of Nym (p. 176), Macmorris (p. 184), and others.
[17] *Henry V*, IV. vii.

social order depends, can yet see in it the reflection of their common humanity. It is this reflection, by which they are ennobled, which has brought them to victory over enemies for whom 'common' humanity is no object of reverence or understanding. If this understanding points eventually to an intuition increasingly tragic in its implications, it is also related to the patriotic purposes which equally prevail in this play.

By the time we reach the opening of the last act, we are in a position to understand why *Henry V* has been most generally popular when imperfectly understood. The concessions made to human feeling in some of the most individual parts of the play are too few, their presiding spirit too rigid, to compel enthusiasm. It ends, as far as the supposedly 'comic' action is concerned, in a decided pessimism which somehow fails to attain the note of tragedy. Pistol, speaking the last word for the cutthroats of the play, leaves us, after Gower's condemnation of him as 'a counterfeit cowardly knave,'[18] with a gloomy and realistic vision of his future which the sober common sense of his companions does not sufficiently lighten:

> Doth Fortune play the huswife with me now?
> News have I, that my Nell is dead i' the spital
> Of malady of France;
> And there my rendezvous is quite cut off.
> Old I do wax; and from my weary limbs
> Honour is cudgelled. Well, bawd I'll turn,
> And something lean to cutpurse of quick hand.
> To England will I steal, and there I'll steal:
> And patches will I get unto these cudgell'd scars,
> And swear I got them in the Gallia wars. (v. i)

The reference to Nell's death and the nature of it are alike significant. They stress, like so much in this play, the passing of the comic spirit so strongly revealed in its predecessors, and relate that passing in terms which look forward to the disillusioned realism of the 'problem' plays. Pistol is the last and least worthy survivor of another world, and his anticipated future looks forward to a very different one to come.

Nor is the political conclusion, which shows peace following on the English triumph, much more encouraging. Burgundy's picture of the benefits of peace and the destruction of war is couched in the decorative vein which we have found elsewhere in what we have called the chronicle matter of this play. True in itself, as far as it goes, its sense is rather public than personal, and its tone makes no pretence to intimacy. The

---

[18] *Henry V*, v. i.

marriage project itself belongs to this order of reality. Katharine of France is, after all, part of the spoils of war; and if Henry woos her with direct simplicity, he has none the less his political purpose clearly and constantly in mind. It is characteristic of him that when he turns to the king of France and asks him to ratify the match—'Shall Kate be my wife?'—his comment when he has received the reply 'So please you,' links his acceptance to the extension of his territorial power: 'I am content; *so the maiden cities you talk of may wait on her:* so that the maid that stood in the way for my wish shall show me *the way to my will.*'[19] It is Henry's virtue, as it is also his limitation, to live entirely, exclusively for the public function which he has accepted as his vocation; and it is therefore fitting that the marriage with which he rounds off his victory is primarily an act of policy.

The nearest approach to a moment of true feeling is that in which the king, in his characteristic, direct prose, contrasts the passing nature of man's decorative virtues with the constancy of 'a good heart':

a speaker is but a prater; a rhyme is but a ballad. A good leg will fall; a straight back will stoop; a black beard will turn white; a curled pate will grow bald; a fair face will wither; a full eye will wax hollow: but a good heart, Kate, is the sun and the moon; or rather the sun and not the moon; for it shines bright and never changes, but keeps his course truly.

(v. ii)

This, at least, belongs rather to Henry's virtues than to the political arrangement being proposed. The same virtues enabled him, on the morning of Agincourt, to unite his followers in the true fellowship of 'a band of brothers.' They are no mean virtues, but that they are mainly dedicated to the public, the political sphere is never more clearly shown than in the manner of this wooing. Henry's approach to Katharine, with its plain and dispassionate honesty, befits what is after all a political agreement undertaken finally in a spirit of sober calculation. It may have satisfied the demands of patriotic orthodoxy at Elizabeth's court; but Shakespeare had the gift of fulfilling obligations of this kind without being deterred from his deeper purposes, and this conclusion, while it confirms Henry's characteristic virtues, limits firmly the range of emotions which he is capable of feeling. Not to have limited them, indeed, would have been to create a figure humanly more interesting but, for that very reason, politically less effective. The inspiration of *Henry V* is, in its deeper moments (which do not represent the whole play), critical, analytic, ex-

[19] *Henry V*, v. ii.

ploratory. As we follow it, and in spite of our admiration for its hero's dedication to his chosen ends, a certain coldness takes possession of us as it took possession, step by step, of the limbs of the dying Falstaff; and we too, as we come to the end of this balanced, sober study of political virtue rewarded by the success it deserves, find ourselves in our own way 'babbling of green fields.'[20]

[20] Theobald's famous emendation has, of course, its difficulties; but in the absence of an alternative which shall appeal both to sense and the poetic instinct we may perhaps be allowed to retain it.